OUTSIDE
THE WIRE

OUTSIDE

edited by
KEVIN PATTERSON *and* JANE WARREN

THE WIRE

THE WAR IN
AFGHANISTAN
IN THE WORDS OF
ITS PARTICIPANTS

foreword by
LGen ROMÉO DALLAIRE

VINTAGE CANADA

VINTAGE CANADA EDITION, 2008

Published in Canada by Vintage Canada, a division of Random House of Canada Limited, Toronto, in 2008. Originally published in hardcover in Canada by Random House Canada, a division of Random House of Canada Limited, Toronto, in 2007. Distributed by Random House of Canada Limited, Toronto.

Vintage Canada and colophon are registered trademarks of Random House of Canada Limited.

www.randomhouse.ca

LIBRARY AND ARCHIVES CANADA CATALOGUING IN PUBLICATION

Outside the wire : the war in Afghanistan in the words of its participants / edited by Kevin Patterson and E. Jane Warren ; foreword by Roméo Dallaire.

ISBN 978-0-307-35631-4

1. Afghan War, 2001–   —Personal narratives, Canadian. 2. Afghan War, 2001–   —Participation, Canadian. 3. Canada—Armed Forces—Afghanistan. I. Patterson, Kevin, 1964–   II. Warren E. Jane

DS371.412.O98 2008   958.104'7   C2008-900313-6

Text design by Jennifer Lum

Printed and bound in the United States of America

10 9 8 7 6 5 4 3 2 1

Dedicated to the memories of

Captain Nichola Goddard
&
Mike Frastacky

CONTENTS

The plight of Canadian soldiers is that they perform the most dangerous of their missions in far-flung lands, and nobody back home—except for those who mourn the dead or suffer along with the wounded—really feels the intrusion of war into the national psyche. In account after account from the trenches of Vimy, the front lines of the liberation of Holland and outside the wire in Afghanistan, we struggle—soldiers struggle—with how to convey the *real* reality. Sometimes even with what *is* the real reality.

In Afghanistan, experiencing the intensity of battle; being the cause of the destruction of villages, of putting people's homes in the target cross-hairs; being able to do little to address the extreme poverty and deprivation of the children; witnessing the burden and abuse of women in this male-dominated social order; hearing the suffering and cries of the wounded, civilian and military alike; seeing the cold and cruel face of death on your enemy as well as on your comrade: these are some of the realities veterans carry back to Canada.

When they arrive home, other realities may shock them: the unseemly opulence of our country; the debates and posturing of politicians wanting to grab the next headline without knowing much about the war; the air of security that envelops civilians as they go so earnestly about their daily routines, detached from any sense of the threat encountered daily by their nation's representatives abroad; the consuming fervour and stress generated by our keen work ethic in this industrialized society; being able to hit the off switch on the remote when the tube projects too much hurt and agony. Is this the mindset the veterans of Afghanistan, and so many of their predecessors, are expected to slip into once again? Is this the *real* reality of life in Canada?

The reality of combat in Afghanistan or the reality of life back home? Which one does the young warrior have to grapple most with? Which actually comforts him most? Which one does the doctor cling to as she faces the passage of wounded people through the Kandahar military hospital? Which does the battle-field humanitarian clutch to his breast as a way to weather the moral and ethical dilemmas of service that are causing intense friction in more and more of his grey cells?

As the adrenalin high of the war zone recedes ever so slowly, the hurt rises in your stomach and buckles your shoulders under the weight of grief and sorrow. You're surprised to feel the deep ache of lonesomeness as you sit once again at your family dinner table—where you longed to be. Though you deny it to the people who love you, the people in your home life who rely on you, you long for extreme emotions: the pounding of your heart in your throat so strong you nearly choke; the perverse exhilaration of defying death time and time again; the intoxicating spasm of raw power you experience among the explosive lights of bursting projectiles, with their acrid smell and deafening blasts; the climax of battle, which leaves you drowning in sweat and relieved to be alive.

How can we—how can they—stay off that drug of combat, that rush into temporary oblivion that has absolutely no equal in the human experience? I can think of no civilian equivalent where one's job is to offer up life and limb for a mission, a cause, a buddy, another human being who is just as human and vulnerable as you. In the aftermath of combat, forever burnt into the wiring of a combatant's brain is another reality, which invades everyday life with a clarity and speed that can surprise, disillusion, depress or elate you all at once. In my experience, no amount of time can dampen this impact on a soldier's psyche.

And so, justly and aptly, some of the writings in this revealing book do not satiate nor temper but instead, with near reckless abandon, describe, feel, explode and pierce the reader with an unbridled energy and clarity that pull at your heart and drive right to your soul. Reading these pages is like hearing voices from the beyond, like seeing ghosts wandering the recesses of all the world's battlefields.

A reader will also encounter the kind of soldiers' stories that wars always produce but that often remain unheard, unread: statements that come out so spontaneously and so to the point. In the field hospital at Kandahar airbase, young Cpl Ryan Pagnacco, having been severely wounded in action, wakes up from his drug-induced torpor to the sound of rocket and mortar fire nearby. As he lies helpless in his bed, the nurse throws a blast blanket over him, and he asks: "Are we being attacked?" The reply comes immediately with calm and serious intent: "Yes . . . go back to sleep." Can one imagine a more suitable response from a caregiver to an anxious patient fresh from the front?

Many serve and so few are recognized or even receive a word of thanks. Often the intensity of the battle prevents its leaders from noticing a *fait d'armes* of heroic proportions. At other times, the leaders themselves are wounded or killed and are not there to pass word up the line of a warrior's feat committed by a private. At other times, the cohesiveness of the group brings about a victorious outcome or a disciplined withdrawal under fire: all are truly heroes, yet all simply feel that they just did their jobs.

It is only when the tired, dirty, hungry and thirsty combatants, caked in dust and mud and too often in blood, find a moment of rest or a place in the shade by their vehicles, that the vividness, the intensity, the adrenalin rush and the steady vise-grip on their stomachs catches them by surprise and replays in digitally clear slow motion the rage, the fear, the sorrow and the extraordinary high of facing death head-on and surviving.

The anecdotes and jokes, the technical and emotional descriptions, the blood-curdling and sad exposés: all are present in these letters home from the battlefield in a far-off land. The human dignity and sorrow, as well as the elation of victory and the emptiness of loss, are laid out in the participants' own innocent, lively and clear prose—the richness of which is incalculable.

—LGen (Retired) the Hon. Roméo A. Dallaire,
OC, CMM, GOQ, MSC, CD Senator

War remains the most divisive and unpredictable undertaking a society may engage in. A failed war has the capacity to topple governments at a stroke. In 413 BCE, the Athenians' ill-judged Sicilian expedition led to the end of their democracy; twenty-five hundred years later, the second Bush era has devastated the American Republican Party through the disastrous occupation of Iraq. And yet. When performed competently and wisely, armed intervention, and sometimes only armed intervention, can rescue whole nations from the abyss. But for the efforts of the British Army in 1999, in the course of the largest United Nations intervention prior to Afghanistan, Sierra Leone would remain a failed state today. The NATO/UN intervention in the former Yugoslavia saved the whole region from descending further into genocide. The Democratic Republic of the Congo faces a future as something other than a tropical charnel house because of the UN's enormous efforts there, while Rwanda has become a byword for murderous spasm because of the absence of a similar effort. Perhaps the only good thing to come of the Lebanese-Hamas-Israeli crisis of the summer of 2006 was the substantial deployment of UN forces to Lebanon. For the first time in thirty-five years, the second-oldest failed state in the world looks to be coalescing into a kind of order, the government asserting its monopoly on force and the influence of foreign powers on local issues in evident decline.

In the wake of the assault by al Qaeda on the West—
launched from the world's oldest failed state, Afghanistan—
thirty years of collective indifference by the West were
superseded, if not by compassion, then at least by alarm. Any
epidemiologist understands: suffering does not localize.
Trouble over there comes here. The United Nations authorized
the creation of a force that would ultimately include personnel
from thirty-seven nations to occupy, pacify and restore a func-
tioning and responsive government to this most martial and
anarchic of societies.

Five years later, there is still a legitimate debate underway
about the feasibility of this deployment. The debate about how
long to persist in the effort is being conducted in parliaments in
London, Ottawa and Den Hague, and on talk radio stations
across North America. Much of the talk involves oft-repeated
nostrums about land wars in Asia, pitted against hand-
wringing about the need to do something. In the anxiety and the
fervour of the debate, our discomfort with the unfamiliarity of
these circumstances becomes clear. What do any of us really
know about Afghanistan? What do the Pashtun really think of
all this? The generals will say one thing. And politicians in
opposition, another.

In the autumn of 413 BCE, a trickle of men returned to
Athens relating how, two months previously, the entire Sicilian
expedition, numbering some twenty-eight thousand, had been
destroyed. The response among Athenians is described by the
historian Thucydides as one of bewildered despair. Nothing in
the reports from the battlefield by generals Nicias and
Demosthenes had prepared the Athenians for the extent of the
calamity. And now the flower of the Athenian navy and army was
gone. Within a matter of months, the slaves revolted, and soon
the Spartans were supervising the Athenians as they were forced
to tear down their own walls, to the sound of pipe music.

We are no less responsible or vulnerable than the Athenians. But we do have access to information that they did not. Embedded journalists may be spun by public affairs officers and partisan politics may intrude between the public and almost every source of information, but this is the information era, and it is possible to read the blogs and emails of privates and corporals and second lieutenants hours after they return from firefights in mountains on the other side of the world. Soldiers in the Second World War were given postcards to mail to their families. Dear _____ , I am (circle one) *fine/happy/ looking forward to seeing you/slightly injured* and will write to you when I *have time/know when I'll be home/have fully recovered.* Nothing like that degree of censorship and control is possible today. Cellphones with Canadian numbers work on the Kandahar base. Hotmail and YouTube and MySpace all flicker on the screens of everyone's laptop. Among the millions of men Britain sent to the front in the Great War, a mere dozen would subsequently become known as War Poets—now, it seems, every man or woman who has trod the Red Desert is one.

The public may make any decision it wants to about the war in Afghanistan. But it may not claim ignorance of what it is that is being done there, in its name.

Outside the Wire collects writing by soldiers, doctors, aid workers and journalists who have worked in Afghanistan. When we solicited these pieces, we asked the contributors to avoid polemics. Neither attacks upon nor defences of the intervention were sought. What was wanted was narrative: "This is what I saw, this is what I did, this is what happened to me." In retrospect, it might not have been necessary to proscribe polemical writing. People yearn to be understood, and this applies as much to the soldiers as it does to the aid workers who appear in this book. No veterans of Afghanistan who submitted writing for this book seemed to be nearly as interested in advancing an argument as they were in simply relating their experience.

Corporal Gordon Whitton's wide-ranging account of his deployment touches tenderly upon how his work affects his family, and then moves on to describe the absurdity, terror and intimacy of combat. Corporal Ryan Pagnacco's surreal account of his time fighting and bagpipe playing and being shot by allies continues the tradition of smart and insightful writing about the strangest and most intense activity that humans engage in. Captain Casey Balden writes lyrically about the battles he experienced, culminating in his own wounding. None of these people went to Afghanistan knowing they would be writing about their time there for the same book, yet, again and again, their paths cross. The late Mike Frastacky knew Maureen Mayhew; they both worked as aid workers, he as a builder of schools, she as a public-health physician. Peter Sherk worked in the Role 3 hospital in Kandahar, together with one of the editors of this book, who writes about a burned boy far from his parents whose loneliness stirred everyone who looked at him. Lieutenant-Colonel Ian Hope was Captain Nichola Goddard's commanding officer; they both fought alongside Whitton. Dead and wounded friends overlap among the writers here; everyone is stirred by the attack on Captain Trevor Greene, who attended a village *shirra*—a meeting of elders—unhelmeted and too trusting. Goddard writes of him only weeks before she was killed in a firefight herself, the first female combat arms fatality in Canadian or NATO history. Her death appears, in its turn, in the ruminations of other writers in this book.

All of which is just to say: in small and closely bonded groups, everyone knows everyone else. There are twenty-five hundred Canadian soldiers in Afghanistan, among thirty thousand from thirty-seven other NATO and allied countries there. And despite the dreadful conditions they live and fight in, none of these have known the least part of the suffering of the Afghans.

There is a legitimate debate about the feasibility of the mission as it has been laid out, whether Western soldiers can be seen as anything other than occupiers six years after the over-throw of the Taliban, whether any solution, however well inten-tioned and planned out, originating from *feringhee* (foreigners) can succeed there. This debate is being decided not in Kandahar and Helmand but in Saskatchewan and Lancashire and Nebraska—through the same political process that the soldiers are trying help establish in Afghanistan. And that political deci-sion, made so far from the battlefield, must be informed by knowledge of it. Which is why these voices have to be heard.

Afghanistan has been a tortured country for longer than any of us has been paying attention. Now that our own injuries have caught our attention, it becomes clear that if we can help pull the country out of the abyss, we must. And, equally, if we can't help, we mustn't make things even worse.

The right thing has to be done in Afghanistan. Whatever that is.

—Kevin Patterson and Jane Warren, editors

Gordon Whitton was born on July 18, 1974. He joined the Stormont, Dundas & Glengarry Highlanders in Cornwall, Ontario, in 1994, and transferred to the regular force in September 1996. He served in the Persian Gulf in 2003 during Operation Apollo. Upon returning to Canada, he served in Reconnaissance Platoon, 1 PPCLI (First Battalion, Princess Patricia's Canadian Light Infantry), and deployed to Afghanistan in January 2006 for Operation Enduring Freedom. He was awarded a "mention in dispatches" for an incident on May 15, 2006, involving a roadside bomb, and returned in August 2006. He is now a member of the PPCLI Regimental Headquarters and lives in Edmonton, Alberta, with his wife and two children.

This is the first of three edited excerpts from the journal Gordon kept while in Afghanistan.

January 25, 2006

The day we've been waiting for, for more than a year, is finally here. Nicole, the kids and I woke up early and got ready to drive to the Lecture Training Facility (LTF) on the Edmonton Garrison to say our final goodbye. It started to sink in before I'd even left our house, I was looking at my wonderful family and home and I knew I was going to miss this more than anything in the world.

We took a few minutes to just hold each other tight on the couch before we left.

When we got to the base, I had some administration to take care of before we got on the buses, so our families could hang around for an hour or so. Landon, Brooke and the other kids were having fun running through all the files of troops on the parade square floor in the LTF. When General Grant (commander of Land Force Western Area) was speaking to all of us, Brooke got lost wandering around in front of him. General Grant stopped in the middle of his speech and asked who owned the little girl in the pink shirt and ponytail. Captain Hamilton knew she was mine, so he pointed her in the right direction; I was almost embarrassed to walk in front of the general to claim my kid.

After a little while all of our admin was complete. I took every chance to just hug my wife and kids as much as I could, it seemed every time I was holding my son or daughter, reporters were all around us taking pictures. My in-laws, Don and Shirley, were also there to say their goodbyes to me, I was happy they could be there to do that, they left about twenty minutes before Nikki and the kids. Landon was just sitting on my kit, he couldn't say much and he seemed depressed, he said he just wanted me to come home. I told him to be a good boy, have lots of fun and Daddy will come home soon, but the truth was seeping out of my eyes, I was having a hard time holding it back. Brooklyn told me she loved me and handed me a penny, which I made sure I put in a safe place. They all just seemed to go silent. I picked up the kids' jackets and helped them put them on, zipped them up and told them I'd walk them out.

Just before they went through the doors, I kneeled down to the kids' level and pulled them both in, I told them I loved them. I stood up and hugged Nikki one last time, I said, "Goodbye, baby, I love you and I'll be home before you know it." I said, "Go, go now, you guys, I love you." They walked through the doors and down the corridor, Brooke and I blowing kisses at each other until they went out of sight. I started to get overwhelmed with some of the stuff I'd been holding in, I had to pull a Kleenex out of my pocket and get a grip on myself, I didn't want to think about it, it just seemed like too much for me to handle. I knew what I had to do and I knew I must get my mind prepared to go out and do it. I made my way through the lines and boarded the bus that took us to the airport where a plane was waiting for us.

A FAMILY REFLECTION OF AFGHANISTAN
BY
SERGEANT RUSSELL D. STORRING

Russell Storring joined the Canadian Forces in 1991 at seventeen years of age. During his career he has been posted to a variety of units across Canada, and he served with the UN in Rwanda in 1994 and with NATO in Afghanistan in 2003 and 2005. He is currently posted to the Canadian Forces Joint Signals Regiment, and resides in Kingston with his wife Nathalie and his children.

Although my family and I have known for a while that I will be leaving again for Afghanistan, I have been so busy helping another squadron get ready to deploy, I haven't really had time to focus on my own departure. Then, at the end of May 2005, when I leave 2 Combat Engineer Regiment to become part of Recce Squadron, Royal Canadian Dragoons, it finally sinks in to Nathalie, the boys and me that, in a couple of short months, I will be headed to Afghanistan for the second time in two years.

We have talked about the danger of serving overseas, and, never keeping anything from Nathalie, I have told her about a couple of close calls from my first tour. It's not really something that comes up over a romantic dinner, just a topic of discussion that sometimes comes out of the blue. When I first told Nathalie about a rocket attack on Camp Warehouse, she worried for a week and kept telling me that she didn't want me to go back. It's hard to explain to someone who isn't in the army that an incident like that, which may seem like a close call to them, is just part of the job to a soldier. It's not that you forget about those close calls after the tour, but because the risk isn't there anymore, they no longer seem like that big a deal.

To ease Nathalie's growing concerns as the days tick by before I depart, I tell her that I won't be heading outside the camp as much as last time, which I know isn't true. I don't really think of it as a lie, but just a way to protect Nathalie and the boys from worrying all the time. Most of what I have been hearing from Recce Squadron is that we will be outside the camp for most of the tour, conducting reconnaissance patrols and convoys for the impending move from Kabul to Kandahar. It's not really something Nathalie needs to know, and it definitely won't help her peace of mind, so I decide to keep it from her.

In June, Recce Squadron heads out to finish our training with a confirmation exercise for the whole task force. It's a little frustrating that just before we leave for a six-month tour, when we want time with our families the most, we have to spend as much as three more months away from home, completing the required training and exercises. I know it bugs Nathalie that I am headed out for a couple of weeks so close to my scheduled departure date, but I assure her that the training will demonstrate to the commander that we are ready for the stresses and dangers of a tour and will also show us that we are as prepared as possible, allowing us to test our skills through a series of drills and exercises that have no actual life or death outcome.

One of the training scenarios that I lead a section through is an urban patrol in "Little Kabul," a small shanty town that has been constructed in the Petawawa training area. My mission is to conduct a presence patrol, and to meet with the local police chief and the town mayor, all the while keeping within mandated rules of engagement. I run my section through orders, and after a quick shakeout, we head into the outskirts of the shanty town. Immediately, the locals (played by Third Battalion, Royal Canadian Regiment soldiers, dressed to the part) start harassing our patrol for food and money, and trying to sell us trinkets. Some are gathered around burn barrels and others simply hang out in their huts watching us walk by. Along the way we are greeted by a variety of locals, from seemingly friendly to indifferent, most just happy to get in our way and make our patrol as difficult as possible. If anyone ever says that soldiers can't act, then they haven't seen the show that 3 RCR put on for our work-up training. Except for the smell and the absence of the smoke that hangs over Kabul, this could almost pass for one of the little gatherings of houses that I saw so many times on my last tour in Afghanistan. The realism doesn't stop there but carries on into first-aid scenarios that involve IEDs (improvised explosive devices), booby traps and enemy insurgents all tied into one continuous realistic training program that both reinforces our abilities and forces us to improvise along the way.

In the second week of my final field exercise, Nathalie calls me from home and tells me that my stepfather, Gerry, is dying. He was diagnosed with lung cancer in late March, and told that he'd probably had it for five years. I already lost my father in 2001, and now before I head out again into harm's way, I'm losing my stepfather, too. I inform my chain of command, and for all the times I've bitched about the army, I have to admit that they move pretty fast in getting me out of the field, back to the padre, leave pass in hand, and on my way home. The army prides itself on being like a family, and the soldiers that I have been working with and for prove to me that they care for me as one of their own.

We consider not taking our boys, Jonathan and Jeremy, to see their Papa Gerry, but feel it wouldn't be fair to them if they weren't able to see him again. With me still dressed in my combats, we make it to the Napanee hospital in record time. In my rush, I forget to thank the police officer who pulls me over for speeding, but, once I explain the situation, quickly lets me go with a warning.

After a short, courageous battle, Papa Gerry passes away on June 17, with his family by his side. As we stand around the hospital bed, and Jonathan and Jeremy realize that they won't be seeing their Papa anymore, I realize that my boys are growing up faster than I want them to. It's sad to have to learn, at six and nine years old, that death is a part of life—it's not that I'd ever felt an impending sense of doom or anything, but Nathalie and I both realize that death is something they should understand. They manage to gather themselves to say their final goodbyes and to kiss Papa Gerry on the cheek one last time, speaking mountains of their own fortitude and courage.

Pre-deployment leave kicks in shortly after we return to Petawawa, and I am on leave from June 30 to July 22, before flying out on July 23. Nathalie's parents come up for the Canada Day weekend, which happens to coincide with Canadian Forces Base Petawawa's one-hundredth birthday. A fun-filled day watching the CF Gun Race, taking in various displays, and enjoying a world-class parachuting display by the Canadian Sky Hawks culminates in a barbecue dinner at our house. While sitting in the living room after supper, my mother-in-law appears with a birthday cake and everyone starts singing "Happy Birthday." I panic, wondering whose birthday I have forgotten, when I realize that the party is for me. Knowing I would miss another birthday at home, Nathalie had planned a surprise one for me, so I could celebrate with my family. I'm not really one for making a fuss over my own birthday, but this time it brings tears to my eyes, reminding me of what I will miss while I'm deployed.

That night, after everyone heads to bed, I realize just how much I ask of my family, how much they go through when I'm not here, and how much they give of themselves to support the life I have chosen. What does a child think when he's talking to his father on the other side of the world, trying to explain his report card or how he's hurt his foot playing soccer, or describing his first trophy? Sharing milestones in a child's life by phone or email, and sometimes with pictures, just isn't the same as sharing them in person. It's hard to console a hurt little boy over the phone, and have him understand that you're not there to make him feel better because you have a job to do helping other people. I'm not sure the boys understand when I tell them that, and every time I return, it seems that they have grown a little farther away from me than when I left them.

With only a couple of weeks left at home, I spend as much time with Nathalie and the boys as possible. We play mini-putt and dodge ball, barbecue all the time and visit the beach. Nathalie and I spend our alone time in the evening talking, making plans for the future, watching movies or walking the dog. This is only Nathalie's second tour as a military spouse, and she amazes me with her strength and steadfastness, especially since most of her friends' husbands will not be deploying with me this time, making it harder for her, reminding her every day she sees them that I am gone and they are still here.

Nathalie finally asks me one night what she and the boys would do if something happened to me in Afghanistan. Being the person that I am, her question doesn't really bother me, but I know from the tears welling up in her eyes that this is something she has been thinking about and keeping inside for a long while. I try to give her the normal answer—"Don't worry, nothing's going to happen"—but she cuts me off and asks, "But what if something does, what do we do?" Really, how is anyone supposed to answer that kind of question? I remind her that she is a strong girl, and would have to be strong for the boys, and that after a while, although it wouldn't be the same, life would move on for them. Lots of people do it, and have done it, but I reassure her again that nothing is going to happen and that in five to six months it will all be over with and I will be on my way home again. I don't think it is a question that really needs an answer, just Nathalie trying to tell me her fears and worries. She tearfully reminds me, "Don't do anything stupid, and don't be a hero," before closing her eyes to sleep.

I lie there for a while with my thoughts spinning and racing. I can't predict the future, and I honestly don't know if everything will be all right, but I know I'm trained, and that I have a damn good bunch of soldiers going over with me. How do you stop a determined suicide bomber? What if there is something like an IED that my driver or I don't see? I could lie here all night running "what if" scenarios through my mind, but it wouldn't help. I know I can react to whatever the Taliban or al Qaeda throw at me, but those unknowns are the scary part. As I finally doze off to the faint drum of a lone helicopter from 427 Tac Hel Squadron flying along the Ottawa River, I wonder how much Afghanistan has changed in the year and a half since I left. The memories of my first deployment start to play through my mind.

My driver, Private Sean Russell, idles our way towards the entrance of the camp behind the lead Bison, while two German Sea Stallions fly in low over the camp, headed toward the helipad, blowing clouds of dust high into the air, drowning out the rumble of the Bison with the slow and heavy beat of the chopper blades. We manage to edge out onto Jalalabad road, missing the brunt of the dust cloud, and head west into the city. It's 1300 hours and the temperature is soaring above forty-five degrees Celsius, without factoring in the added heat of body armour and the heat generated by a steel-armoured vehicle. The wind blowing by my face as I remain low in the Bison crew commander's hatch is anything but refreshing. There is no natural wind today, so what is generated as we cruise along Jalalabad road at sixty kilometres an hour is simply stifling. Despite the heat, I don't mind being out and about now, as most normal people tend to avoid the hottest part of the day.

Today should be a relatively simple mission, as I am heading up to TV Hill, above Kabul, to pick up a couple of people going home for their HLTA (home leave travel assistance). Depending on the traffic, I should be able to get there in just over an hour, spend thirty minutes loading up, and then get back in an hour and a bit, which should land us just in time for supper. The lead Bison is crew-commanded by Master Corporal Dan Walker, and my driver knows to keep him within twenty-five to fifty metres, and to try and not let vehicles in between us.

As we near the first traffic circle, the roads start to get congested. As we make our way around the circle, I swing my C-6 GPMG (general-purpose machine gun) over to cover our right side, and the stench of the city hits us. It's a nauseating smell generated by a mixture of garbage lying in the streets and gutters, human waste from the open sewers, animal feces, and the result of burning tires, wood and anything else flammable. It's not just a smell, but something that hits the back of your throat and stays with you like you swallowed it, and if you don't have a strong enough stomach it can make you nauseous. It doesn't cover the whole city, as the city centre is kept relatively free of markets, garbage piles and squatters, but as we drive across the city we hit pockets of stench.

Each time we reach an intersection, we slow down to make sure other vehicles see us, and then proceed through, covering left and right as we go. At some intersections, the local police try to direct traffic, but most of the time, the drivers just ignore their hand signals and go whenever they see a chance. I'm certain the size of our vehicles and the machine guns mounted up front are a factor in usually securing passage when and where we want it on the roads.

The trip up TV Hill begins with a drive through a small, crowded side street, overflowing with people and shop stalls. On the left are a number of meat stands with cow, chicken and I'm not sure what other parts, hanging in the daytime heat waiting for a buyer. On the right are a number of vehicle repair shops, where fathers and sons (who should be in school) work together to keep the city's cars on the road. Their ingenuity and ability to keep these old things running simply amaze me.

As we slowly move past the shops, a large graveyard appears on the left, empty, as always, of people. For the next fifteen minutes, as we wind our way up the switchbacks, we constantly have children running beside the Bisons, shouting out for food, water and candy, with their hands outstretched towards the vehicles. I'm always afraid that one will stumble and fall under our wheels, but they jump nimbly over the rocks and holes in their paths, keeping pace beside us. The second half of the hill is too steep and rocky for houses and we continue up the remainder of the hill unbothered by running, screaming children.

Despite what we see as we drive through the city, the view from TV Hill is amazing and, on some days, a thing of beauty. When we stand on top of the bunker, we can do a complete three-hundred-and-sixty-degree turn and look out over the whole city, and make out the mosques, the new buildings, the roads, the embassies and the military bases. If we listen carefully we can pick out people yelling, honking their horns, animals braying or barking, and the constant drum of airplanes and helicopters leaving and arriving at KIA (Kabul International Airport). On a clear day, the only thing that stops our view is either our own eyesight or the snow-capped mountain peaks that surround Kabul. Not every day is the view so majestic, and quite often the city is covered by a haze of smoke and dirt. I have stood on top of TV Hill and actually watched a dirt storm roll across the city, a towering wall of dirt hundreds of metres high, like something out of a movie, literally hiding a city of a million-plus people from view.

Today is one of those clear days, and I take the opportunity to snap a few pictures of the surrounding hills to send to Nathalie and the boys. As I take the pictures, my driver tells me we are going to be delayed for at least an hour due to an incident near Camp Souter, the British camp, which is on our way. He doesn't have many details, and when I scan the city with my binoculars, I can't see anything out of the ordinary happening. Of course, everything here is out of the ordinary compared to life in Canada, but you learn to recognize which explosions and gunfire are normal and which aren't. Not seeing anything unusual, I shrug and put the binos away and look over at Pte Russell. "I'm going to sprawl out for a bit here on the bench till they let us move. Wake me up if something happens, alright?" I tell him. He laughs, "You mean if something else happens?" TV Hill is a secure area, so I drop my flak jacket on my seat, and shoot back, laughing, "You know what I mean." As I stretch out on the Bison crew bench, my feet hanging over the seat onto the rear ramp, and my rifle tucked in beside me, Pte Russell takes over my crew commander's seat so he can man the C-6 and the radio. I reach up and tap him on the back of the leg, and he looks down. "Wake me up in a half hour so you can crash if you want," I instruct him. He mutters something in response, but I don't catch it, and I turn over and close my eyes. I've known Pte Russell long enough to know he won't wake me up unless he has to. With the sounds of the city far below, coupled with the oven-like conditions in the back of the Bison, I quickly doze off, noticing that at least up this high it doesn't smell.

These memories creep into my dreams a year and a half later, and when the alarm goes off in the morning, for a moment I think it's one of the alarms in the Bison. Sitting up, I wonder why Pte Russell hasn't turned it off yet. My feet hit the hard-wood floor before I realize it's not one of the Bison alarms, and I haven't been sleeping on the crew bench. It's 6:45 and I am standing in my bedroom reaching for the alarm clock so it doesn't wake Nathalie up. The heat in the house is stifling because I forgot to turn the air conditioner on last night, and though Petawawa in mid-July is not Afghanistan, it's definitely one of the hotter summers that I can remember. Nathalie is still sleeping, so I head into the kitchen to make some coffee and let the dog out.

We are down to my last week at home, and I try to spend as much time with Nathalie and the boys as I can. Up until now, even though we all knew I was leaving, it seems like it hadn't really sunk in. The boys have tears in their eyes now when they talk about me leaving, and ask why I have to go again so soon. I explain as best as I can that it's my job, and everyone has to take turns leaving, but that this tour should be it for a couple of years. I once again promise them that I'll make it up to them when I get back, and promise myself that I'll make sure I do.

On my last night at home, we allow the boys to stay up until nine. I tuck them in and they do their best to keep their tears in, telling me to be careful. I promise to call them and email them as much as I can. I spend the rest of the night lying awake beside a fitfully sleeping Nathalie. I wonder what's on her mind as she lies there, but she has kept most of her thoughts to herself this time around. I know she is still worried, probably more about the troops' pending move to Kandahar, but she has handled this deployment much differently than the last one. I guess I have, too, as we both have a better idea of what to expect.

In the morning I get up, and after I'm dressed, I just sit on the couch with Jeremy, Jonathan and Alex (Alex being my fourteen-year-old son from a previous relationship, who has come to see me off and help with his half-brothers). I remind them to help out as much as they can, to listen to Nathalie and not give her a hard time. We had decided that only Nathalie would go with me to the bus, as the boys took it too hard last time, so at nine thirty, I stand up and say it's time for me to go. We take a few pictures together outside, and I give them each a hug and a kiss, and tell them to be good and that I love them. Jonathan and Jeremy are both crying now, and I tell them not to worry, that it will be over before they know it. I stay as long as I can, then tell Alex to take them into the house. Nathalie and I head off to the Silver Dart Arena (where we will depart from), and as I walk down the street holding Nathalie's hand, she reminds me one last time to be careful and not to be a hero.

Halfway down the next block, I hear Jonathan yelling "Dad!" and I turn and see him standing barefoot at the end of our street, crying and waving. It breaks my heart and I motion for him to catch up. When he gets to us, I give him a big hug, and remind him that he's a good boy, and that it will be over soon. I send him back home, and we continue the short walk to the arena as I wipe my eyes.

Nathalie and I spend our last forty-five minutes waiting outside the arena for the buses to show up, and when they finally do, we say our own goodbyes. We tell each other we will be alright, and I promise to call as soon as I can. I wipe away Nathalie's tears and kiss her one last time before I head for the bus.

The trip is as long as I remember it, but I spend most of the fourteen-plus hours of flight time reading *Shake Hands with the Devil* by Roméo Dallaire, and catching the odd catnap. The final Herc (CC-130 Hercules) ride into Afghanistan isn't quite as horrible as I remember the last one being, and I don't feel like I'll be sick as we hug the contours into Kabul.

When we disembark from the plane, I'm almost expecting the same fanfare as when we arrived for Roto 0 back in 2003, but we make the walk across the tarmac unobserved, save by our own Recce OC (officer commanding) and sergeant major. The short trip from the Kabul International Airport is exactly as I remember it. The dust permeates the armoured Bison that six of us are crammed into, and the stench of Kabul is not far behind it. It's not a smell easily forgotten, and for a few brief minutes, I think it might actually make me sick this time, but it quickly passes.

Arriving at Camp Julian, I notice it doesn't seem as hot now in Kabul as it did on Roto 0. Maybe it's because of the extremely hot weather in Petawawa before I left, or maybe I just know what to expect. A thick layer of dust has settled over the camp, making it look much older than its two years. The camp is also now shared by a host of nations, such as the United States, Slovenia, Hungary, Norway and Italy, with Romanian troops scheduled to move in shortly.

I manage to phone Nathalie and the boys a couple of times in the first two weeks, and we are actually surprised at how quickly time is going by—and hopeful that the rest of the tour goes as fast as it seems to be going right now. Before we know it, I will be headed to Kandahar, which brings me that much closer to coming home. It's a little ironic that, when you're at home before you come over, you tend to think about what's going on over here, and when you're here, you think about what's going on at home and when you get to go back.

In the meantime, we both do our best not to worry the other with our separate lives, Nathalie always telling me that the boys are being good and listening, and that she is doing fine. And I'm always telling Nathalie that I'm not leaving the camp as much as I do, and that there is never any danger.

When it's all over and we're back together, the truth will come out—my stories of danger and close calls, and Nathalie's of the trials and tribulations of being a single mom to two boys. Time has a way of dulling the memories and all those close calls and dangerous times will be trivialized and won't seem as bad, until the next time I prepare to deploy, and all those feelings and memories come rushing back again. Till then, we will keep each other close, making up now for time we will certainly lose later.

TWO DAYS IN PANJWAYI
BY
CORPORAL RYAN PAGNACCO

Ryan Pagnacco was born on September 7, 1979, in Simcoe, Ontario. He joined the 1596 Highland Fusiliers of Canada, Royal Canadian Army Cadet Corps, and at age nineteen, joined the Canadian Forces Primary Reserves with the Royal Highland Fusiliers of Canada. In 2005, Ryan applied for a tour in Afghanistan, on Task Force 3-06, and deployed with 8 Platoon, Charles Company, First Battalion, Royal Canadian Regiment, in August 2006, as part of the reserve augmentation to the regular force battle group. He now lives with his wife in Kitchener, Ontario.

I had been in Afghanistan for only three weeks when one span of forty-eight hours changed my life forever, and very nearly ended it halfway up a mountain on the south bank of the Arghandab River. I had thought a more opportune time for my demise would have been the day before, during the battle of Panjwayi, or even during the previous two weeks, when my platoon repeatedly encountered the enemy during patrols and convoys. But, to my surprise, my brush with death came just after breakfast on September 4, 2006.

And when I thought the end was near, my life didn't flash before my eyes. I didn't cry. I didn't pray. I didn't try to repent, and I wasn't angry or even upset. Only three thoughts went through my mind:

"I'm not dying here . . . not like this."

"I wonder if my bagpipes survived the attack." And,

"I wonder how funny it would be if I asked the medic to draw a curly moustache and pointy beard on my face with that Magic Marker."

I was a reservist from the Royal Highland Fusiliers of Canada, based in Cambridge, Ontario, and one of only ten in that regiment selected to serve overseas. Only four of those ten were then attached to a regular-force rifle company. It was a great honour to be selected. I was attached to 8 Platoon, Charles Company, 1 RCR (First Battalion, Royal Canadian Regiment), augmented by reservists to bolster the number of soldiers in Afghanistan. Charles Company was one of three combat-infantry companies in the battle group, and was at the tip of the sword every day we left the wire.

We spent two weeks in Kandahar, moving from forward operating base to patrol base to open desert and back again. We were in and out of firefights with the enemy, surviving only on rations and with one set of clean clothing. After those two weeks, we finally returned to Kandahar Air Field for supplies, ammunition and a change of clothing, and we even managed to get in some downtime.

Three days later we headed back into the Panjwayi district, where we had spent the last two weeks, to conduct Operation Medusa. This was to be the biggest multinational operation in Afghanistan since the beginning of the war, and was the biggest operation Canada had participated in since the Korean War. It would include air support from the U.S. and British Air Forces, as well as support elements from just about every other nation in theatre.

The goal of the mission was to increase security in the Panjwayi district by routing the Taliban from the Arghandab Valley greenbelt and the surrounding villages. To ensure this security, our engineers would build a road linking two major highways straight through the village of Pashmul, providing a secure route for the locals, as well as a supply route to a central forward operating base in the middle of this former Taliban stronghold, manned by soldiers from the Afghan National Army.

Charles Company's role in Operation Medusa was to secure the village of Pashmul from the south side of the Arghandab River, rout the Taliban, and then provide security for the combat engineers as they ploughed the road through. First ones in, and that's the way we liked it.

On August 30, we received our orders and began preparing for the mission. For the first few days, our LAVs (light-armoured vehicles) would engage the enemy from a distance, while our air support would pound hard targets with guided bombs. At least that was the plan.

In the wee hours of the morning of September 1, we mounted up into our LAVs and made our way back out to Panjwayi. But this time, it wasn't out to an FOB or a patrol base; we headed to a position in the middle of the desert, where we would prepare to move into a firing position overlooking the Arghandab River valley and the Taliban-occupied village of Pashmul.

When we arrived at our first position, we parked our vehicles in a circle, facing outward, in what we refer to as a leaguer, to wait out the first phase of the mission. While we waited, the coalition air force was dropping leaflets over the greenbelt, warning civilians to leave and letting the Taliban know we were coming. Reconnaissance teams, snipers, unmanned aerial vehicles (UAVs) and other air assets surveyed the area awaiting our arrival, while we spent the day taking turns in the LAV turret, watching the surrounding mountain ranges for insurgent activity, and relaxing on the warm sand.

Along the road beside our position, we watched as vehicles full of women, children and old men fled from the direction of the Pashmul valley. On their way out, they passed more vehicles full of what we describe as fighting-age males—men old enough to fight, some as young as sixteen years old—heading directly into the valley. We knew we would be seeing these men again, only next time, it would be in battle. But for now, they were unarmed, and in accordance with our rules of engagement, we did not fire.

Traffic on the road stayed constant throughout the day. We watched and waited.

The day was broken up by one-hour shifts in the LAV's turret, weapons maintenance and cleaning, and lots of rest and relaxation in the shade of the vehicles. We moved around the LAV, chasing the shade as the sun crossed the sky. It was hot. When the wind blew, it blew hot sand. The sand had the texture of talcum powder and stung when it hit skin.

The sergeant gave us the word, and we began to police up our garbage and personal kit. Once in the back of the LAV, things were calm. Everyone was in his place, and we were ready to roll. The LAV's engine roared and we fired up the CSAM (crew situational awareness monitor) so we could see what we were heading into.

The radio crackled over the PA system in the back of the LAV. "All call signs three-two, this is three-two." The order to roll came down from the platoon commander. The two air sentries in my LAV stepped further down into their holes in preparation to move.

BOOM! The blast shook the side of the vehicle. Our air sentries dropped into the seats they were standing on. Dust poured over the open air-sentry hatches.

"That was close! Was that mortar or an RGP?" I asked our bird-gunners, but they knew as much as I did.

The troops in the back of the LAV were shaken. But we were ready to fight.

After a few moments of confusion, the radio came to life again. "Call sign three-two, our platoon headquarters' LAV has backed over an anti-tank mine." They were all okay—only minor injuries to one of their air sentries—but their LAV was immobilized, having lost two wheels off the right side of the vehicle. We dismounted and began drills for minefields, searching the area around our vehicle and providing security for the soldiers of the damaged LAV as they prodded the ground with their bayonets in search of more mines.

Before long, the combat engineers arrived to recover the damaged LAV and to search the area with a mine sweeper for more hidden gems. The rest of us stood shifts in the open desert providing security. I tried not to think about this. I tried not to think about everything I had learned about minefields during training. I especially tried not to think about how we cover our minefields with machine-gun fire, and how although Canada doesn't use anti-personnel mines, a lot of other countries do. Russia, during their campaign in Afghanistan, used a lot of them, and the Taliban surely wouldn't hesitate to do the same. I tried not to think of all this because now, as the sun set and darkness fell, I was standing in the middle of what we believed to be a minefield.

We were lucky. There was only the one mine, and the engineers gave the all-clear. We were now down a LAV and all the firepower associated with it, particularly its powerful 25mm Bushmaster cannon. All of the remaining LAVs were now burdened with the extra equipment, rations, cases of water, ammo, soldiers and personal kit from the damaged LAV.

Plans had to change to accommodate this incident. We would spend the night in the middle of the desert.

We slept in the sand with all of our gear on, just in case, with the warm blowing sand as a blanket. Even after the excitement of the day, I slept fairly well. I took my turn in the turret at midnight, and at 0330 we were told to prepare to move to the assembly area. By 0345, we were on the road.

We had only gone a half-hour down the road when we came under fire from a small group of insurgents. We stopped and the LAV gunners and air sentries returned fire. A few weeks ago, this would have shocked me, but we had all become used to the sound of RPGs (rocket-propelled grenades) and bullets flying over our vehicle. The convoy stopped only long enough to deal with the ambush, and then we were on our way again.

Once in the assembly area, all we could do was wait. There was no getting out of the boat now: we were too close to the enemy. The back of the LAV felt even tighter, and to add to the tension, we were all anxious to get into position. The gunners had been given fairly liberal "open-fire" orders during the briefing; the air force had been dropping leaflets for the past few days, so whoever was left in the valley was "not friendly" and would be considered an open target. From what we saw moving along the road, the Taliban were the only people left. We couldn't wait to see the light show.

The order came across the radio and we were moving. When the vehicle came to a stop again, all we could hear was the 25mm firing. *Thump, thump, thump.*

We watched the battle on the CSAM. We might as well have been watching a war movie, with the explosions, fire and tracer rounds zipping all over the screen. We cheered on the action.

A few hours passed, and we were now out of the LAV with only our ballistic vests on, relaxing in the shade of the vehicles, or in the ruins of the village of Bazaar-e-Panjwayi. And the LAVs battled on. *Thump, thump, thump.*

Occasionally, the British or U.S. Air Force would drop something big. When we heard word come over the radio, we'd grab our cameras and wait patiently for the flash, the plume of smoke and the delayed thump. We knew what they were hitting: there were very few targets that deserved to be hit so hard. Three of the targets were the source of mortars fired at our base in the previous weeks; they were also the same three places where soldiers from previous tours took fire and lost lives—the White School, the Yellow Building and the Mosque.

These were the main fortifications used by the Taliban in the area. The White School, once a school for eager children, was now a stronghold for insurgents, and the Yellow Building was being used to house weapons for the fighters who came into the area unarmed. As for the Mosque, the Taliban knew we would hesitate to fire on a religious site, and so they would take refuge there, appearing only long enough to fire mortar bombs at us. After watching bomb after bomb drop on these targets, I wondered how anything could survive. I figured that when we went in, we'd be walking into a ghost town.

As the air force and artillery bombarded the area, we relaxed and rotated through a machine-gun position on the top of a small mountain beside our firing line. This location became the best vantage point for the platoon's amateur photographers. I took pictures of the valley, the river, the ruins of the village we occupied, and the other small peaks and dusty valleys that surrounded us. The rocky sandstone mountain ranges we sat upon provided stark contrast to the lush green fields and bright blue-green flowing water in the valley.

While we sat on the side of the mountain, relaxing in what little shade we could find, away from the LAVs as they fired, something seemed different. No one said anything about it at first, but then, as we all lay there in the shade, we all felt it . . . and smelled it. The wind blowing across the mountains was cool and smelled sweet, like flowers. It was a very welcome change to the normal hot blowing sand and stench of feces we'd experienced everywhere else. We basked in it, joked about it to each other, and enjoyed the surreal moment: explosions, smoke, the thump of the 25s, and the sweet, cool breeze from the valley below.

It was then, as we lay on the side of the mountain, that we first heard the roaring sound we would never forget. It would be burned into all our memories that day and then again the next. It was the sound of the infamous 30mm chain gun mounted on the nose of the U.S. Air Force A-10 Fairchild Thunderbolt II Warthog ground support aircraft. We watched this spectacular plane weave and turn across the sky, line up to fire and, when in position, unleash hell. A trail of smoke escaped from the front of the slow-moving bird, but there was no sound yet. Along the ground, ahead of the jet, a trail of sparks danced as the high-explosive incendiary ammunition exploded like grenades on impact. The sound came from the ground first, like popcorn, then, a moment later, the muzzle report from the aircraft echoed across the valley. The targets on the ground were much closer to us than the jet, so with its every pass we would see and hear the effects first, and then we would hear the burp of the gun, a sound best described by a fellow soldier: "It's like the gun is ripping the sky a new asshole."

And that was the sound: a roar, a rip, a belch. However you choose to describe it, it was the sound of raw, awesome destruction. And we cheered it on.

The sounds of battle, which first excited us, now became background music while we continued to rest and wait for orders. We were told this would be a three-day bombardment, so we settled in.

As the sun began to set over the valley, our platoon warrant officer, Frank Mellish, called me over to our platoon's G-Wagon jeep. He had a green backpack in his hand. In the pack was my set of bagpipes. I had pulled them out of my barracks box back in KAF (Kandahar Air Field) specifically to bring them on this operation. This was the first time I'd brought them out since I had been in country.

While on work-up training, I had been made the unofficial piper for 8 Platoon and then Charles Company. WO Mellish had asked me to play many times while in the field during exercises, even when we conducted training back in CFB Wainwright, Alberta. Some of the troops in the platoon loved it; some of the troops hated it, especially when I played reveille early in the morning.

That evening, when WO Mellish handed me my pipes and asked me to play, I felt as though I were following in the footsteps of the combat pipers of my great-grandfather's generation. It filled me with pride. I made my way to the edge of the ridge, beside the LAVs as they fired into the valley, overlooking the battlefield with the enemy less than half a mile away. I pieced the pipes together, brought them up and began to play. I expected the troops to complain, as it woke many of them up. I expected someone to yell, as I was out in the open with no protective equipment on and no weapon in hand. I expected the catcalls and hoots I had received from the troops in the past. But there were none.

The sound of the pipes echoed across the valley, broken only by the sound of the 25s firing. The troops watched, took pictures, and cheered after each tune. Even the U.S. and ANA (Afghan National Army) soldiers watched, and some took pictures as well. This was the first time I had played my pipes in Afghanistan.

After a few sets of tunes, I stopped for a sip of water.

"PIPER! 'BLACK BEAR'!" yelled Mellish.

"Black Bear" was his favourite tune, and every time I played, he requested it. Unfortunately, I don't know it well. I set down my water bottle and played "Black Bear," or at least the first part of it, as that's the part everyone seems to know so well. I continued to play right into a set I had often played with my home regiment's band that went nicely with "Black Bear": "Scotland the Brave," "Wings" and "Flett from Flotta." I ended my impromptu concert with a sombre slow air, a farewell to the setting sun, and then packed up my pipes.

As the sun set over the Arghandab Valley and the cool, sweet-smelling wind drifted across our position on the side of the mountain, we settled in for the night on the sandy slopes, under the protection of the LAVs, snipers and air supports. It seems odd to me now, thinking back, how comfortable we were as we lay down our heads, while only a few hundred feet away the enemy sat, waiting in bunkers and mud huts, close enough to strike at any time.

That same cool breeze brought a slight chill with it at night, and I found myself requiring a blanket to be comfortable, which was rare when sleeping out in the desert. Throughout the night, the air strikes and LAVs only let up a bit, and occasionally the flash of a large bomb detonating in the valley would wake me up. And if it wasn't the flash, it was the thunderous boom that followed. After the first few blasts, I covered my head with my ranger blanket and put in my earplugs.

My dreams that night were vivid. This was partially due to the reality of my situation and partially due to the anti-malarial medication we had taken, which is known for its nightmare-related side effects. I dreamed my platoon left in the night without me, leaving me with only my rifle and equipment and my bagpipes. So I played. I played until I was surrounded by Taliban. I would awake in a panic from these dreams, watch the light show in the valley for a few moments, then drift back to sleep.

At 0400, we awoke with orders to eat, police up our gear and be ready to move. We were going in ahead of schedule. Three days of bombardment had been reduced to one day. Needless to say, we weren't very happy with this plan, but ours is not to question why.

By 0500, we were in the back of the LAVs and on our way to the assault line. I looked around at the boys: we were ready, we were anxious, we were good to go. And we were all a little scared.

This wasn't going to be a ten-minute roadside contact with the enemy; this wasn't going to be a few mortars, some AK-47 fire and a couple RPGs; this was going to be combat.

We crossed the Arghandab around 0630. This was supposed to be the biggest river crossing since World War II and was to include a bridging effort by the combat engineers; when all was said and done, however, only the bottom two inches of tread on the LAV's huge tires got wet, as the river was only about that deep. It looked much bigger on the map, I suppose. We manoeuvred into position on the north side of the Arghandab, in the Pashmul village, and provided cover for the combat engineers as they began ploughing their road through the fields.

We dismounted and began our cordon search, as practised many times in training, and then took up defensive positions. I looked around at the field I was kneeling in—the vegetation was harvested and the field was freshly ploughed, but I could still find remnants of what was growing there: poppies. I found a few petals first, and then, buried under some dirt, I found the flower. We were in poppy fields, like the fields our great-grandfathers fought in during the Great War.

Also scattered across the ground were the many different leaflets dropped by the coalition. I gathered up as many as I could while I covered my arcs. I soon realized that if something was going to happen, it would be here, and it would be soon. I looked around again, and I found myself standing out in the open, the farthest person away from the LAV.

We were recalled to the LAV and moved into another position as the engineers manoeuvred around the field. We conducted our cordon again, and again I found myself farthest away from the LAV. To my left was a forest of marijuana plants, each about ten feet tall, and in front of me was the compound, an eerily quiet and empty collection of mud huts with thatch roofs. The old cliché went through my mind: It's quiet . . . too quiet. I pulled out my digital camera and started taking pictures. I took shots of the compound, the forest of weed, and the empty poppy fields.

Again we were recalled to the LAV to move. The engineers were breaching into a new area and needed cover. Once in our new position, we dismounted again and took up defensive positions close to the LAV. I thought of an old army expression: "On the bus, off the bus."

At 0730, the calm was broken. The sound of a whistle and a flare fired from the direction of the infamous White School signalled the attack. Within seconds, we found ourselves in a well-planned and well-executed U-shaped ambush. We were under fire from all directions, except the way we had come in. The enemy came out of the compounds and the dense fields of marijuana that, only five minutes before, I had been taking pictures of while they used it as cover to move around us undetected, waiting until we were in the right place.

I heard the sound of AK fire and could feel the bullets zipping past my head. We opened fire immediately. They were close, some as close as sixty feet. Cpl Bruce Moncur, the other reservist in my section, and I laid down fire: Bruce with his C-9 light machine gun, and me with my C-7 assault rifle. Other members of our section were tasked to help support other sections on the flanks and protect the C-6 machine gun. At the height of the battle, there were only three of us at our section's LAV, besides the crew in the vehicle—the sergeant, the other reservist, and me. Everyone else had been tasked to help fight elsewhere.

We kept firing, and they kept coming.

The battle raged on for a few hours, during which we all had our close calls. A thousand-pound guided bomb, which was supposed to be dropped "danger close" (roughly three hundred feet from our position), ended up falling about eighty feet in front of our platoon. Luckily, it had disarmed once it had wandered off its course, or I wouldn't be here to write about it (and neither would the rest of my platoon, or the platoon to our right flank).

As the fighting continued, the casualties mounted. Although we were fighting very effectively, we were still surrounded and grossly outnumbered by about ten to one. We had already lost two soldiers in the opening shots of the battle, and the wounded were multiplying at the casualty collection point. We went in with two platoons and engineer assets: roughly eighty soldiers. We faced an estimated four hundred to eight hundred insurgent fighters who had waited, and planned, and dug in. After hours of fighting, we knew we would have to withdraw if we were to remain a combat-effective company. We finally left with four killed and at least ten wounded.

During the withdrawal, my section's LAV was used to collect the casualties, so I rode with another section, with about ten of us crammed into the back of a vehicle designed for seven. When the ramp lowered again, we were in a *wadi* (dry river bed) beside the Arghandab River. I jumped out and went looking for my section. Along the way, I learned that a LAV from the other platoon, 7 Platoon, had been hit and damaged and left on the battlefield. I also learned that Cpl Rodney Grubb, another reservist, and a close friend from my home regiment, was in the LAV when it was hit. I didn't know if he was dead or alive.

After searching around the *wadi*, I found my LAV and my section. As I approached, the ramp dropped. The inside of the LAV was covered in blood. And there on the benches and floor lay two body bags and two stretchers, each holding the lifeless body of a fallen comrade.

I grabbed a corner of one of the bags, assisted by three others from my section, and we carried it over to the casualty collection point. Inside was the body of WO Nolan, the platoon warrant officer of 7 Platoon. He was one of the first killed in the battle, as his G-Wagon was hit by an RPG. We returned to the LAV to grab one of the stretchers. On it was the body of WO Mellish, who was killed by an RPG as he went to help WO Nolan, his friend, during the battle. I couldn't believe Mellish was gone. It all seemed so surreal, as if he was going to wake up and yell at us for jostling him around too much as we carried him. But he didn't.

The other troops brought the bodies of Sergeant Stachnik, an engineer I had never met, and Private Cushley, who I only knew casually from parties in the barracks back in Petawawa. All were excellent soldiers. They will all be missed by many.

The adrenalin had worn off, and I felt drained, physically and emotionally. As I walked back, I heard the sergeant who had taken over for WO Nolan talking to the section commander whose LAV had been left on the battlefield. The sergeant asked if he had accounted for everyone. The section commander said he couldn't find Grubb, my reservist friend from my home unit. I couldn't believe what I was hearing. I tried to compose myself before returning to the LAV. There was still work to be done, and this was no time to lament.

We began resupplying the LAV, making trips back and forth to the supply truck for water and ammo, while the artillery and air force continued bombarding the Taliban positions. We weren't out of danger, though, we were still close enough to take fire, and the rounds kept coming in. On one trip over to the supplies, with my spirits down and no energy, I heard a familiar voice. A group of medics and a sergeant were standing around a solider sitting on an ammo crate and holding a bandage to his face. It was Grubb!

I walked over to him, but couldn't say anything. I couldn't even begin to express the things going through my mind. I just stood there with a box of ammo on one shoulder and another in my other hand, and stared at him. He looked up and smiled and gave his usual greeting: "Hey, buddy."

I grumbled and swore and walked away. All I could think was, "That son of a bitch." He was supposed to be dead or missing, and I'd felt so bad about it, and all that time, he was fine. Just a few nicks and scratches. I was relieved and angry at the same time.

Once we finished loading up the LAVs, we mounted up and withdrew back to our original firing positions on the side of the mountain, south of the Arghandab. When we stopped again, the ramps dropped and so did all our gear. Not a word was spoken. We set up camouflage netting to provide some shade from the midday sun. The reality of the battle set in, and we all felt the losses as we reflected on the day. We ate, or at least we tried, and we slept. Or at least we tried.

The company commander gathered us, by platoon, and we discussed what could have been done better and what we did well. It is normal, after an operation, to conduct an AAR, or after action review. But this one was fraught with angst and sorrow due to the losses. Phrases such as "It would be nice if," common in AARs after training exercises, were replaced with "It should have been." And there was much heated discussion about what should have been. Through it all there was the sense of loss and sadness.

We were given the rest of the day to reflect on the morning's events and relax while our leadership formulated a new plan for the next day. Meanwhile, our support elements, air and artillery, continued to bombard the insurgent positions in the valley. This continued into the night as we slept.

I don't remember dreaming that night. I was so exhausted from the day that sleep came easily. I woke up only a few times, usually to the sound of the bombs and the flashes of light, like the night before. But I returned to sleep quickly. The next morning was no different from the morning before. We woke up at 0500 and had breakfast. We had become very sick of IMP (individual meal pack) rations, so we resorted to junk-food meals every once in a while. That morning my breakfast consisted of a bottle of water with juice crystals and a Pop-Tart, which we seemed to have an abundance of, as we had swiped a few large boxes of them from the kitchen in KAF.

We were told to burn our garbage, as we had nowhere to store it and we couldn't just leave it in place, since it could potentially reveal tactical information. The morning air was chilly, so the garbage fire served two purposes: warmth and garbage removal. I stood by the fire eating my breakfast, chatting with a fellow soldier, Mark Graham, in the dark, cool hours before dawn. I'd only really gotten to know Mark during the last two months in Petawawa for work-up training, and I admired him greatly. He was not only an excellent soldier but also a former Olympic athlete. I threw my garbage in the fire and started to make my way back to my weapon and protective equipment to prepare for the day.

I made it no further than five feet from the fire when I heard what sounded like popcorn popping. Then sparks flew past me. People started yelling, "Who put ammo in the fire?" But it wasn't bullets cooking off, we were being attacked. My legs went numb and I fell forward. I'd been hit. I couldn't feel my legs. I didn't look, but if they were gone, I didn't want to know. I pulled myself up with my arms and tried to crawl to my weapon; if we were under attack, I'd have to fight, wounded or not.

The attack kicked up so much dust that I couldn't see much around me. Shadows ran all around, and I could hear people yelling. I kept crawling. Then I heard it. The same sound we had cheered the day before now made us shudder in disbelief. It was the roar of the chain gun on the nose of the A-10 Warthog. We had been hit by friendly fire. After hearing that sound, and realizing what had happened, I felt my heart sink and I stopped trying to get to my weapon and gear. Now all I could do was fix myself up and help others around me. But I had two problems: I didn't have my first-aid kit, and I couldn't move my legs. It was also becoming apparent that I had been hit in the right arm, too, as it was going numb.

A fellow soldier from my platoon came over to help me. At first he thought I was someone else and kept calling me this other person's name before rolling me over. Once I was on my back, he could see that I'd been hit pretty badly. He applied tourniquets to both legs and my right arm and called the platoon medic over to double-check my condition. By this time, the dust had settled, and we could see the extent of the damage. The badly wounded soldiers were being treated by soldiers who were also wounded. And those who could were treating themselves.

Once the bleeding stopped, I was loaded onto a stretcher and taken over to the casualty collection point to wait for evacuation to the hospital at Kandahar Air Field. All the wounded were categorized by priority: Priority One included those who required immediate medical care; Priority Two, those with severe wounds but who did not require immediate care to survive; and Priority Three, the ambulatory (walking wounded) and the deceased, as they required little or no treatment other than what had been rendered on site. When the medic first conducted triage, I was categorized as Priority Two, as my wounds had been stabilized. Once I arrived at the CCP (casualty collection point), the medic noticed I was now lying in a pool of blood, and rolled me over to search for more wounds. He found two in my lower back, and bumped me up to Priority One.

While we waited for evacuation, the medic periodically checked the wounds and eased, then retightened, the tourniquets. Each time a tourniquet is applied, or reapplied, the time has to be recorded to ensure that it's not left on too long, which could cause necrosis of the limb below the tourniquet. The normal procedure is to record the time on the forehead of the casualty with a marker. As we waited, and as the medic continued the rounds of the wounded, I collected more and more markings on my head and face: the time, crossed out over and over, my ZAP number, a means of quickly identifying soldiers over the radio, and my blood type, all scribbled on my face.

I looked around at those who were tending to me. They stood over me with the most serious and depressing looks. I looked around at my fellow wounded soldiers, some conscious, some not, and my thoughts turned dark. I was cold, but it wasn't the weather. I couldn't stop shaking. And I still couldn't feel my legs. I wiggled my toes and looked to see if they moved. They did. I lifted my right arm and wiggled my fingers. They moved, too. But I noticed something I hadn't before. Something was dangling from the tips of my middle and ring fingers on my right hand. It looked like some kind of material soaked in blood. I looked more closely: the material was the tissue of my finger tips. They had been chewed up by shrapnel. Under the dangling flesh, I could see bone.

The fingers began to hurt, as did everything else. The medic applied morphine.

The troops around me asked me what I needed, and it wasn't long before I had a blanket over me, but I still couldn't stop shaking. I thought about the attack, and then it dawned on me: my bagpipes were still in the G-Wagon. I wondered if they had survived. Then I wondered if I would survive. I was tired, and cold, but I didn't want to close my eyes.

The morphine kicked in, and suddenly everything seemed way more serious than it needed to be. Everyone seemed to be looking at me as if it was going to be the last time they'd see me alive, but they didn't want to tell me. I could hear the choppers coming in to get us.

The medic came back to ease and tighten the tourniquets one last time before I was evacuated. She wrote the time in what little space was left on my forehead and was about to leave to check on the next casualty. I don't know if it was the morphine or just my sick sense of humour, but I thought if I had her draw a curly moustache and pointy beard on my face, it would lighten the mood a little. I asked her, and after much debate, and some peer pressure, she finally gave in. It seemed to raise the spirits of the troops standing over me. I giggled and shivered.

In the helicopter, as well as in the hospital at KAF, I got the same response: the medics and doctors would laugh, and then ask me who had drawn on me. I had some fun with it, at first denying any knowledge of it, and then, after a good laugh, telling them that I was responsible. And, of course, out came the cameras. The nurses and doctors even crowded in for a group picture at one point, but I have yet to see any photos.

After multiple X-rays, CT scans and other tests, I was rushed into surgery to have the shrapnel removed and the wounds cleaned. As they wheeled me into the operating room, I asked the doctor if he could save any pieces of shrapnel they removed so that I could keep them as souvenirs. I thought this was a fairly morbid request, but it turns out it is very common. So common that the doctor was going to save them anyway and present them to me after the operation.

Unfortunately, all the shrapnel that was removed was either too small or disintegrated as it was being taken out, but thanks to some very deep wounds in my back, I was able to "keep" two pieces.

When the rounds from the A-10's gun had hit the ground, they'd exploded into small shards of hot liquid metal that flew everywhere in little sparks, along with fragments of other debris from the impact area. These pieces of shrapnel had pierced my right arm through my inner bicep, exiting near my elbow, as well as my left leg, entering through the back of my thigh and exiting very close to my femoral artery, leaving a gaping four-inch hole.

I was lucky, the damage could have been much worse. During training, we had learned that a wound to the femoral artery, if untreated, could result in death within five minutes, due to loss of blood. Other pieces of shrapnel had chewed up my left calf, the backs of my left and right thighs, with holes in both going right down to the bone, and had nearly taken off the tips of two fingers on my right hand.

The two pieces in my back had made their way in a zigzag pattern all the way down to my kidneys. Those pieces were so perilously positioned that any attempt to remove them could have permanently damaged the surrounding tissue and organs. So there they'll stay, to set off metal detectors and prevent me from ever being able to have MRIs, until the pieces either surface or cause enough problems to warrant going in after them.

They're my souvenirs from Afghanistan, courtesy of the U.S. Air Force.

The hospital was chaotic for the rest of the day, treating as many as forty wounded soldiers from both the friendly fire and the ongoing battle in Panjwayi. After my surgery, I was wheeled into the hall to await transfer to a recovery area. Seeing some of the other wounded in the emergency ward, I remembered how many other soldiers had been around the fire, as close as I had been to the point of impact. Soldiers from my platoon walked by, and I reached out from my gurney to ask if they knew what was going on. The heavy doses of morphine made this difficult, but I grabbed on to someone and started asking questions. I asked him if everyone was okay, and if anyone had been killed.

The soldier's face went pale. He didn't want to tell me.

I asked again, and his only response was, "Mark Graham."

I confirmed with another soldier: Mark Graham had been killed by shrapnel. He was a good friend and an inspiration to all who knew him. He will be missed. The news of Mark's death saddened me greatly, but all I could do was lie on the gurney and stare at the ceiling.

Our company sergeant major, who had been wounded the day before in battle, made his rounds of the hospital, visiting briefly with the troops and trying his best to raise morale. With him was our company commander, who was also wounded in the friendly-fire incident. When they got to me, the CSM asked all the usual questions—"How are you doing?" "Can I get you any-thing?" et cetera, et cetera. But his next request broke my heart. He asked me if I would be able to play my bagpipes at the ramp ceremony for our fallen troops the next day.

I couldn't feel anything below my right elbow, and when I held my hand up, the wounds in my fingers still looked as bad as they had when I was first hit. I would have played from the gur-ney if I could have played at all. But I couldn't move my fingers. I couldn't even vocalize a response, I just held up my hand and felt a tear run down my cheek. I wept not for my hand, or my legs, or even my kidneys, but because I wasn't able to pay my last respects to my fallen brothers. I couldn't play the pipes for them.

I spent the day lying in a puddle of blood and plasma that leaked from the wounds in my legs. I was alive though, and that was the most important thing. The next day, those who were severely wounded, including me, were to be flown to Landstuhl, Germany, to a U.S. military hospital. Our injuries were consid-ered serious enough to warrant further medical attention out of theatre. And this was very apparent with some of the other wounded, some of whom had suffered severe head trauma or injuries that could not be treated or recovered from in Afghanistan. I was very disappointed. As much as I missed home, I didn't want to leave my platoon.

While I rested in the hospital in KAF along with more of the wounded, a nurse came around with a cordless phone so we could call our families before they learned of the attack through non-official channels. When she handed me the phone, I asked her what time it was in Canada. It was three o'clock in the morning. I refused to call my family at 3 a.m. to tell them I had been wounded. I chose to wait.

When I did finally call, about four hours later, I first phoned my fiancée, who took the news surprisingly well, and then I called my father. His reaction was exactly what I expected: he was calm, and we even joked about it to lighten the mood. The sense of humour runs in the family.

It wasn't long before I had my first visitors. A friend of my sister's, Jason "Kooch" Kucherawy, worked in KAF as a civilian, and once he had learned of my injuries, he came to the hospital to visit me. The commanding officer (CO) of my regiment, who was also on tour in Afghanistan, came by shortly after Jason did to see how I was doing. Seeing both of them lifted my morale greatly, even though, from what I'm told, it had the opposite effect on them.

Before I drifted off to sleep, I asked the nurses to wake me up for the ramp ceremony the next morning. But they couldn't agree to my request, as my wounds were too severe to have me wheeled anywhere but onto a plane headed for Germany. I protested. Their response came in the form of a sedative.

Sometime in the night, I awoke to sirens. I thought I had heard a blast or even the shriek of an RPG. One of the nurses threw a blast blanket over me, while another wheeled one of the other less wounded to a bunker.

"Are we being attacked?" I asked in a daze, thinking it could have been just the sedative and the morphine.

"Yes . . . go back to sleep," the nurse replied, and I did.

When I next awoke, it was only briefly as they loaded me onto a stretcher rack on a plane bound for Germany. And when I awoke after that, we were being loaded from the plane onto an ambulance bus. The air was cool and fresh, and everything around us was green. It almost looked like home. We were greeted at the hospital by Canadian and U.S. medical personnel, padres and media—lots of media. The care in Germany was, quite easily, the best I've ever had. We were treated quickly and efficiently, with dignity and respect. The nursing staff seemed to anticipate when we would be in pain and were quick to respond to the call button.

I celebrated my twenty-seventh birthday there, on September 7, only a few days before I was scheduled to return home to Canada. The Canadian medical staff at the hospital in Landstuhl had organized a surprise. The rest of the wounded soldiers were gathered in my room, originally just for a meeting, but after the meeting was over, a nurse brought in a Black Forest cake and a jug of locally brewed beer, both of which had been donated by a nearby inn.

Once back in Canada, I spent a week and a half in Sunnybrook Hospital in Toronto, then another week in St. Mary's Hospital in Kitchener, after which I was released for home care and physiotherapy. At that time, I was just happy to be alive and home. But it wasn't long before I began to miss my brothers back in Afghanistan.

I tried to keep myself busy, which was hard, as I could barely move around on my own. So I read everything I could about what was going on in Afghanistan, and wrote down everything I thought and felt about what had happened. I began to feel guilty about leaving my friends and wished nothing more than to be with them again, and I spent a lot of time trying to figure out a way to get back over there. I barely slept. When I did nod off, my dreams were full of visions of what had happened over there, and they kept waking me up.

I was able to keep in touch with the other wounded soldiers, and occasionally they would pass on information about the troops still overseas. I spoke to the families of the fallen soldiers occasionally, and we shared in our grief. I tried to see everything in the most positive light, but it was always clouded by my feelings of guilt.

The months passed, and I was given some amazing opportunities, as people seemed to think I was some kind of hero. I was invited to parades and dinners as a guest of honour. I was presented with a signed football from the Toronto Argonauts and was invited to watch a London Knights hockey game from a private box. The media were in constant contact, and I was interviewed several times, so much so that my fellow wounded soldiers up in Petawawa gave me the nickname "Media Whore."

Even my sister and my fiancée got in on the excitement, and began a fundraiser to replace the set of bagpipes I had been playing for eight years. These pipes, which had been on loan from the military, had travelled with me to Afghanistan and back, surviving battle and then one last Remembrance Day before being replaced by an ornate and expensive set of my very own, donated by McCallum Bagpipes of Scotland.

Nothing I could possibly say or do could ever express my gratitude to all these people for their attention, kind wishes, generous offers and thoughtful gifts. But as all this was happening, I could only think of the troops who were still over there while I was at home, enjoying my time with family and friends. I had never felt more sad and happy at the same time.

As time went on, my physical wounds began to heal, but the nightmares continued. My fiancée and I bought a house, to give me more room (and privacy) to recuperate, and we moved in on December 1, 2006. I also had a nice vacation in St. Lucia the last week of April, where my fiancée and I were finally married.

The past eight months, between getting wounded, home ownership and a wedding, have been an emotional roller coaster. Even now, in May 2007, I am thrilled to be at home with my wife. But I just can't get over the feelings of guilt and sadness, and the yearning to get back to Afghanistan.

But I guess those are feelings that I will have to deal with forever.

Our brotherhood of warriors, the finest of men, has been forged in battle: baptized by fire and quenched in tears. We became, and will always be, a fraternity of blood with a bond stronger than death.

I will remember always those few days when I truly lived and nearly died.

LETTERS HOME FROM
CAPTAIN NICHOLA GODDARD

Captain Goddard was born on May 2, 1980, in Papua New Guinea, and raised in Canada. She was a member of the Royal Canadian Horse Artillery, based in Shilo, Manitoba. She served in Afghanistan with the First Battalion, Princess Patricia's Canadian Light Infantry, from January 2006 to May 17, 2006, when she was killed during a firefight in the Panjwayi district. Below are four of the letters that Nichola Goddard emailed from Afghanistan up until two weeks before her death. They have been reprinted here with the permission of her parents, Tim and Sally Goddard, and her husband, Jason Beam.

Week 2

Hello Everyone,

I am writing from my bunk bed—we have moved up in the world and now live in a BAT (which stands for Big @$$ Tent) which is pretty cozy. There are about 200 people in each tent. There is also power, which is awesome!! I got a top bunk, so I'm happy☺ I haven't really had time to appreciate living inside a tent with power, though, because I have been so busy.

Overall, the quality of life in KAF is improving daily. The females now have their own bathroom, which is really nice. There's a lot to be said for having your own cubicle☺ Each bathroom/shower room has its own water supply. Because there are far fewer females, we always have hot water and lots of it. That is really nice, because the guys still complain about running out all of the time. I think I mentioned that in the last letter—but it's worth saying again.

I also bought a little mat for my feet in the morning. It covers up the big gravel chunks so it's not quite as bad to get off my bunk. The bunk beds are pretty little. My Sgt is 6'4" and he has to sleep diagonally—Jay would hate it! They are also quite flimsy. I almost knocked mine over climbing in without the Sgt down below to anchor me. We have a SOP (standard operating procedure) established now so there haven't been any other incidents. My crew all gets to sleep right beside one another, which I really like. The only thing to really complain about is the smell. 200 men in one tent after a busy day rivals the cess pool outside. I don't think my nose hairs will ever be the same again☺

I can't believe that we have been here for only a week. The days are all so full, time seems to fly by. On the other hand, you are never far from my thoughts. I got a letter from Victoria today (thanks! My first one). It was great to have news from home. I find that I am very cut off from the outside world. I have absolutely no idea what is going on outside of Afghanistan and even my knowledge of Afghanistan is very restricted to the Kandahar area. So—any news articles or stories would be really appreciated.

My crew is doing really well. Our morale is pretty high and we are keeping very busy. It is an amazing feeling to get out and actually do our job. I knew that we were well trained, but I didn't realize quite how well until we started actually doing road moves and patrols. I am very confident in my crew and in our equipment. Don't worry Dad, confidence does not equal carelessness. We are very careful. I find our trips "out of the wire" very tiring mentally. We are all keyed up and super alert for the whole thing, so we're all really tired when we get back. But, it is great to get out there and see the country.

Leaving KAF (Kandahar Air Field) is like moving to another world. First, we cross about 2 km of garbage. The field of garbage always has people "shopping" as Mum would say. It is quite sad. There are a couple of apartment buildings that have half collapsed. When you get to the other side, you see that they don't have a back at all. Apparently, they were hit by 500-lb bombs sometime ago. They are filled with people. The kids all run out to watch us drive by. Sometimes they wave and smile, but other times they swear at us and throw rocks. I still find it pretty shocking to see young children so full of hate at us being here. But others wave and smile and seem to want us around. It is hard to know who is right. I just have to believe that we are doing a good thing, especially when I hear our intelligence updates about the widespread violence and I see the terrible poverty.

I have seen several herds of wild camels. I'm still trying to find a tame one so that I can go for a ride. I think that must be one of those "gotta do it" things. The opportunity hasn't come up yet, but I'm only in week 2☺ Other bizarre things—the donkeys are hobbled. Their front legs are tied so close together that they can't even walk—they have to hop. Gundy would be horrified. I found it very sad to watch. On the other hand, these people have so little, it is easy to understand that they don't want their only donkey to run away.

I can't begin to describe the poverty that I have seen here. It actually makes me sick to my stomach to see how little these people have. In the countryside, there are lean-tos made out of old tarp and almost see-through cloth. It seems like dozens of people fit into them. We went to practise shooting our weapons and the locals all gathered around to watch. That was fine, but as soon as we were done, they came to scavenge the area. They collected all of the used casings from our weapons. They were actually pushing and shoving each other to get at it.

I have also never seen so many people maimed and wounded. People with crutches and people without who should have them.

I have seen about 100 men in our trips and easily double that in children, but no women so far. I don't think they realize that I am a woman when we drive by, which is fine by me.

I can see why people dream about visiting here. It is stunningly beautiful in areas. I got to see the Red Desert to the south—it was amazing. I don't think any description or photo could do it justice. It was silhouetted on both sides by the mountains to the East, and the plains to the West. It stretched South for as far as we could see. It wasn't flat, like the deserts in the movies. Instead, it was rolling and a blood red colour. The sand was so fine, you couldn't even pick it up. I will find you a cool rock, Tory, don't worry!

So far, my most interesting stories involve the insects and animals that I have seen. Still no camel spiders or scorpions, but I did see a wild stick bug—it looked just like they look at the zoo. It must have been a baby one, though, because it was very small. We've also seen some pretty cool lizards and spiders, but all small. I've got to say, I'm not really disappointed.

It has been getting steadily hotter. It reaches about 35°C in the afternoons, but drops down to about 5°C at night. As soon as the sun goes down, the temperature drops completely. I am definitely working on my tan!! We have air conditioning in our vehicle, which is awesome. Anything without our vehicle sucks more than I could ever describe. My personal protective equipment weighs about 40 lbs, plus the weight of a rucksack (between 40–60 lbs) . . . that is 2/3 of my body weight and I feel every pound of it. "Living the dream" as we all say☺

I've got to admit, the LCF (look cool factor) is pretty good. I will take lots of pictures.

I guess that is it—hopefully, the weeks continue to fly by. I trust that all is well on the home front. I miss you guys—

Nich

Week 5

March 4, 2006

Hello All,

I am afraid that this week's letter will be neither long nor particularly cheerful. There is a lot to say, but most of it is pretty serious and depressing. But, you are all in with me for good or for bad, so I'll launch into this week.

This week started off quite slow. My crew and I went out for a couple of routine patrols around the area. They were uneventful. We got to fire off some mortar rounds at one of the ranges and generally had a good time being gunners.

Early this week, I attended my second American Ramp ceremony. The service was virtually identical to the first one, except that it was emotionally much harder because the feeling that this wasn't going to be the last one was unavoidable. I'm not sure exactly how many American soldiers have been killed in theatre (between here and Iraq), but I know that it is in the mid-2500s . . . it was difficult to accept how matter of fact they were about the whole thing. It was also harder because this time it dealt with a normal soldier, just like us. The time before it had been for American special forces guys—it is easy to think of them as different from "us." But this soldier was just like any one of us, and it was horrible. I was in the first row behind the

American troops that were lining the route, and I could hear a couple of them crying. That was really tough.

Two days later, we attended the first Canadian Ramp ceremony held in theatre. This time, it was a soldier that I had lived near and worked with in Shilo. This time, I knew the pallbearers, and I was one of the soldiers lining the route. Our service was longer then the American one, but I found it very moving. The casket was driven onto the parade, and soldiers from his section acted as pallbearers. The four Canadian Padres serving in theatre said a brief blessing and short prayer, and the procession moved onto the plane. I ask that your thoughts and prayers go with the young man's family. He is survived by his wife and two young daughters.

This week was also notable in the several IED strikes and confirmed rocket attacks against coalition vehicles/convoys. Overall, it was a very emotional and high-stress week.

Fortunately, the other personnel injured in both the vehicle rollover and attacks seem to be recovering well and we finished off the week without any other serious injuries. On a more personal note, I received my posting message to Wainwright, Alberta. Jay and I will be going on a house-hunting trip on my leave in June, looking at moving sometime in August. I will start work as the Operations Officer in the Canadian Manoeuvre Training Centre in mid-September. Jay and I knew that it might happen, but it is now official. We are very excited, as are our "boys" at the thought of owning our own house☺

I don't want you to feel that I am depressed or defeated. Far from it. The longer that we are in theatre and the more that we actually interact with the Afghan people, the more I feel that we are serving a purpose here. I think that these people, through the Afghan National Army and Afghan National Police, are trying to achieve something that we in Canada have long since taken for granted. They lay down their lives daily to try to seize something that is so idealistic it is almost impossible to define. It goes beyond women wearing burkas and children being taught to read and write. The Afghan people have chosen who will lead them. Their new government is striving to make Afghanistan a better place. I had never truly appreciated the awesome power of a democratic government before. We are here to assist that legitimate and democratically elected government. It is easy to poke holes in that statement and say that the system is corrupt and that violence and poverty make people easy targets for our own agendas. Those statements are true; however, we have to start somewhere. With the best of intentions, we have started in Afghanistan. There is nowhere else that I'd rather be right now.

It is not the critic who counts, not the man who points out how the strong man stumbles, or where the doer of deeds could have done better. The credit belongs to the man who is actually in the arena, whose face is marred by dust and sweat and blood, who strives valiantly . . . who spends himself for a worthy cause; who, at the best, knows in the end the triumph of high achievement, and who, at the worst, if he fails, at least he fails while daring so greatly, so that his place shall never be with those cold and timid souls who have never known neither victory nor defeat.

—Theodore Roosevelt

Nichola

Weeks 6–8

March 25, 2006

Hello Everyone,
I am afraid that this letter will be a long one, so go and get a coffee (Tim Hortons if you can swing it; I really miss my Single Singles☺) and pull up a chair. There is so much to say, I am not

even sure where to begin. The good news is that you can feel free to skim if your eyes start to glaze over.

I just got back from Operation Sola Kowel (Pashto for Peacemaker). I was deployed north of Kandahar city for the last two weeks. It was an incredibly challenging and rewarding experience. I feel like a poster child for why people should join the military—it was an amazing 15 days.

We did not stick to any type of routine, as hard as that may be to believe for those who know me well. One of the biggest challenges here is trying not to set a pattern. The local informant system is better then any CSIS network imaginable, so we try not to give them any more help than necessary. We make sure that patrols always go out at unpredictable intervals and that our routes change at bizarre places. This is not as challenging as it sounds, as a vehicle breakdown (very common) or road on the map that doesn't actually exist (happens all the time) force us to change our timings and routes frequently. The big joke is that there is no way for the bad guys to guess our next move, because we aren't sure yet, either☺ One of those "funny because it's true" statements☺

Anyway, our mission was to move into isolated areas, either by foot or with our vehicles, to meet with the local elders and conduct *shirras*. *Shirra* is the Pashto word for "meeting" or what we are calling "leader engagements." Essentially, a group of 30–50 soldiers shows up on the outside of town. A smaller delegation of 5–10 soldiers and 3–5 Afghan National Army (ANA) soldiers (depending on the size of the town) goes forward under the remainder's watchful eye. They ask to speak to the village leader and/or elders. In every village that we visited (I lost track after 10), this was absolutely no problem. A group of 3–10 men would show up, with one designated leader. They would sit down somewhere in the open, watched by the remainder of the men in the village. We would watch our emissaries very closely for security reasons. Then, the *shirra* would begin. In most of the villages, after about 10 minutes of pleasantries, the chai (sweet tea) and bread would be brought out. They would also bring out candy and sometimes soup. Then, the real business would begin.

I was honoured to be invited to 2 different *shirras*. I really thought that the whole female thing would be a huge issue. It was, but not in the way that I thought it would be. The first time, it was an ANA commander who insisted that I be included. It was not that my leadership was excusing or excluding me—as an artillery officer, I was set in a position of overwatch doing my job . . . the infantry officers were involved in the actual *shirra*. Anyway, I had to climb down from my precarious perch on the side of a mountain to drink chai. I am not sure how serious the discussion was before I got there, but once I arrived it quickly centred on my marriage status. The big shock was not that I was in the army, but that I was married and in the army. The fact that my husband was not also a soldier was even more disturbing (don't worry, Jay, I said that if you were strong enough to handle me, you didn't need to be a soldier, too☺). The remainder of the discussion revolved around my inexplicable lack of children. The elder offered to go inside and get me some milk and bread, as diet was probably the issue. He was 67 and had 2 wives and several children under the age of 10 . . . I said that my husband would definitely say that one wife was enough. He thought that was hysterical, and I was a hit.

The second *shirra* that I was invited to was quite large. About 15 elders turned up with close to 20 children. We are always relieved to see children, as it means that the meeting will probably go smoothly. Anyway, here the issue was not my lack of children, but my availability. My boss was apparently asked if I was available to marry one of the elder's sons who looked to be about 15. After we'd established that I was already married, the issue turned to the all-important one of baking bread. When I confessed that I could not make the delicious flatbread that they serve (like a flat naan bread) the elder asked "Can you at least boil water to make chai?" I was quite indignant in my response "Yes!!" which amused them all☺

Working with the ANA and interpreters was eye opening to say the least. I am always astonished at the way that the military acts as a great equalizer. It doesn't matter where you are from, or how much money you had growing up or the size of your family. It doesn't even matter what country you're from or your level of education. Once you're out with other soldiers, doing your thing, we are all the same. We respect each other based on ability, not background. We value a positive attitude, determination, and a good sense of humour. The ANA possessed all of those qualities to a high degree.

The ANA soldiers are very professional and very competent. They are also in amazing physical shape. Watching them run up and down the mountains with all of their gear was phenomenal. Seeing how proud they are of their country and how determined they are to work towards peace was inspiring. They are paid very little and do very dangerous work—it is not rhetoric for them. They really do want to get rid of the Taliban and al Qaeda to make their country a better place.

The interpreters are even more idealistic. They are paid quite well by local standards, but many of them risk their lives by coming out with us. Some don't want to go into specific areas, because of past family conflicts. One interpreter was born in Afghanistan, but his family fled to Pakistan in the mid-70s. He came here two years ago to be an interpreter, as he feels it is his way to help Afghanistan. He spoke Farsi, Pashto and English without any problems at all. He invited my Sergeant and to the interpreter's home for dinner sometime in the future—that should be very interesting!

I think that my proudest moment over the last 15 days was after a 10 km march with a 2000-foot altitude gain. I was carrying approximately 100 lbs of kit. It was a lot. It was the most physically challenging thing that I have ever done—and I've done some crazy stuff. There were two points where I almost gave up. After we had done the climb up, and were coming down through the valley, one of the ANA soldiers came up to me with an interpreter. The interpreter said "they want me to tell you that all of the ANA are talking about you, because you have done this march with us." I said, "tell him that I am talking about them, because they can run up and down the mountains." After this message was translated, the ANA soldier came up to me and said in broken English (better than my Pashto): "I fight Taliban. I fight al Qaeda. You fight also. *Dersi. Mananna*" (*Dersi* is Pashto for "very good" and *Mananna* is Pashto for "thank you').

Another proud moment—we were in a village and were just getting on our kit to walk to the next town. I had attracted a crowd of 5 men aged 15–60 who were watching me. It is kind of funny, I can sort of see why the Afghan women cover up their faces. The men are pretty bold. I am not sure how I am going to feel walking through a town without attracting a crowd—it will be quite humbling after all of the attention that I am getting here☺ A man that must have been at least 60 came over to help me put on my rucksack. He almost took a knee lifting it up, but he did it. It was really neat☺

Anyway, the interpreter came up and had a 2–3 minute conversation in Pashto with the 5 men who were watching me. Then he turned to me and said, "Please excuse their staring. They are just very surprised that you are a woman working with all of these men. I have told them that you climbed over the mountain with us with your heavy bag and that you had no problems. They think that you must be very strong. I explained to them that you are just like the men, and that you can do everything that they can do the same as them." It was perhaps the greatest statement of equality that I have ever heard—and it was given by a Pakistani-raised, Afghan male in the middle of an Afghan village that is only accessible by a 5 km walk up a mountain. It just goes to show that anything is possible and that stereotypes are often completely wrong.

I have skipped over the media. We had what we call "embedded media." Embedded media are media personnel who get to live and work beside us for a specific length of time. In addition to the privilege of going without running water and plumbing, they get to experience the news stories as they happen. I have to say, their drive and focus is noteworthy. I don't think that our media person really knew what she was getting herself into, but it was pretty impressive to me that she stuck it out. She and her cameraman were out with us for 4 days, and then they went to another company for the remaining 4 days. For those of you who have lost track, that was a total of 8 days out of the 15 that the rest of us were deployed. 8 days without a shower or any plumbing whatsoever is a pretty big chunk of time for anybody, let alone someone without any real "hardship" training. I was impressed.

Lisa LaFlamme was the reporter, I don't know the name of her cameraman. Anyway, Lisa latched on to me right away because she felt that I would be a "good story." For those of you who don't know my take on media, I'll just spend a second to say that I agree that they serve an important purpose. I agree that soldiers are often misrepresented, and the only way to fix that is to get media onside and to give them honest stories. But I'd much rather that someone else be the one talking. Anyway, my crew was pretty excited, because every time she filmed me, they were there but they didn't have to do any talking. I was interviewed several times.

I am afraid that I was a dismal failure on the interviews. She interviewed me right before we left. She kept on asking me if I was scared or apprehensive. I said "no." This last trip out was my crew's 13th time "out of the wire." (We're no longer keeping track.) She said "well, this is a much bigger operation for a much longer period of time through less travelled areas." I agreed, but said that what we do doesn't change, regardless of the length of the operation or its location. Our drills are the same, as are our preparations. She then asked me what my biggest concern was. I said that it is that I will make a poor decision that will hurt someone unnecessarily. That is my biggest fear, and something that I think every leader struggles with all of the time. All I can do is try my best and hope that I will do the best possible thing for my guys. I don't think that was really moving enough for her, which was kind of ironic because it is almost all-consuming to me.

She also interviewed me giving orders. I tried very hard not to swear, but I don't think I was successful. I'm sorry, Dad. I guess that if it makes it to the documentary, they'll cut out the swearing part or beep it over or something.

A couple of days later, she asked me if I was finding the conditions really rough. I said "Not really. We are getting more sleep then we get back in Canada on exercise, and the weather is nicer." She asked if I was really stressed about hearing of the IED (improvised explosive device) attacks that had happened that day. I said, "No. We all know it could happen to anybody. I am just glad that everyone is okay." That was the last time she interviewed me. I'm afraid that my 15 minutes of fame will be more like 15 seconds. The only story that might make it on is when I called in a "contact" of two men carrying rifles. It turns out that they were two guys with umbrellas . . . false alarm. That will probably make it to the documentary☺

Most of the areas that we visited were accessible by a dirt road or, more often, through the dried up riverbed that served as a road. We would see the odd truck or motorbike; however, it was quite unusual to see vehicles. For the most part, people walk from place to place or they ride camels or donkeys. I saw a couple of horses in the wealthier towns, but they were not common. Occasionally, we would see one tractor that obviously served the entire town or sometimes towns. That was it for machinery. No running water. No electricity. No generators. Nothing.

The towns were beautiful. The homes are made out of packed mud with small doors and tiny windows. I think that this must be to conserve heat at night and keep it cool during the day. It must take a LONG time to build the houses, as the water has to be carried to the location, mud has to be made, then it has to be packed, then it has to dry . . . and the process repeats itself. Along with mud houses, each home is fenced in with high mud or sometimes rock walls. The walls then make a compound, giving each family unit privacy and space. It is interesting, the human desire to claim something as their "own." In the middle of nowhere, a single house will have a wall around it, claiming that space.

There are gardens everywhere, and they are terraced with an irrigation system that would do any civil engineer proud. We walked around a town that was about 5 km in circumference. There was a series of gardens terraced up the mountainside with irrigation and drainage systems interconnecting the whole thing. It was kilometres long . . . all done by hand. Not to mention the planting, weeding and harvesting which is all done by hand. I can't wait until the summer when everything will be in bloom. I wish that I had my Dad's gift with a camera to capture the colours properly.

We passed hundreds of nomads. The Pashto word is *Koochi*. The men wore the traditional Afghani dress of dark browns and blacks, but the women wore beautiful bright-coloured clothing. Unlike the rest of the women we saw, the Koochi women did not cover up their faces or hands. The families travelled herding hundreds of goats and sheep. I don't know how they could possibly keep them all together. They had dogs that looked like Great Danes crossed with horses—beautiful, massive things. They also had camels. Lots and lots of camels. Our interpreter said he'd try to get me a ride on one next time. I'd love to ride a camel☺ I can't even fathom that lifestyle. Moving each day, setting up a tent shelter in a likely area. Spending a few days there, then moving on to the next place. They took our presence in stride and just carried on doing their thing.

A few other highlights that I should mention. Last week was the Afghan New Year. I, along with about 15 other people, was invited to the Afghan National Army New Year's celebration while we were out. They slaughtered three goats in celebration. I'd never had goat before. It tasted sort of like chicken . . . just kidding☺ It was actually quite good. They roasted it over an open fire and served it wrapped in the flat naan-style bread. Then there was the soup. The soup was like a chicken broth except that it smelt and tasted like you had just dug the goat up from under a rock. I was lucky enough to get an extra serving of fat in mine. Wow. The only thing that I can even remember tasting as bad was the dead seal that we had in the N.W.T . . . and that had been left decomposing for days. It was completely disgusting. I don't know where I got the intestinal fortitude to finish it off, but I drank my cup without making a face or anything. It took about 12 hours for me to get rid of the taste, though. Ugh. Talk about memories that I'll never forget☺

Hopefully, all of that gives you a little sample of what the last few weeks were like for me. I am going to do better on the next Operation out. I will take a notebook and actually keep a day-by-day journal so that I don't forget anything. There are so many things to write about and share with you all.

I keep thinking about my grandparents, and what they must have gone through in World War I and II. This is nothing compared to that. I have an end-date. I know that I'll be home sometime in August. I have the ability to come back to a warm tent and call home to hear my Mum's voice. I have the ability to check email and send a message instantly. I am so proud of all of the veterans that I know, but especially both of my grandfathers and grandmothers. I am in such good company in uniform. It truly is an honour to be wearing a uniform overseas.

I want to talk about the importance of family and friends. I think of you often, especially when I see especially different or funny things. When I got back there was a stack of mail. I'm not kidding. Like, over 25 envelopes. I've written back to about half of the people now, and hope to get through the rest of the letters tomorrow. It means so much to me that so many people have taken the time to email/write/mail newspapers and letters. Thank you.

Home sometimes feels very far away. Especially when it is Saturday night and we have deep-fried catfish at the mess, because our mess is an American one and they eat some strange stuff . . . your letters make me feel that much closer. Thank you.

Finally, I ask that you all think, pray, meditate, whatever it is that you believe works, about Captain Trevor Greene, the soldier who was attacked by an axe at a *shirra* several weeks ago and seriously injured. His condition remains serious but stable. Please think of his family and of him. He is an excellent person.

Nichola

"Don't be afraid to take a big step if one is indicated. You can't cross a chasm in two small jumps."

—David Lloyd George

Weeks 9–12

May 3, 2006

Hello All,

I am feeling a certain amount of performance anxiety as I sit to write the latest letter . . . I have received so much positive feedback from the other letters, I don't want this one to be a disappointment. I know that I have been gone for a while, so I will try to recount the last month's activities as accurately as possible.

On the 29th March, a soldier from Charlie Company, the infantry company that I work with, was killed in action in a forward operating base (FOB). 3 others were injured. The Ramp ceremony was especially moving, as it was the first time in a long while that a Canadian has been killed overseas in a firefight. I was in the front rank, standing beside the three injured soldiers as we saluted someone who epitomized everything that Canadians in Afghanistan represent. Private Costall was killed in a firefight, defending the FOB from over a hundred Taliban soldiers. The gate that he died defending has since been renamed "Costall Gate."

Three days after Private Costall's death, my party, with the remainder of Charlie Company, moved into the forward operating base (FOB) to assist in its defence. We were told that we would be going for 1–7 days. 29 days later, we came back to KAF☺ This latest letter will be about my time in the FOB.

Although the FOB is not physically that far from KAF, it took us 30 hours to reach it. We had intended to leave at first light from KAF, but the powers that be conspired against us, and we had a hard time tracking down all of the interpreters, medics, etc that are "must haves" prior to rolling out of the wire. Finally, we were ready to leave . . . just in time for the Sunday afternoon market in Kandahar city. Our vehicle convoy was huge, almost

50 vehicles. To make it a little more manageable, we left in 5 packets of 8–10 vehicles. I was in the second packet.

Just prior to my packet hitting Kandahar City (or K.C., for those who are in the know), packet 1 hit and killed a donkey. They were unable to properly secure the area, so they pushed on, directing packet 3 to deal with the donkey and owner. My packet took a different route. I can't quite describe what it is like moving our huge armoured vehicle through a city teeming with people, kids, donkeys, dogs, carts, shops and cars on streets that are designed for small cars. To mitigate the risk of suicide bombers cutting between our vehicles, we drive very close together and move quite quickly. My hat goes off to our drivers—mine kept us within 5 feet of the vehicle in front for the hour that it took us to drive through the city—amazing.

Anyway, just prior to my packet getting out of the city, packet 4 discovered that they had taken a wrong turn and were now about halfway up a one-way street, going the wrong way. To make matters worse, packet 4 was made up of the guns and gun trucks . . . about 70 feet in length per truck. There were 2 of them, plus the other vehicles in their packet. A 3 point turn was not an option! I was impressed by the Lieutenant who came over the radio and said, very calmly, "Um. We seem to be going the wrong way up a one-way street. We are trying to convince the traffic in front of us to turn around. Any security you could send us would be appreciated." That took about an hour to sort out. In the meantime, my packet was stopped on the edge of K.C. . . . not a great place to be. That was when the intelligence hits, reporting a suicide bomber in a white Toyota Corolla heading our way, started to get sent in.

As we knew we were going to be stopped for a while, we pulled over to the side of the road and started marshalling vehicles. They had to be quickly searched and then allowed to pass through. K.C. has a LOT of vehicle traffic, and we were trying to do a thorough job without holding up people . . . a big traffic backlog is the worst PR move ever, as you big-city readers can appreciate. After about 10 minutes, we realized that we had pulled over in front of a boys' orphanage. There were about a hundred boys of all ages outside, ostensibly playing soccer. I couldn't count the number of times they kicked the ball over the wall and had to come out to get it, en masse. It is funny to me that boys are boys, no matter where you are☺

Anyway, as the threat of suicide bombers continued to escalate, every second car seemed to be a white Toyota Corolla with one person in it and suspicious packaging in the back. Everyone remained calm, and once again, I was amazed at the professionalism of our soldiers. We had been moving traffic for about an hour when packet 4 eventually met up with the rest of our convoy . . . only to discover that one of their vehicles was incapable of going more then 5 km/hour . . . recovery had to be called. Packet 3 had also met up with us at this point, after unsuccessfully trying to locate the dead donkey and owner. I'm not sure why the guy wouldn't have stuck around for 2 hours, waiting for more military people to show up and question him about his donkey . . . although I understand why we can't just pay off guys when stuff like this happens, it makes the remuneration process very long and frustrating for everyone involved. Recovery arrived about an hour later for the downed vehicle, and then we were ready to roll.

We had moved about 20 minutes outside of K.C. when the next incident happened. You have probably all seen pictures of the LAVs and the cannon on the front? Well, we have the ability to traverse the cannon in all directions. When we are driving, we usually alternate sides that we are pointed at, to maximize coverage. For example, my vehicle will take from 12 o'clock to 3 o'clock. The vehicle behind will take from 12 o'clock to 9 o'clock, etc. Anyway, one of the LAVs passed too close to a truck, hitting the truck. Fortunately, the truck was static, and no one was in the front of it. The turret was knocked right around, hitting the two soldiers standing in the back. Both were seriously injured and were sent back to Canada for reconstructive surgery—but both will be okay. The highpoint of that was the one guy with a smashed-in jaw, concussion, broken nose and serious whiplash who said to the medic, "Doc, my head really hurts." To which the medic replied, "no $H!T, buddy."☺ They were airlifted out, and will both be okay.

We were then ready to carry on . . . oh! I should mention at this point that I then saw my first honest-to-goodness unmarked minefield. It really wasn't that exciting. It is hard to believe that such small and inanimate things can cause such pain and destruction. The mine was an anti-tank mine, and definitely off of the road, so it didn't cause us any difficulty.

At this point, we were ready to carry on. We stopped to refuel, and then began our last 30-km cross-country portion around suppertime. We thought it would take us about 3 hours. 15 hours later, we rolled into the FOB. Why did it take so long, you may ask . . . well, let me tell you☺

We were going cross-country, which wasn't too bad. The area was hard-packed sand with rolling hills, and was quite easy to drive on. It was just getting dark as we started, so we had to slow down a fair bit when it got dark. We were driving without any lights, using our thermal and night-vision devices to see. It worked okay. We had been going about an hour when someone realized that we had lost a vehicle. As in, it had completely disappeared off the face of the planet. To make it even more bizarre, it was a big truck about the size of a semi-trailer that we had "lost." We started to look for it, and ended up getting two helicopters to come and help us do a search. 2 hours later, we found it. I guess that when everyone else turned left, these guys turned right. They then drove off a 10-foot drop, where they scared the crap out of themselves. As perhaps anyone would do in this moment of crisis, they then turned off the engine and all the lights, and sat in their vehicle, waiting for help . . . finally, we found them.

As we started to move forward again, the vehicle in front of me hit a huge hole, scaring the crap out of their driver. Their communications gear was also knocked out. They stopped and sat there. This might sound stupid to you, but please keep in mind that we had been travelling through pretty stressful ground for about 20 hours now, and tempers were wearing a little thin. As everyone who knows me well can attest to, I am quite patient and understanding of indecisiveness in others, especially when I am tired and hungry and just want to get to the end point. I must confess to using words that would shock my parents as I climbed out of my vehicle to go and sort out the vehicle in front of me. It was at this point that we started seeing the tracer fire . . .

My Sergeant started to yell at me to "get in the f*c!ing vehicle," as I was busy yelling at the vehicle in front of us to start "your f*c!ing vehicle" . . . if only Lisa LaFlamme had been there for that one! Anyway, what the tracer fire didn't do for the vehicle in front, my—ah—words of encouragement seemed to do the trick, and they started up. The tracer fire really wasn't aimed at us, so that was okay . . . we think it was likely being used as a way of signalling between the villages that we were en route. Anyway, no one was hurt by it, which is the important thing. We carried on . . .

The rest of the trip was pretty uneventful. Well, aside from the 3 vehicles that got stuck, but we could self-recover those, so that wasn't a big deal. The only really funny thing to add was that the Americans who were leading us kept on falling asleep at the stop points . . . as in, completely unconscious. I managed to scare the crap out of one of them, as I drove up my vehicle (much bigger then a Hummer) and pretty much nosed them forward, until they woke up☺ I must say, that restored my good humour☺

Finally, we arrived at the FOB . . . which is where the adventure truly begins☺

I can't talk about the security of the FOB, or its exact location, or its name. But I can tell you that when the 150 of us showed up, there were 2 toilets. Oh, the toilets were also communal (i.e. No walls around them) . . . that was it for amenities. The toilets were also like the ones in *Jarhead*, where some unfortunate soul gets to burn the contents of the bucket once a day. Needless to say, a high priority for everyone was to build more toilets. They were completed by the 3rd day there, which was awesome. Showers came about 2 weeks later, as we settled into the realization that we were there for the long haul.

The area itself was beautiful and the wealthiest area that I have seen yet in Afghanistan. Houses had basements and some even had second storeys. Some would not have looked out of place in downtown Brandon; it was amazing. Most houses had electricity, virtually every house had a generator and reliable water source. I saw my first poppy fields, and was amazed at how beautiful they are. They also don't look anything like the poppies that we wear on Remembrance Day, in case you were curious. They grow like tulips, very tall and very straight with big flowers. Not that I am an expert, but I can now tell you which ones produce the best heroin . . . it was an interesting few weeks!

It was a lot warmer in the FOB then back in KAF. It got up to 57°C at one point—I kept on telling myself that it was a "dry hot," but I'm not sure how much that helped☺ I think that the worst was that we had no way of freezing anything. We were drinking bottled water, but by lunchtime, it would be at least 50°C . . . you were so thirsty, you had to drink, but it was almost too hot to drink. Crazy. We experimented with keeping it in the shade, in a wet sock . . . but it was still gross, warm water.

Two highpoints that are worth mentioning at this time. We had been there about 2 1/2 weeks when a team of specialists came up from KAF to check out the area. They flew in by chopper (no 30-hour road move for them!). The officer asked me how I was finding things, I said that they were pretty good as we now had showers. I pointed with pride to the 4-stall shower booth that the Engineers had built for us. The officer said "wow, that would be amazing. Do you have a towel that I can borrow?" I stared at him in stunned disbelief, and then responded, "Buddy, I came out here with 4 sets of clothes. I have been here for 20 days, and I don't know when I'm going back to KAF. Even if I had a towel, I wouldn't let you use it." I didn't see him again after that.

Another high point—we were on hard rations throughout, which is about as exciting as it sounds. Anyway, we had been there about 2 weeks when a couple of Americans came over. They had a refrigerating unit with them. Apparently, they had thawed out some steaks, but they had thawed "way more than they could eat." They wanted to know if we wanted any. We, of course, said yes . . . they were delicious! I don't think that I've ever had steak that good☺

We left the FOB basically every day or night, depending on the scope of what we were doing. The area that we were in had not seen any mechanized coalition forces before. The last mechanized forces that they had seen were the Russians. Understandably, they weren't too fond of us—at least not initially. It was really encouraging to see the difference between the locals' reactions when we first showed up to the last few days. Kids were starting to wave, and elders were coming forward of their own volition to talk to us—it was wonderful. I wish that we could have stayed there longer, but it was not to be.

The trip back was, if anything, longer and more exciting then the trip out. I won't go into all the details . . . basically, take the trip out but add a couple more serious vehicle breakdowns and an IED strike that didn't hurt anyone, double the length . . . and 3 days later we were back☺ All in all, quite a month.

TALK TO ME LIKE MY FATHER
BY
KEVIN PATTERSON

"There is no security threat to Canada that the United States would not be ready, willing and able to help with. There would be no debate. There would be no hesitation. We would be there for Canada—part of our family. And that is why so many in the United States are so disappointed and upset that Canada is not fully supporting us now."
—Paul Cellucci, former ambassador to Canada, on Canada's declining to participate in the invasion of Iraq

It's an unexpected pleasure, this bit of humour: en route to Kandahar, Canadian military personnel stop at a Middle Eastern facility called "Camp Mirage" that sits on a clear desert highway and even shimmers in the early afternoon heat. It serves as the airhead for Australian, New Zealand and Canadian forces in Afghanistan and the Persian Gulf. Befitting its name, it exists, and yet apparently does not: the Host Nation does not acknowledge it. Sensitive to the population's discomfort with armed unbelievers on its soil, it forbids its mention publicly. Uniforms must not be worn off the camp, nor may taxis be hired to bring personnel back from shopping trips in the closest city.

The faux secrecy of it all smacks of Cold War—era posturing. All documentation refers to the "HN," even the sign in the base convenience store, informing visitors that both American and

"HN" currency are accepted, as if nobody there knows exactly where they are. In the transients' accommodation, there is a little booklet outlining the prevailing cultural norms in the "Host Nation," even a brief outline of the recent history of the "Host Nation," with a circumspect discussion of the power politics of the "Host Nation" and the lingering influence of the old families.

The preposterousness of all this pretence sets me back into nostalgic reminiscence. Thirteen years previously, I had been a captain in the Canadian Army, a medical officer in an artillery regiment, and bored to the point of catatonia. I had enrolled in the army partly in an effort to pay for medical school, but I had been drawn, as well, to the fantasy of distant deployments and UN peacekeeping, anything to get me out of dusty and pre-dictable Manitoba, where the idea of "exotic" exists only in the context of dancers in Saturday afternoon bars.

In the event, nothing I could have done would have inserted me more deeply into the Manitoban blow-dust. I was attached to the Third Regiment, Royal Canadian Horse Artillery, in Canadian Forces Base Shilo, a vast, arid base of whitewashed clapboard huts tossed up during the height of the Cold War. When I was there, the base housed the Royal Canadian Artillery Battle School; the Third Regiment, Royal Canadian Horse Artillery; and several German Panzer regiments filled with a steadily rotating cadre of blond conscriptees in training, all longing for their *weissbier* and civilized conversation. We used to watch them as their buses from Winnipeg pulled in, their hol-lowed eyes gazing out at the long, narrow shacks in which we worked—*Gut Gott* their faces said, but they were only ever there for a few months at a time. And though they might have known more than we did of café culture and what constitutes ambition in a restaurant, it had escaped none of us residents that Canadian Forces Base Shilo really was a dreary place to live.

In other contexts, desolate places can be easy to love—the sea, for instance, north of the horse latitudes, is grey and ill-tempered and relentless; and the arctic shores of Hudson Bay—but these places are lent dignity by the struggle necessary to work and travel there. The arid desolation, however, was the least part of CFB Shilo's dreariness. A peacetime army, possessed of resources greatly disproportionate to its requirements, is defined by its underemployment and by its need to manufacture purpose. I was twenty-five when I arrived there, and had four hundred young men and a small clot of aggrieved women to care for. They were none of them sick. If they were, any one of them would have used their illness to insist on a posting to a city. My day's work was often done by 9 a.m. The rest of the day, I napped on my desk. The left side of my face, I worried, threatened to develop calluses.

Purposelessness and peacetime armies: the problem was left behind by Western militaries six Septembers ago. The tiny Canadian Army is now deployed in Afghanistan, almost to the limits of its capabilities. The list of combat deaths is steadily rising and hundreds of disabling injuries can be counted among its 2,500-strong battle group; most of these have been sustained since the Canadians assumed responsibility for Kandahar province, and the risk of such calamities, per soldier in theatre, exceeds even what the occupying forces know in Iraq.

Armies exist to fight. When peace prevails, they wither. It will not be the most engaged among us who are drawn to enrol in peacetime armies. The doctors who thrive there will be less interested in taking care of sick and wounded soldiers than they are in administration, the volume of which will be undiminished by the absence of battle injuries. Combat-arms officers in peacetime expend great energies persuading themselves, and those around them, that they would be equal to the challenges of genuine combat, knowing that there is no way that the experience can be recreated in exercise, that the difference between flash-bangs going off nearby and that of mortar shells is the difference between play-fighting and incontinence. The requisite chest beating creates a culture of pretense. The men attracted to peacetime armies, especially the officers, it seemed to me as a resident at CFB Shilo, were fantasists and poseurs, drawn to the power that combat-arms officers are accorded over their men, even in those more settled times.

A troop commander in my regiment told me, "It's hard not to think that the world would probably be better off if we just didn't come to work in the morning. One less 155mm round going off, one more school bus bought." He and the regimental chaplain were my friends. The three of us used to drink sacramental wine together in the priest's tent during quiet times in deployments. The padre was from Argentina and missed his *yerba maté*. He had some shipped to the regiment in the field, and asked the machinists to make him a *bombilla*, a metal drinking straw capped with a wire-mesh filter to keep the lawn clippings—like mat of maté out of the straw. The machinists, young men fresh from adolescences in Edmonton and Toronto and Montreal, had little doubt about what they were in fact making, and the priest's request for a Spanish hash pipe only elevated his status among the men.

Such playfulness would not be countenanced now, I thought, as I stood among the payload masters on the airfield at Camp Mirage. I was flying in to run the ICU in the Kandahar Air Field hospital for six weeks; accompanying me on the tarmac were elements of the First Battalion, Royal Canadian Regiment, including a company of infantry. There was an air of taut and humourless anxiety I could not recall from my own days in uniform. I wore a Kevlar helmet and body armour over my jeans and sweater. The other two civilians were an agitated bouffant-going-grey foreign service officer and a lithe man in a goatee who, when I asked him what had brought him to Afghanistan, replied, "This and that." He could have been a hairdresser or a software engineer but for a certain exaggerated yet quiet attentiveness. He said his name was Greg. The foreign service officer asked him how long he was going to be in. "Two, three months," he said. She nodded, and began telling animated and self-congratulatory stories of her last spell in Kabul. He did not pay her much attention.

The infantry boarded the C-130 Hercules, the soldiers by turns anxious and bored. We three civilians boarded last, carrying our boxed lunches under our arms like schoolchildren. The loadmaster gave the perfunctory safety briefing and the airplane rumbled forward and up into the night sky. The master corporal sitting across from me ate his lunch as soon as we were airborne. When he finished he asked me if I was a reporter. I shook my head. "A doctor," I said. He nodded. The engines were too loud to permit much conversation. Crates of 5.56mm ball rifle ammunition were stacked in the plane with us. The master corporal put in earplugs and went to sleep. Down the two rows of infantry, young men sat, sleeping and thinking as the airplane growled into the midnight sky. It became hard not to miss the more adolescent and ineffectual circumstance that I had known better.

The hurtling-at-the-earth, prostate-squeezing tactical landings that were once the most striking experience in a tour in Kandahar are no longer performed. The Taliban are not known to possess surface-to-air missiles—though the number of unaccounted-for Stinger missiles provided to the mujahadeen by the CIA in the 1980s gives every operational commander fits—and anyway, as the loadmaster explains, "If we'd have kept that up we'd have worn out all the planes by now." Our landing is anticlimactic, and as we emerge from the aircraft into the night sky, the devastated Russian-built hangar looms over us. We are ushered into the building, from the roof of which hang long tendrils of shattered metal. Great holes in the roof gape widely enough that stars can be seen through them. Mars glows red through the largest. A partially ruined yellow-brick building referred to by consensus as "Taliban's Last Stand" stands beside it. A company sergeant major approaches me and asks who I am. "Well, why hasn't the hospital sent someone for you?" The foreign service officer walks around in tight, quick circles directing pointed questions into her BlackBerry. "Greg" had slipped away quietly.

Detecting little in my bewildered response to satisfy him, the sergeant major strides away, barking into a telephone. A few minutes later a medic comes to pick me up and drive me to the hospital.

The hospital is constructed of mostly unpainted plywood. The aesthetic sensibility is construction-site-ATCO-trailer. The toilets are mounted in a shipping container. There are two operating rooms and the only CT scanner in the province. Two surgical teams work alongside one another: one Canadian, the other either Danish or Dutch. Each includes OR nurses, a supply team, an anesthetist, and a general surgeon and an internist. The Dutch alternate with the Danes, cycling surgical teams in and out every four months. Among these are British, Australian and American doctors, nurses and medical assistants; at morning rounds the next day, the place has the sort of internationalist air that Madrid might have had in 1936, or, more optimistically, that an operations centre in the Gulf War may have had. NCOs (non-commissioned officers) don't bother saluting officers here—no one can figure out the myriad of rank insignia present on the base. In the DFAC—the dining facility run by the ubiquitous Kellog, Brown and Root (KBR) Corporation—Estonian, Romanian, Spanish, Jordanian, New Zealand and French soldiers eat alongside the NATO soldiers, and together they form one polyglot mass of blinking and farting martial vigour.

In Kandahar, the International Security Assistance Force (ISAF) is principally the Canadian battle group, though the Dutch and American presence is strong as well. The Tolkeinesque-sounding Uruzgan province to the north is mostly Dutch, and to the west, the British are responsible for Helmand. But Afghanistan remains primarily an American theatre; they are responsible for security in Zabul, Paktia, Ghazni, Paktika, Logar, Wardak and Nangarhar provinces to the east, near Pakistan. There are twenty thousand American soldiers and airmen here now, and it is to them that the small armies look for leadership. And for air support.

Genuinely multinational combat armies are uncommon. Historically, one nation dominates an effort and bit players stand around for show: the British directed Sierra Leone; the French, Congo; the Americans, the Gulf War and Korea. The defeat of the Nazis really was done in concert, however: two of the Normandy beaches were American efforts, two were British, and one was Canadian. And the Nazis themselves had Romanian, Italian and Hungarian divisions on the Eastern Front. But these exceptions only prove the rule. Those in uniform are unsettled by non-uniformity, and discrepancies in codes and procedures and firing orders between different armies can lead to catastrophe. Yet the variations on the theme of desert-brown khaki present in Afghanistan are multitude. Thirty-seven nations are here now, each with its own command centres and political masters. One pities the generals in charge of making them work together. But they do. The British are dying in Helmand, the Dutch in Uruzgan, and the Canadians in

Kandahar. Nobody dies as much as the Americans do, but it remains: they are accompanied.

Major Dawn Graham, a U.S. Air Force ICU nurse working among the Dutch and Canadians, spent four months in Iraq, near Kirkuk, before coming here. She is careful with her words but her expression betrays her impatience with amateurishness. When a chest-shot Afghan is undergoing a CT scan I ordered, the Canadian master corporal CT technician makes a small and officious fuss about the amount of oral contrast the patient received, and Major Graham's temporal arteries pulse visibly. Over coffee at Green Beans—a sort of downscale Starbucks that has become as regular a feature on American military bases as Starbucks is in gentrified urban cores—she explained that she is accustomed to a more professional atmosphere. "If you have sick people to care of, you just don't have time for that sort of thing." She would like to say more. She sets down her cup of coffee (double, house) and then closes her mouth. She picks it up and shrugs. Later, when we're discussing the blood bank, she comments on the doctrine that requires American soldiers to receive only American blood products, even in this, a Canadian-run hospital: "I understand that the Dutch platelets aren't screened as thoroughly as our American blood is." Bristling, I tell her that Americans had for years paid people to donate—attracting high-risk populations for hepatitis and HIV—and that, historically, the infectiousness of their blood products has surpassed that of any other developed nation. She bit her lip. I was sorry the moment the words were out of my mouth.

The interaction between all the nationalities in theatre is interesting. Hanging over it, at all times, is the trouble in Mesopotamia. Were it not for Iraq, the easiest thing for all involved here would have been for America to assume its traditional role as the military substance in Afghanistan, leaving the other nations to provide symbolic support with well-photographed arrivals of exotic uniforms. Were it not for Iraq, the winnable war would have been won by now. And the tiny armies would still be unbloodied.

It is unfair to lump the British in with the rest of the small armies. They remain, for now, in Iraq alongside the Americans and they provide their own air support with their Harriers. In Afghanistan, one may detect an assurance in the Brits less comfortably worn by the Dutch and the Canadians. Helmand looks to be the hot spot this year, and the *New York Times* reports that the British have killed 490 Taliban in the previous nine days. Musa Qala, which is sixty miles to the northwest of Kandahar, had been seized by Taliban forces recently, in defiance of a mutual withdrawal agreement made with the British general responsible for the area several months earlier. The British promptly killed the Taliban commander with an aerial strike when he unwisely drove out of town to inspect his perimeter.

The Royal Air Force Regiment—an infantry battalion composed of airmen—is deployed in Kandahar to provide airstrip security—a task shared with the Romanians, who have quickly acquired a reputation both for aggressive patrolling and for a certain erratic quality to their response times. Opinion varies over which characteristic predominates. People want to like strangers with common purposes. And they want to feel superior to them.

The Romanians are still armed with Warsaw Pact—era AK-47s. The rest of the troops in Kandahar carry, for the most part, versions of the M-16; the British use their bullpup model, but NATO-standard .223 calibre ammunition works in all of them. But the Romanians cleave to the .30 calibre weapon favoured by dirt fighters everywhere in the world. Some soldiers opine that the heavier .30 calibre round is better suited for desert fighting, where range is important. Weaponry is at all times on display here. Soldiers may not be fed in the DFACs if they are unarmed—though neither are they permitted entry if they are carrying a bag of any sort. I asked one of the soldiers in line with me waiting for breakfast why this was. "In case a Taliban in disguise," he nodded towards one of the Jordanians, "wants to blow us up." He suggested I just stuff my camera bag in a jacket pocket. We were behind a private from the perpetually deployed American Tenth Mountain Division carrying an M-203 grenade launcher; in front of him, the Jordanians stood in their jungle-green fatigues, M-16s slung casually over their shoulders, spare magazines full of ammunition jutting from their pockets. War fogs, rather than clarifies, thinking about both security matters and xenophobia.

The Romanians keep to themselves. They've built a little church that appears to have been lifted whole from the shore of the Black Sea. In the enormous halls of the KBR dining facility, the tables, viewed from the entrance, appear as a kind of fabric mosaic: the Americans and Canadians in their pixellated browns and greys, the Australians in their cartoon-bunny-ear-patterned beige, the British streaked by sawgrass-coloured fronds, and the Romanians in their own yellowish brown uniforms. Floppy camouflage-pattern hats that are currently the trend in military millinery—the Canadians, Dutch and British all sport variants—make them look rather like lifeguards in mufti. A month previously, Romania had entered the European Union, and undoubtedly their presence in Kandahar was influenced both by their application to join and by their expectation that they would be accepted. I tried but I never succeeded in engaging any of the Romanian soldiers in conversation. Everyone commented on how much they ate, great heaping mounds of chicken and potatoes and steaks stacked like flapjacks. Still, their comparatively gaunt faces seemed half the size of their corn-fed brethren's, dark eyes under shaven heads gazing around at such foreignness. And all the food you can eat.

—

The majority of the patients in the hospital are Afghan nationals: Afghan National Army soldiers, Afghan National Police and civilians who have been caught in crossfire or who have wandered over land mines. Coalition personnel who are wounded in Afghanistan are evacuated expeditiously either to the American military hospital at Landstuhl, Germany, or to Birmingham, England, and so the bed census remains overwhelmingly Afghan most of the time.

The interaction between the hospital staff and the Afghan patients is characterized by silence. The patients will not complain—of pain, about the food, their missing limbs or the fact that they have been shot inadvertently by Canadians.

This happens every couple of weeks or so. One man was riding a motorcycle and approached too closely to a checkpoint without slowing; the 5.56mm round fractured his tibia, but it was preserved. A tibial nerve contusion left him with a foot drop, however, which would prove debilitating. Another man, an ANA soldier riding in a truck, approached a Canadian military convoy from behind; he was recognized as ANA by the rear vehicle and waved forward. This was not communicated to the gunner of the lead vehicle, however, and he opened fire, killing the driver and sending six rounds into the soldier's evidently robust body armour and another into his right arm. He suffered a broken bone and a severed ulnar nerve, but in the hospital he underwent nerve grafting, and in six months or so it will be possible to know if it worked.

Blue-on-blue fire is a topic of some urgency among the Canadians. Three times, at least, they have been attacked by American aircraft. The first was April 18, 2002, when an F-16 at twenty thousand feet flew over them and saw the Princess Patricia's Canadian Light Infantry on a night-fire exercise. The pilot concluded that the tracer fire indicated he was under attack. Invoking the right to self-defence, he dropped a five-hundred-pound bomb, killing four and wounding another twelve. In September 2006, an A-10 attack bomber machine-gunned members of the Royal Canadian Regiment, killing one and wounding thirty; later that month, another five-hundred-pound bomb was dropped on the First Battalion, Royal Canadian Regiment—fortunately, it didn't explode.

Everyone understands that friendly fire—the military prefers the "blue-on-blue" appellation because it is so decid-edly not friendly—is inevitable in war. This exists as an abstracted lesson from every previous conflict, but the emotion it generates today is heightened perhaps because we are consti-tutionally less prepared for the fog of war. Cellphones work in Mogadishu, the Hubble telescope can make out the distant wob-bles of planets ten trillion miles away, and radar and GPS can define any terrain through the darkest night or the most opaque mist—and yet, frightened and overeager soldiers and airmen seem nearly as likely to shoot one another as they are any recog-nizable enemy. In Afghanistan, and in Iraq, presumably, any shooting not involving uniformed allied personnel seems con-sidered justified, at least retrospectively. The shootings of ANA and coalition members present a thornier problem.

Soldiers maintain it should be easy to know what portion of bullet wounds are friendly and which are not: NATO countries use 5.56mm ammunition and an AK-47 uses 7.62mm ammuni-tion. But the local allied forces—the ANA, ANP—use AK-47s too, as do the forces of the former Warsaw Pact—the Romanians, the Estonians—and anyway, when bullets strike bone they usually shatter, spraying shards of metal through the body like a satellite breaking up on re-entry. And if they don't strike bone, these fully metal-jacketed rounds are designed to keep going, on and out the other side. Doctors usually don't have any idea whether a wounded person was shot by his confederates or by an antago-nist, except by what is claimed. We don't even try to figure it out, most of the time. Doubtless, more times than we could guess, we don't want to know the answer.

An Afghan National Army soldier, who had been shot in the chest, came in to the KAF hospital. The call from the aeromedical team said that the entrance wound was in his mid-thorax and we wondered why they were even evacuating him—here in Kandahar where there is no cardiac or vascular surgeon. When he arrived, his wild-eyed look proved to be a product of simple fright. On exploration, the bullet was palpable in the tissue overlying his sternum; the shooter must have been at extreme range. The bullet was excised under local anesthesia by Lieutenant-Colonel Casse Reeuvers, a Dutch surgeon who smiles all the time. When he plucked the .30 calibre bullet out from under the man's skin, the patient and the surgeon exchanged amused grins. The surgeon then told him to buy lottery tickets, but neither the translator nor the patient understood. "Go to the casino," the surgeon tried. Still only agreeable but baffled nods. The soldier went back to his barracks that night and we didn't see him again.

I was standing at the memorial to the Canadians who have died here when the first rocket flew into the camp. A granite slab with Captain Nichola Goddard's picture etched into it smiled out from among the other forty-four. She was an artillery officer from Shilo, my regiment, who was working as a forward observation officer when she was killed by a rocket-propelled grenade strike on her vehicle. At the memorial site, my roommate, Major Steve Masseours—we'd been captains together in Ottawa a dozen years earlier—was standing beside me. He's an orthopedic surgeon now, and he was in the hospital when she came in, in May 2006. "She had terrible luck," he said. "Fragment of shrapnel flew in under her helmet, over her armour, at just the wrong angle, and went into her head." She was the first female combat-arms officer of any NATO country killed in action. Twenty-four years old. Open faced with a good-natured grin. Almost beautiful. Beautiful, in fact. "We started to resuscitate her but it was pretty clear it was hopeless," Steve said.

The rocket whistled overhead then, a short, thin stream of red light trailing behind it. Steve was already ducking low when it exploded in the military police compound, a hundred yards from where we were standing. A fraction of a second later, another. The attack siren went off and we lay on the concrete pad among the pictures of the fallen—smiling, large-toothed men and one woman, all self-conscious in their posed portraits; the common elements: shoulders and acne. After a few minutes we stood low and scurried over to the nearest bunker. These bunkers litter the camp, and in ours we were joined by soldiers, just arrived from Canada and Holland, who were laughing nervously. Among them were the Americans, who do fifteen-month tours rather than six, and who were long ago inured to these drills. "That's the helicopters going up," one lanky Texan said, to the thumping sound filling the air. And when it next was possible to be heard, he added, "Give them thirty, forty-five minutes and y'all can go back to work." I nodded more times than was necessary. He was entertained. The all-clear signal rang out and we walked quickly to the hospital. There was only one casualty— an American military police sergeant who had been picked up and tossed by the explosion. He had suffered abrasions on his back and exhibited a talkative, agitated demeanour that belied any attempt to minimize his alarm.

A little later, in the DFAC, we ate with Major Sanjay Acharya, an anesthetist of Gujarati stock by way of Newfoundland, who speaks with the rolling lilt of that island, almost Irish in its gregarious musicality. He possesses most of the personality evident among the doctors present. "What this represents, gentlemen," he declares, indicating the salmon on his plate, "is creeping mediocrity." Island peoples have high standards for fish. He will allow that he is also rattled by the rocket attack and as a consequence may be more critical than usual. "I'm not here blowing any of them up. Bastards are probably off giggling like it's some fucking game of knock-knock Ginger." The Texan had described how the rockets are set up with a block of ice holding down the release lever—allowing the Taliban to get many miles away by the time the helicopters find the launch site.

Acharya is the institutional object of amusement at the hospital. He sleeps heroically when the wounded are not coming. The nameplate on his room reads "G. Assman." When upright, he lays out his plans: to start a cult called the "Church of the Spiritual Redeemer," modelled on Scientology—"I've already got that Eastern mystic-yogi-guru thing down"—to attend law school, to leave the military when he becomes eligible for a pension. In an organization committed to the cultivation of zeal, he has proved to be barren land. He tells us about the time he was charged for disobeying a lawful command, after antagonizing his superior into apoplexy. But by simply failing to co-operate with the court martial, by refusing to give a statement or to use the military-appointed lawyer, he stopped the charge in its tracks. The functionaries, it is plain, are baffled by him. At home, in Ottawa, he keeps workaholic hours—a hundred on-call nights a year in critical care and anesthesia. But the rocket attack has helped him make up his mind about remaining in the army. "It's just not safe here, in the war zone," he says, eyes twinkling, smirk just below the surface.

The CH-47 Chinook helicopter had twenty-two American Special Forces soldiers on it. It was flying among the mountains of Zabul province when it developed engine failure—first one engine collapsed, prompting the pilot to radio in his concern, then the other, preventing him from landing his bird safely in the snow. The aircrew, including the pilot, were all killed immediately, as were several of the soldiers, eight dead in all. The fifteen survivors were three hours in the snow waiting for the weather to allow them out. The notification of a MASCAL, or mass-casualty situation, reached us long before they arrived at the hospital, and the staff of the hospital had time to walk in comfortably from the barracks, buying coffee en route from the open-all-nite Green Beans. The month prior to this had seen a slow trickle of battle-wounded—ANA and ANP, as always, predominating—and there had been warnings that the pace would pick up imminently.

The rescue helicopters brought them in by groups of three and four; they were all terribly cold and shattered. Cold blood will not clot appropriately and so they bled briskly—from minor wounds as well as major ones. The blood bank began releasing the first of the two hundred units of blood needed that day. The wounded had fractured spleens, broken spines, punctured lungs and broken-open pelvises. There were representatives of every important long-bone fracture.

One man had not a mark on him, but had struck his helmeted head so hard he had been found unconscious at the scene and had remained so thereafter. A CT scan showed hemorrhaging and bleeding and, most of all, swelling. He was given medicine to reduce the swelling in his brain, and preparations were made to evacuate him. We were told that it would be no less than seven hours before the American evacuation aircraft and medical crew could get here from their bases in Iraq. Then there would be a ten-hour flight to the hospital in Landstuhl, Germany.

A sergeant came in with an obviously broken femur. He insisted he felt well, that he could wait to be seen. A chest X-ray showed his right chest to be half full of blood. At that point an American Special Forces surgeon appeared—we had thought we were the only doctors in the camp—and helped with the resuscitation. As he put a chest tube into the man's thorax, the patient began coughing blood. A Special Forces nurse-anesthetist was also there, and I told him to intubate the man as I put another chest tube in his other side. His blood pressure fell further. I started large central lines in his femoral veins. He became difficult to bag and his blood pressure dropped further. I put a large needle into one side of his chest and then the other. Great flumes of blood-tinged air spurted from the needles—bilateral tension pneumothoraces: air had built up around and compressed the heart until it couldn't pump. The surgeon and I looked at one another quizzically. Shouldn't have happened with chest tubes in place. Still, the needle had worked. His blood pressure rose and the nurse-anesthetist reported that he was suddenly much easier to bag. All around us: other doctors and nurses, struggling with their own assignments of fractures, lacerations and hemorrhage.

The management of battle trauma was changing quickly, the Special Forces surgeon told me, as we worked on the man. He had just spent a year in Iraq doing trauma resuscitation full time. "We're going right away from crystalloid [saline]," he said, "and using larger volumes of blood products up front." (He meant plasma, packed red-blood cells, platelets, frozen concentrated fibrinogen and recombinant Factor VII, an important clotting protein worth five thousand dollars a dose.) "We're also very aggressive about warming them, and we're using whole blood more and more often."

We worked the rest of that day together, the surgeon and I and all the nurses and other surgeons and anesthetists, resuscitating those men. The man with the head injury deteriorated despite our medicines and his right pupil grew very large and unreactive as his pulse slowed to thirty-five. Four of us convened at the foot of his bed. We'd discussed a decompressive craniotomy earlier—opening the skull to relieve the pressure on the brain—but in blunt trauma, this is a desperate measure and there is little data to suggest it works. No one could think of anything else. The oral surgeon took him to the OR and began drilling holes in his skull.

Another man had an unstable pelvic fracture that had torn the web of veins in front of the sacrum. It took fifty units of blood to stabilize him and then he developed an abdominal compartment syndrome—his belly grew so taut from the bleeding in it that the pressure squeezed the blood out of its vessels—and he had to go back to the OR. He had come back, improving, when Dawn Graham asked me to look at the abdomen of the man with the chest tubes. "I think he's got one too." And he did. When I went to get Colonel Reeuvers from the operating room, where he was helping take out a spleen, he thought I was talking about the first man, "What more do you want me to do, his belly is already wide open!?"

I blinked at him. "Come see him," I said. I led him to the second abdominal compartment syndrome and he just shook his head. "What a day." And he took him to the operating room.

The man with the fractured femur and chest tubes was still unstable, still hemorrhaging, and we had run out of cryoprecipitate. The Americans maintain walking blood banks among their soldiers—men and women who are pre-screened for hepatitis and HIV, and who have volunteered to be available in such circumstances. I asked the nurse in charge to activate the blood bank, and within an hour, forty soldiers had donated blood. We ran this whole blood into the man with the chest tubes and also into the man with the broken pelvis, and, finally, for the first time that day, both began to stabilize. The Special Forces surgeon walked by, removing a gown and gloves, and nodded. "I love whole blood," he said. I agreed, but thought to myself it might be time for him to spend a few months someplace other than Iraq or Afghanistan. He moved on.

The man-with-the-fractured-femur's respiratory diffi-culties, clotting problems and kidney problems were so severe that we thought he might have fat-embolism syndrome, where marrow fat is pushed into the blood stream by the violence done to the bone. It then becomes lodged in the brain, lungs, kidneys. It was a strong argument for stabilizing his fracture before mov-ing him anywhere.

Sanjay Acharya and I brought him to the operating room, where Sanjay prepared to give him anesthetic. Moments after we moved him to the operating-room table, the oxygen content in his blood fell critically low (oxygen saturations of hemoglobin are normally 95 to 98 per cent; his fell to 38 per cent, which is incompatible with life). The sergeant turned the colour of an aubergine. This is an anesthetist's nightmare—and still Acharya spoke levelly, moved quickly but unhurriedly. We bagged him hard, adjusted his ventilator settings, and slowly his saturations picked up. Steve Masseours lifted his eyebrows. We all breathed in on the sergeant's behalf. Finally, his saturations rose to 90 per cent, and Sanjay nodded for Steve to begin. I stepped out of the operating room to stretch my arms, and looked around as if for the first time that day.

In the hospital now was carnage: puddles of blood under most of the stretchers, Dutch, American, Canadian, Danish and British nurses and doctors, all working madly, calling for more blood, calling for more hot blankets, more IVs, another CT scan, more blood, more blood, more blood.

From the emergency entrance, breathing the now-evening air, I could seen the tents housing the primary-care clinics. A long line of American blood donors stretched out of one of the tents, sleeves rolled up. In that tent, among the phle-botomies and flying paperwork, was a boy, Abdullah, twelve years old, who had been burned when he started a fire with brush he had gathered, which contained an illumination grenade. When his father had arrived to see him, after a week, the boy was sedated and still being mechanically ventilated. His father had visited for a few hours, and then began the long journey home to the rest of his family in Panjwayi District. Now Abdullah was awake and free of the ventilator, and every night he wept to see his father. Another boy in the hospital, whose family lived closer to Kandahar, had lost a foot after stepping on a land mine. His father remained by his son. Later, according to the interpreter, Abdullah rolled over and called to the old man, "Please, come talk to me like my father."

The account of that exchange was passed among the doctors and nurses and medics over the subsequent days, and on its telling, in every instance, the listener caught his or her breath. The boy's confused and disoriented loneliness resonated with every one of us. Just when we thought we had grown accustomed to the madness of the place. The old man sat with Abdullah and mourned his own son's shredded foot. He and Abdullah whispered to one another and nodded. None of the translators could say what they talked about.

And the slopes of Ghare Kalay glowed orange in the setting sun, just as the west-facing Coast Mountains do on the shore of British Columbia during late winter afternoons such as this. All of them—Abdullah, the Dutch, the Danes, Americans—so far from all of their homes.

MARCH

BY

CORPORAL GORDON WHITTON

This is the second of three edited excerpts from the journal Gordon kept while in Afghanistan. He was deployed from January 2006 to August 2006.

March 1, 2006

Last night at 1950 hours, Reconnaissance (Recce) Platoon's 2 Section was providing a convoy escort for a group of vehicles traveling from Camp Nathan Smith to KAF. As they were travelling south through IED alley on Highway Four, an IED went off prematurely in front of the first vehicle of the patrol. AK-47 fire and two RPG rockets followed, one of the RPGs skipped off the road in between the two front G-Wagons. Cpl Brad Kauffeldt was the turret gunner in the first G-Wagon and found himself under a giant cloud of dirt falling from the sky, Johnny Ghostkeeper was in the second turret and had actually seen the flashes from the RPGs launching, so he was quick to respond with a long burst of C-6 fire. 2 Section's patrol commander, Sgt Janek, was in the first vehicle and he told his driver, Cpl Barnes, to punch through it. The entire nine-vehicle patrol made it through the ambush unharmed. I was sitting there in our tent when 2 Section walked back in, they had smiles on their faces but at the same time they felt very fortunate they made it through unharmed. It was obviously hard for them to sleep, so we just sat around listening to each of their perspectives on the ambush. I'll never forget what Jeremy Barnes said that night: "I can't believe someone is trying to kill me." That made us all laugh hysterically.

Later that night, everyone in my tent was woken up by CSM (Company Sergeant Major) Zack, at 0200 we were marched out to the runway for a ramp ceremony for an American soldier who was killed by an IED in another province. I don't mind attending ramp ceremonies for these men who die in Afghanistan, and I don't care what country they're from either, I just wish we could get a name and hometown of the fallen soldier, it would give me something to think about as I salute the flag-covered casket when they slowly march him up the ramp of the Galaxy as they play those beautiful bagpipes. What I do think about is how much of a shame it is to lose such young, strong, brave men, and how it is too soon to go. I have no idea what my fate is over here. I sure hope I'm walking on that plane at the end of my tour, there is so much I want to do with my life, it would be such a shame.

March 2, 2006

There never is a dull moment around here, this morning I walked over to the computer shack to check my email, but the computers were all down. Someone walked in and told us there was a communication lockdown on camp. I'd heard about communication lockdowns and I knew the computers might be down the entire day. I decided to walk over to the meal line because some buddies of mine were standing at the end of it. Sgt MacDonald was there and told me a Canadian soldier had gotten killed, a LAV had rolled over three times, losing its turret, killing the gunner and injuring everyone else in the vehicle. He also said another soldier is clinging to life. Later in the day, we learned that Cpl Paul Davis of 2 PPCLI (Second Battalion,

Princess Patricia's Canadian Light Infantry), Bravo Company, was the man killed in the rollover.

Tonight we sat through a detailed set of orders for a three-day mission that was to take my platoon up north for a little Taliban hunt. We were all pumped and ready to go until Major Smith, our company commander, walked in the tent and told us the mission was squashed because we'd lost our Afghan army guys to some other mission. They were going to be a major part of our mission, so when our higher-ups learned we would not have them, they were forced to make the snap decision. During the orders, a rocket zipped through the air above the tent, we heard an impact far off in the distance and we just looked at each other and laughed. Sgt MacDonald smiled and said, "Those bold fuckers." Losing the mission is not a big deal, we all know there is enough fight to go around for everybody, it just prolonged the inevitable. Tomorrow morning we do a ramp ceremony for Cpl Davis.

On the morning of the third, Cpls Willetts and Nevell from Reconnaissance Platoon were working out on Highway Four conducting a checkpoint with the Twelfth RBC (Régiment blindé du Canada). The two men were parked on the side of the highway in a G-Wagon when a convoy of vehicles from our task force came through. As this convoy was passing, a white Toyota drove up the shoulder attempting to pass a LAV and get to the G-Wagon. MCpl Loewen was the crew commander of the LAV and he was waving at the vehicle to yield. Just as the Toyota was beside the LAV, Cpl Hayward, who was driving the LAV, ran him off the road. The car exploded into a million pieces. The blast wounded the two men in the turret, Cpl Greg Davis took some minor shrapnel to the hand but MCpl Loewen's arm was almost severed. Pte Nigel Williams was up doing air sentry and was thrown down below, he thought he was wounded, and he recalls quickly feeling every limb to make sure it was still there. His ballistic sunglasses were matted with residue from the blast; it was a miracle he made it through that without a scratch because he was staring right at the car when it blew. This is the same Nigel Williams that played pro football for the Washington Redskins and nine seasons with CFL teams in Montreal, Toronto, Edmonton and Hamilton, he is kind of a celebrity amongst the troops. If the VBIED had made it to the G-Wagon we would surely have two dead guys in Recce Platoon.

Cpl Willetts was standing outside the G-Wagon looking on as all this unfolded. He and Pte Williams walked over to the remains of the suicide bomber and, to their surprise, his body was in rather good shape, considering his car was completely destroyed. The explosives were all packed behind the driver's seat; when it exploded it sent the suicide bomber out the front windshield like a human cannonball. He landed several metres away with only an arm missing. His death was more slow and agonizing then he had hoped for, I'm sure.

March 5, 2006
I never did get to do that ramp ceremony for Cpl Davis; instead I was doing battle procedure for another mission. This mission was to insert a seven-man team with a .50 calibre McMillan sniper rifle on Three Mile Mountain because of all the shit that's being going on in that area lately. There was a funny moment when Sully, Jack and I met up with the four snipers we'd be working with and joined 9 Platoon for Captain Alcock's orders. The three of us were the only ones in the tent with cam paint on our faces, some of the NCOs got a kick out of us and I felt like an idiot. Orders and timings were quick, so we had little time to adjust our kit for dismounted mountain operations.

We departed KAF on the night of the third, our seven-man team all crawled into the back of a LAV from 9 Platoon, C Company. From the beginning I didn't like the mission, it just seemed we were too exposed in an area that had too many sets of eyes. The American LRSD (long-range surveillance detachment) guys told us they once put an observation post on No Drug Mountain and they got compromised. As we were driving north on Highway Four, a rocket flew right over our LAV, Sgt Ingram and Cpl Nolan were up doing air sentry; they ducked down below and looked at each other and said, "Holy shit, did you see that, man?"

The four LAVs from 9 Platoon, C Coy, were to do routine patrols on trails around Three Mile Mountain. They stopped at our insertion point on the north side of the mountain at 2245 hours, and one of the vehicles faked a blown tire as a distraction for my seven-man team and Sgt Patrick Tower's section to crawl into a *wadi*. Sgt Tower's section was only there in case our patrol ran into trouble on the way up, we also suspected there might be an enemy observation post up there, so we needed the extra firepower. Once our position was secure, they would climb back down to be picked up and we would carry on for a mission approximately thirty hours long. So after the four LAVs continued on, we did a ten-minute listening halt, it seemed so quiet after the vehicles left us, so alone. We needed to get up that mountain undetected and find the quickest route to get us in place before first light.

Under the cover of darkness, Sgt Tower's section led the way up, it felt more like he was running us up because we were carrying almost one hundred pounds of kit, those guys were only wearing their fighting order. The climb was more miserable than it was dangerous. I actually thought climbing that mountain would be a walk in the park, but it was one of my hardest humps ever. I soaked my uniform with sweat even though the temperature was almost freezing, sometimes it was so steep we were using all four limbs to get over a ledge. I remember looking back down the mountain at times and you could vaguely see the place where we were inserted, we just kept on going up, it seemed like it would never end. In a way I needed that hump, so next time I had a mission like this, I'd know to have way less kit. I was already carrying ammo, ten litres of water, rations for three days, a Sophie (a thermal viewer that can see just about anything in the dark at super-long distances, it looks like a set of binos on steroids), extra radio batteries and a Claymore (a command detonated mine). Every time we halted, I would feel my homemade deer-antler knife on my hip and think, "I'm never taking that thing out on another mission." I remember the Americans telling us "ounces make pounds," and I would start thinking of what else I could get out of my rucksack.

After climbing up the north side of Three Mile Mountain for four hours, the point man reached the summit, which is like a razorback. We established an observation position looking down on a stretch of Highway Four and a village just to the south of the mountain. Dave and Miles spent over an hour looking for the perfect position for the .50 calibre. Sgt Tower's section turned back down the mountain and got picked up with no problems. That was one of the coldest nights I did in a long time, I was soaked with sweat so when my heart rate slowed down I began to shiver, and the only trick I could think of to keep warm was taking deep breaths. So many times in my military career I can remember being out on cold nights waiting for the sun to come up, we soldiers call it "the heat tab in the sky."

We had to lie up on that mountain until first light; we then waited all day in the hot sun because the ambushes have been happening in the evening. Our plan was to catch the Taliban red-handed setting up an ambush along Highway Four and see where they came from, we also noted all suspicious activity with as much detail as possible. Jack and I took turns doing sentry on his C-9 light machine gun to the west. The entire day I could hear the people in the village at the bottom of the mountain going about their daily business, we had such little cover up there we had to piss lying down. The faint sounds of the tractors and jingle-truck horns made me nervous for some reason; it seemed the longer we got into this mission, the more nervous we became. As I was lying down near Jack's machine gun, I noticed a pebble-sized black human skull in the dirt. The thing freaked me right out. I rolled over to Jack and said, "What the hell is this, man?" and he said "It's one of my patrol beads that fell off my vest, they sell them in the kit shop, where have you been, man?"

After almost a full day of our roasting in the sun, the sounds of tractors and jingle trucks started to decrease. It would soon be dusk and we knew that's when the bullshit usually happened. I was sitting against a rock close enough to Sully to whisper in his ear, when Miles looked over at me and made the signal that someone was close to us. I gave Sully a shake and we put our fingers on our triggers. Jack was facing west on his C-9, I looked back at Miles and you could tell he was looking at someone approaching by the way he was looking and slouching down like a cat. All of a sudden this kid stumbled right onto our position, he let out this horrible scream and continued to scream and cry all the way down the south side of the mountain. We immediately threw our rucksacks on and Dave, the patrol commander, reported the incident to call sign zero. They gave us a "wait out," so we sat in place hoping we would get orders for an immediate extraction, we had plans of our own to extract ourselves to an alternate pre-designated position. The village at the bottom of the mountain was going nuts, women and children were fleeing, it was evident that our jig was up. After about ten minutes, the unthinkable happened.

We had established an all-around defence; the alternate position didn't have the vantage point this one had to see the base of both sides of the mountain, so we had decided to just stay put. I was covering to the north looking down the mountain when I saw impacts near the base of the north side of the mountain, the sound immediately followed and I was in disbelief, it was so loud and those impacts were so big it was just unbelievable. At first, "RPG" came out of my mouth, but after those initial four impacts, more started coming in, they were creeping up the mountain towards us. We were being mortared and they had us for line, they were simply walking the mortars in towards us. We all jumped to our feet, Miles yelled out, "Down the face of the mountain!" Miles and Cory briefly stayed in position, attempting to locate where the rounds were being launched from, but they had to move. Just as we started to run down the south face I felt the shock wave from one of the impacts, a round impacted right where Jack, Sully and I had been lying and someone's rucksack flew by me. Looking down that mountain, I wondered where the hell we were going to go, our extraction point was back on the north side where the mortar tube could see us and the village was at the bottom of the south side. Falling rocks were becoming a danger, so we quickly found a re-entrant where we could spread out in another all-around defence and call in the contact to call sign zero. We could tell that whoever was dropping mortars on us had lost sight of us because he seemed to be dropping them all over the place now. As Dave was radioing grids and situation reports, Cory, who is one of the snipers, was observing the village on the base of the south side of the mountain, all the women and children had fled and men were gathering, there was even traffic being directed towards the village from the highway. I remember asking Cory if he could sugar-coat those SITREPS for me, he said, "No. Sorry, man." If we could just hold out long enough for an Apache to get to us, we could get off the mountain under the cover of darkness.

The mortars continued to impact on the mountain. They had someone calling the shots because it now seemed like we were being bracketed, a round would land east of us, then less than a minute later one would land west of us, every round getting closer. The guys on the mortar tube could not see us but someone was calling their shots, probably by a cellphone on the south side of the mountain. Those rounds make such an eerie sound before they impact, the more rounds that came in the angrier I was becoming. Once the rounds started getting too close to us we would pick up and move locations, the guy calling the shots and the guys on the mortar tube would have to start bracketing all over again. It was hard for the sniper on the radio to communicate while on the move, so we would stop and spread out, we also had to send a new grid reference every time we moved. We could hear the sound of a chopper, which reminded us to turn on our infrared strobe lights on our helmets; the chopper found us quickly and we asked him to do a thermal sweep of the mountain just to ensure we were up here alone. Those bad guys were so bold, every time the chopper would turn to face south another round would impact. All the men that had gathered at the village seemed to disappear when the chopper showed up and we had an armoured convoy en route to a grid that Sully eyeballed beside the town. It was just about dark enough to use our monoculars and the mortaring was tapering off, so we started our slow descent. I was starting to think we were going to survive.

The descent was faster than the climb the night before, we were more at risk of injury but we all knew how important it was to get ourselves off that mountain. It had become so dark that we could only see with night vision, this was to our advantage. Everyone had their finger on their laser, which you can only see through your monocular. It was kind of funny to see all the lasers scanning every suspicious-looking rock on the mountain. We encountered this cave and I swear we almost blasted the shit out of it. It only took us about an hour to reach a safe little ditch at the bottom of the mountain, but we were basically in someone's backyard. We heard our rescue convoy driving around trying to get to the grid Sully gave them, they got on the radio and told us we must walk to them, they were parked on the other side of the village. It was the final leg of our journey; I quickly pulled out my two-quart of water and passed it around, Miles turned around and said, "This is it, boys." We walked through that village with our weapons at the ready, it seemed like a ghost town it was so quiet, but it wasn't, we could feel the eyes looking at us. They knew the night belonged to us and they probably didn't want to fuck with anyone brave enough to walk through their village like they owned it, especially after what we'd just gone through. Once we cleared the village and a cemetery, there it was, our armoured convoy waiting with their ramps down.

It was such a relief to crawl into the back of a LAV, I knew the mission was over and I could take my guard down. It was a convoy from A Company that just happened to be driving back to KAF from up north, Pte Simpson looked down from the air sentry hatch and said, "Gordo, is that you, man?" Jack was sitting beside me and I asked him if he wanted to go for a coffee with me later because I sure feel like one. It was one of the best rides I've ever been on. I thought I was dead up there, when those first rounds impacted my mind went somewhere else for a split second. It was weird because I saw my kids, I also saw every happy moment I've ever had with them, my overall feeling was, what a shame.

As soon as we dismounted back at our compound, our entire platoon was there to meet us, they were marshalled up the whole time waiting for the word to extract us. They wanted to hear what happened but I didn't know where to start, all I could say was, "It was fucked, a damn kid." They all knew we got mortared, but they'll never know how close we came to being dead. What they may never know is the feeling you get when you're being hunted, it's the freakiest thing I've ever experienced, and something I hope I'll never experience again. I thought for sure I was going to be on Al Jazeera television and all over the Internet, being dragged all over town behind a truck as everyone beat my dead body. My seven-man patrol walked over to call sign zero for a mission debriefing, we were in their orders room with many of the task force officers. Dave and Miles did most of the talking, giving the information we had gathered, including where we thought that mortar tube had been firing from, we guessed it was no more than half a mile northwest of Three Mile Mountain. I wasn't ready to give any type of briefing, I needed to defuse for a couple of days, but they were planning a bigger mission. What I did like was the pizzas they had waiting for us, though.

Later on, when I was taking the Claymore out of my rucksack and cleaning the Sophie at our platoon sea container, Jeff walked over to me and said, "A Company was conducting a *shirra* up north today and some freak came up behind one of our officers and hit him in the head with an axe." I said, "What the hell are you talking about?" He told me how Lieutenant Trevor Greene from Vancouver's Seaforth Highlanders was in serious condition after he had an axe buried in the back of his head. The A Company guys standing there shot and killed the axe attacker immediately and all hell broke loose; they came under fire but took no more casualties. I said, "What the hell is this place coming to?" The Taliban have claimed they are starting their spring campaign early, I would believe it from the amount of shit that's going on around here every day.

Last night when I went to my bed there was a letter sitting on my pillow from Nikki, it was good to read some of her nice words. She was telling me about their day and what they did; they all wanted me to know how much they miss me and how much they love me. Nikki did tell me in the letter that she hopes I'll never have to go on another tour, it's just too long. I can't argue with her there, it must be so hard being at home with the kids and having your other half in Afghanistan.

This morning when I woke up I looked at Jack and said, "It's a new day," so we went over to the mess hall to get some bacon and eggs in us. Sully caught up with us and asked if we were fucked up over our experience on the mountain last night, of course we said no. Some of the other troops in the platoon thought it was cool and considered it a good experience; they even wished they had been with us. When we got to the mess hall we met up with some other buddies from the battalion, the word was spreading that the second man that was beside Cpl Paul Davis in the turret during the LAV rollover a few days ago had passed away in Germany. I immediately knew it was a buddy of mine, MCpl Timothy Wilson of B Company, 2 PPCLI. He passed away with his family at his side. I had the privilege of doing my sniper course with Tim in Dundurn, Saskatchewan, last summer, I also caught the odd bit of conversation with him around here when we first got our boots on the ground. Tim was a good man with lots of family that loved him, he will always be missed.

KALAKASHAK KONIM (LET'S PEEK)

BY

MAUREEN MAYHEW, MD, MPH

Dr. Maureen Mayhew is a Vancouver-based public-health physician with a focus on health public policy. She first visited Afghanistan in 2000, during the Taliban regime. She has since returned three times, spending a total of almost three years in the country. Her first two visits were to Western Afghanistan with Médecins Sans Frontières (MSF) and involved identifying health priorities and establishing maternal and child health clinics in rural areas. The last two visits were based in Kabul, with travel to other provinces, where she worked with Johns Hopkins University in health-care research and health-policy development. During the past several years, she has visited fifty-three countries and participated in emergency relief efforts in Asia and Africa.

My first memory of Afghanistan

After the small aircraft landed outside the city of Herat on a desert runway littered with battered Russian helicopter gunships and a crashed plane, the absence of women seemed peculiar and tension was tangible. We entered the destroyed airport through a sea of stern, bearded men wearing turbans and carrying Kalashnikovs. The scene suggested a world where women, including me, were ghosts. None of the men seemed to notice us, yet magically a path appeared through them, leading us to an immigration official. Not once did he look at us—he just stamped our passports and pointed to the exit. It was easy to feel insulted. Fortunately, another foreign woman from the flight, with thirty years of experience in Afghanistan, coached me to take the lack of attention as the highest form of respect, an idea that struck me as perverse at the time. She explained that their interpretation of the Koran viewed any interaction with women as defiling them. Included in these "interactions" were eye contact and conversation. Burka-clad ghosts accompanied by men, boys and other burkas punctuated our drive through Herat. These women appeared to have no interaction with their surroundings. Of course, this observation was erroneous, but a common one for foreigners when first exposed to Afghan culture.

Bala Morghab

Surprisingly, women in rural areas appeared to have more freedom than their city counterparts. I lived in Bala Morghab, a village with a population of five thousand, where women often walked in groups, surrounded by brightly clothed children. They chatted animatedly, burka covers flipped up to expose their faces. When men passed, the face screens came down and the laughter vanished. Some women continued talking while covering and uncovering their faces numerous times, as if it were a game. Frequently when we conversed, I felt at a disadvantage because women in burkas could read my face, whereas my view of their faces was limited to two dark spots, hidden eyes. After work, as I walked the local streets, women often appeared on rooftops, in doorways or windows, or peeking from behind chimneys, curtains or laundry. If my male companion, with whom I was obliged to be accompanied, looked away, they exposed their faces, beckoning to me. His glance caused them to shrink into the shadows, immediately reappearing when he looked away again.

Inside the women's houses, we spoke of marriage, children, origins and family. An offer of tea, supper and spending the night inevitably followed. Sometimes a village man joined my companion and me during our walk and invited me into his compound to meet his wife and the rest of his family. When we reached the man's compound, my companion either made arrangements for the stranger to walk me home or came back later to fetch me. Most visits were enjoyable and only once did I witness injustices towards an older wife. This solitary occurrence saddened me—a younger wife, decorated in jewellery and fine clothing, ate with me while suckling her newborn son, and the worn, older wife, wearing rags, sullenly scoured pots outside, after having cooked the meal and baked the bread over a scorching hot tandoor oven. The older wife was introduced only after I had expressed concern about her depressed appearance. When I left, the younger wife confessed that her own cooking skills were inadequate, but that the older lady refused to teach her. Of course, discordant households like this one could have been common, but I was unlikely to be invited into them.

Lessons in Dari . . . and more

I'd learned Dari, an Afghan version of the Persian language related to Farsi, from our night guard, who, although not formally schooled, was exceptionally intelligent and inquisitive. Most of my evenings were spent creating a phonetic dictionary of Dari and English with this brilliant twenty-seven-year-old male Pashtun who spoke little English and had four sons and two surviving wives. We began by pointing and miming and eventually used a Persian dictionary to supplement conversations on cultural differences and current events. One evening, each of us bundled in blankets, our breath visibly frozen in the air, he said, "So, you have been earning money as a doctor for fifteen years, yet you have no home; you don't wear jewels, and you have no children. What did you do with your money?" I replied, "I do have possessions that I store to use when I return." He asked why I would have things that I don't use if I had nowhere to put them. Who uses them now? I began to comprehend his perspective and I chuckled uncomfortably; as a single person, I had more possessions than he and his family together. "They are stored in a small rented wooden room in a locked, guarded building." A discussion of cost followed. He asked if I could sleep in the room. After he learned that the storage locker cost me several days' wages per month, he looked at me incredulously, saying, "You spend that many days' wages for a room to store stuff you don't use and you can't even sleep in it?! You should buy a house." Sheepishly wondering about my gluttonous behaviour I said, "Yes, it is different in Canada." Cultural rules dictated that my meetings with the night guard were unacceptable, so they remained a well-kept secret until my return the following year.

Home visits

It was Friday afternoon, the men were at the mosque and we women were satiated, having just finished mounds of rice, mutton and aubergine in yogurt sauce. I sat on a thin mattress, leaning back on an intricately embroidered cushion of numerous fluorescent colours. A ten-year-old girl with kohl makeup, brightly coloured lips and gaudy, chipped black nail polish fanned away the flies. Mesmerized by my foreign characteristics she snuggled up, putting her face in front of mine. It was hot; her mother scolded her, sending her to fetch tea. A younger girl took her place. They noticed every small droplet of sweat on my body, and set to work drying it up with fans. Sometimes this took two fans. They fed me sweets as the tea was poured. "Why don't you have children?" they asked. "Because I'm not married," I replied, not having the heart to say I didn't want any, since raising children was the essence of their lives. Silently they contemplated their tea, trying to decide how far they could probe. "You are a good woman, and smart. Why don't you get married?" they enquired, secretly wondering if I had some incurable problem. "Because I have yet to find an interesting man who will tolerate my world travels. If I were married and had children, I wouldn't be here. In my culture, being single is not difficult like it is here. I enjoy my life," I said. An older woman nodded knowingly, even though she had not set foot outside of her village since the day she was married at fourteen years old. The boisterous young matriarch with many children looked at me as if I was hiding something: "You work so much and spend so much time alone that we worry about you. How can you be happy? If you had a husband, you wouldn't have to work. He would keep you warm at night." Many nodded. A beautiful, round girl of sixteen, just married, began to dance—intricate footwork, twisting hands, beautiful posture—to the soothing beat of the drum, the lilting song. A three-year-old girl mimicked her outside the circle of women.

Later on, as we departed, burkas were donned. I tried one on, and imagined how I would walk in high heels like they did when I couldn't see my feet. "Yes," they said, "sometimes it is awkward but it is normal for us. If we don't wear a burka people stare like they stare at you. It's hard to live that way." One woman whispered that proximity to most men made her so nervous that she felt faint. In her *chaderi* she felt invisible, free from leering men. Unlike Western culture, where breasts and thighs are erotic, in Afghan culture, the face, hair, ankles and forearms are tantalizing. Breasts in this culture appeared to be functional. While women covered their faces, their breasts hung out of their dresses, ready for feeding. In the following days, I experienced this difference when, while teaching a man how to take blood pressure, I exposed my whole arm and his eyes nearly popped out of his head.

A village wedding

In the heat of my mud office, I struggled to balance a budget, distracted by drumming at my neighbour's house. My interpreter told me it was a wedding, and that as a neighbouring woman, I was welcome to attend the women's party. I walked outside into an oven-like temperature and started to sweat even more. Mud houses with thick walls, domed roofs and Afghan air-conditioning—a chimney that funnelled wind through thorns dampened by water—were a lot cooler than fancy cement dwellings. The compound was full of women jostling each other to get food or conversing with friends. They marvelled slyly at me as the single foreign woman, pinched my cheek, cupped my breast and then took my hand to lead me to the bride. I sat beside her, a demure young woman who seemed a little sad. I learned later that she was effectively a showpiece for three days, during which her sombre mood was expected, in part out of respect for her mother, whose house she was leaving forever. Maybe she was anxious about moving in with a man she didn't know, and perhaps losing her virginity. I couldn't ask. Oddly, after about fifteen minutes, all the women disappeared. Thinking it bizarre that a wedding would end this way, I returned to the compound to discover that the women had all gone to the groom's house for another party. So I walked over, arriving late. Men waited outside like guards. In the inner courtyard was a festival of several hundred women shimmering in sunshine. Dancing had begun. Women sang and clapped. I tried to take a photo but a hand shot up to cover the lens. Photos were forbidden, in fact illegal, during the Taliban regime. They encouraged me to dance. In shyness, I insisted that a woman dance with me so I could mimic her loose-jointed foot, shoulder, neck and hand movements.

Lunch with the governor

We had invited the governor and his entourage to lunch, a courtesy invitation to maintain good relations between the local government and our organization. As lunch began, the invited men and our staff determined that the Swiss midwife and I, the two foreign females, could be included in the feast as well. We arrived late to sit on the floor around the tablecloth with the governor, his eight black-turbaned Taliban supporters, our translator and our English co-worker. There were no greetings or conversation; they just ate. A little bored, I decided to ask the governor about river fishing, an activity I knew he enjoyed. He'd throw bomblets in the river and scoop up the floating fish. Looking at my plate, I asked my question in Dari, wondering if he would answer. Our translator smiled encouragingly. After a slight hesitation, the governor responded. An odd conversation began with each of us gazing at our food as we spoke, since it was unacceptable to look at each other. Eventually, I glanced up to notice that he would watch me as I spoke, but never as he responded. And so this bizarre conversation continued for several minutes.

When our guests departed we were once again courteously ignored.

Three worlds—of men, of women and of families

One early evening, after I had lived in Bala Morghab for several months, the evening guard took me out for a walk and, after jumping across a canal, we encountered another guard harvesting wheat. After exchanging numerous mandatory greetings, we spoke of crops and animals. I had visited both men's homes and wanted to thank the second guard for a scarf his wife had made for me. I began, "Thank you so much for lunch a few days ago . . ." Afghans have extraordinary non-verbal communication, and his eyes stated, "Enough!" But he said, "We so much enjoyed having you." My evening guard had courteously stepped away to speak with his son. After the conversation, when I was again alone with him, he said, "We don't mention our wives to each other. He does not know my wife's name, nor do I know his." I apologized for my ignorance and mentioned how fortunate I felt to be able to see the different worlds of men and women when he was unable to. "Yes," he said, with a knowing smile that suggested I had learned yet one more lesson in how things are in Afghanistan.

Straddling these worlds was awkward, for although both were open for me to view, I was a guest in each. Later on, I was invited to our guard's home to share a Friday meal. The meal began with the guard and me eating together in private, served by his oldest son. The rest of the family was in another room, which made me feel like I was being interviewed for the position of third wife. I asked him where everyone else was eating and why they hadn't joined us. He suggested that I ask them in, so I ended the uncomfortable situation by fetching the rest of his family. From that point on, every time I visited, the whole family sat together.

Returning to Afghanistan

I returned to Afghanistan in December 2001, after the fall of the Taliban, driven by a desire to help the wonderful people I remembered. After travelling across Turkmenistan by night train and then carting our belongings across the border, where the border guards' guns pointed at the three European MSF workers and me, Afghanistan looked strangely familiar and friendly, a desiccated, brown uncultivated land where crossing the border meant slipping back in time by several centuries. Chronic war had prevented advancement. Electricity, pavement, fancy cars, availability of goods, Western clothing, women's faces, alcohol, telephones and televisions all disappeared at the border. Opium, however, was abundant.

When I arrived in Herat, evidence of war still existed. Each house I visited was decorated with white plastic spoons and foil pouches hung on nails, remnants of unused food packets dropped by the military. Children picked up bomblets resembling toys and ended up in hospital with missing limbs. Cluster bombs were the same colour as food packages; both had been dropped from the sky. Mazlakh camp, where MSF worked, was overcrowded with people seeking food, shelter and safety. Snow leaked through the tents and latrines overflowed. On the road to the camp, twenty Russian military tanks waited for deployment. One day they were gone. A bomb exploded about two kilometres away. The shock wave blew our office doors open, causing everyone to flee to the basement. Children often followed me, pushing each other and occasionally throwing rocks. "*Khorije,*" they chanted—foreigner. "*Americai hastid*"—are you American? American bombs had killed their friends and destroyed their homes.

Cultural rules in flux

Within a month of my arrival, previously clear gender rules became hazy as both Westerners and Afghans pushed to change them. International non-government organizations (INGOs) had come to town bringing the West with them, and most expatriates were first-time visitors to Afghanistan who hadn't known Taliban rules, so they dressed in tight *shalwar kameez*, resembling prostitutes but thinking themselves conservatively dressed, or wore jeans covered by a shirt the length of a miniskirt, not nearly long enough by Afghan standards. Our Afghan staff began arriving at the office with cellphones and cars. The movie theatre opened and the staff asked questions about love scenes they had witnessed in Western movies.

Satellite dishes proliferated. President Karzai announced by radio that all Afghans should dress in Western clothing while working. Western dress was interpreted in different ways. One employee, previously covered in a *shalwar kameez*, came to work wearing gold chains and a basketball singlet that barely covered his muscles. He had proudly shaved off his beard and changed his hairstyle. In secret, he told me he had tasted vodka. Families celebrated with picnics in the surrounding countryside. The euphoria was tangible.

Taking risks

Our Afghan administrators, who had previously always advised conservative behaviour, were suddenly taking risks. We women sat in the front seat of vehicles, travelled more freely with Afghan men and ate together at one tablecloth. Some women even drove their own vehicles. I was encouraged to walk the five minutes to the hospital by myself. Walking alone for the first time, I felt incredibly free, but was surprised by a sense of vulnerability. If after a few months of always being accompanied I was feeling tentative about walking alone, imagine how difficult it would be for someone who had been accompanied in public for her whole life and was just now being asked to change. Men in the shops stopped their work and stared. Boys in the roadside store shouted, "*Khorije!*" I had to walk cautiously but with confidence. Relief came when a small girl with green eyes and dirty hands greeted me. As if sensing my discomfort, she took my hand and accompanied me to the hospital. Somehow this small gesture helped me gain the confidence to gaze openly at the village men and greet them. Each time I was met with smiles, and eventually my five-minute walk became a normal part of village life. Soon people became aware of my language ability, and small conversations began with groups of women who walked in the streets as village women had the previous year. Finally I was able to look beyond burkas, seeing the eyes within.

Flirting

Flirting seemed natural in Afghan society and single women were fair game to pursue. My driver and I had spent many long trips together and I completely trusted his advice on security, code of conduct and planning trips through remote areas. He described his enjoyment at watching women as we travelled from village to village, and boasted about how much he could tell about a woman despite her *chaderi*, a coy game played by both men and women. As he drove by a woman, she looked quickly, then covered herself; often, however, she looked again, and the canny fellow would catch sight of her in his rearview mirror.

Inadvertently, I facilitated this game by being an appealing subject for Afghan women to gaze at, so they delayed covering themselves. Sometimes a woman would uncover herself enough to show a wrist. Men described how they identified a beautiful woman—by her face, her shoes, her ankle lace, her fingers, her silhouette or her agility. The strong yearning of both genders to see one another was evident in daily life, each tantalizing the other, a dangerous game where too much tempting could result in family shame and violent retribution.

Dancing at a wedding

Weddings in Western Afghanistan were still gender-segregated affairs, and, as I discovered, played a key role in selecting mates for other members of the family. On the day following a wedding I had attended, some of our male employees, whom I hadn't seen at the wedding, sang compliments about my dancing. Talented female dancers were noticed, and so, of course, were foreigners.

Although many other factors were considered when choosing a wife—family status, education, personality, beauty—dancing ability was important. Trying to understand why, I assumed that it must reveal self-confidence, music appreciation, fun, eroticism, beauty, litheness in body and some degree of aptitude for learning.

Several months later, the day before I was leaving for Canada, I received a proposal of marriage, as second wife. Whether this offer hinged on my dancing ability remains a mystery. The proposal came during a visit to my driver's father, a sick man who commanded respect in the gentle way of someone who has successfully yet lovingly negotiated tough situations. He lay on his bed with the whole family congregated in front of him. After our discussion about his medical condition, he began to speak in earnest. "You make my son so happy. Ever since he began working with you, he is a changed man. You have done a lot for him . . . perhaps you would marry him." A little shaken and unprepared, I replied, "This is a grand offer and I would be honoured, but tomorrow I must return to my mother and father in Canada. My family expects me and it would disappoint them were I not to return." More insistence and resistance occurred, but the proposal was eventually settled without shame, and his son drove me back to my compound. The whole way he marvelled, "Did you hear what my father said? Did you understand? You will come back soon?" Maybe his father's request had surprised him. He certainly seemed excited.

Time in between: 2002–2005

Between my trip in 2002 and the following ones in 2005 and 2006, many Afghans and foreigners, including aid workers, had been killed. Five Médecins Sans Frontières employees had been shot while working in one of the few clinics in Afghanistan that diagnosed and treated tuberculosis. MSF had started this project in 2002. The project closed in 2004 and the organization has not yet returned. The rash of killings was said to be a random event but I wondered if, as social norms were redefined, unarmed INGO workers, like military soldiers, had become targets.

Competition with men

In 2005, I revisited Herat in a different role, as manager of a survey of health facilities in Western Afghanistan. It began with a week-long training session. A male physician from the Afghan government and I trained twenty-two men from remote areas in the west. During the training, one man responded to a question by arguing minute details in a competitive way, as if having a say in the discussion was more important than the points raised and the resolution achieved. Another disagreed. Then multiple people chimed in, each person speaking louder than the previous one. Finally we banged on the table, only to have the arguing start all over again. On the fourth day of training, the seating order had changed. The most argumentative man, a surgeon, sat next to me. During the talk he leaned over to look at my computer screen, awfully close. He asked me a few questions and came closer. I made an excuse to move away. In the afternoon, his friend sat there. He too sat closer than necessary, subtly sniffing my perfume. He giggled, resembling a self-conscious rule-breaking schoolboy. Patience, I thought. I never knew whether they came to challenge me or to be close to a foreign woman, but I did learn not to wear perfume. Gender issues constantly disturbed effective working relationships. It was exhausting to be possibly these men's first and only platonic female relationship. Throughout the week, my Afghan counterpart became more strained and, for reasons he refused to disclose, left early.

Abdul, as I'll refer to the Afghan physician who replaced my colleague, told me that in Afghan custom I was now his responsibility and therefore obliged to disclose my whereabouts at all times. It became apparent that this protector role was important to him, and since my job would have been difficult without him, and I had already lost one man, I acquiesced. Oddly, I felt more restricted when dealing with these educated men of Kabul than with the amicable village men from rural areas.

Skeptics

Abdul was skeptical of platonic activities involving men and women. Swimming fascinated him. He wanted to know if we wore bathing suits, whether men and women swam together at the same time, and whether "anything" transpired between genders while swimming. He had never set foot in a swimming pool. Platonic relationships between men and women were foreign to him, perhaps unimaginable. Similarly, our driver had questions about the yoga classes I attended in Kabul. As he dropped me off for the second class, he asked with a grin what we did in the huge room full of men and women, having taken note of this strange sight the first time he'd brought me. Each time I returned from class, he had gathered more information from observations and discussions with other Afghan drivers while they also waited for the class to finish. He described how he had seen us moving up and down in unison and wondered if we were praying. If so, why was this being done by women in spaghetti-strap tops and tight pants? I latched onto this misunderstanding and explained that yoga was a combination of sport and prayer.

Working with women

During my last trip to Afghanistan, I worked mainly with women, a different experience from working with men. Habitually, when I entered the office I shared with two colleagues, they were drinking tea and chatting about the previous night—they had not slept because of their children, or because someone had died, or because of a wedding or because they had stayed up late cooking for guests. Further delays in starting work happened because a new *chador* had to be modelled, or the women were worried about delays in someone's marriage. Computer chatting was a fascinating new toy. They constantly spoke of worry about family, friends, health, money, losing what they had accumulated in recent years, wanting something different, or moving to a new place, but no personal decisions were made. I understood their desire to rest away from constant family demands, but it was difficult to motivate and mentor them when they appeared so unaccustomed to working. Exceptions existed. One midwife, with whom I worked while accrediting midwifery schools, was so motivated that she began an association of midwives that spread across the country. On good days she was a dream to work with, but her non-productive days were full of depression as she relived painful memories of difficult battles and deaths of loved ones. The most difficult part of working with educated women from Kabul was the magnitude of their pain and their never-ending depressive thoughts. They had witnessed many deaths and much violence; they had endured constant uncertainty about surviving another day and serious financial losses. They had quickly grown old in times of war. None of the women with whom I travelled went out in the evening. They preferred to rest. Sometimes I needed to escape.

Kabul

Kabul was strikingly different from the rest of the country, flaunting higher education levels, a rapid population growth, a large expatriate population and a boomtown-like aura. After 2002, millions of refugees had returned, and many others had moved to Kabul hoping to reap the benefits of international aid. Traffic congestion and road rage were common. Beggars filled the streets, congregating near international compounds and bazaars. Few women walked in the street, since it was considered safer to be driven. In general, Kabul was viewed as a dangerous place where women and children required protection. Usually our visits to homes excluded foreign men so that we could all eat and drink tea together. Feasting was common, but dancing and drumming were activities usually relegated to children, except during weddings. In my experience, educated women made only marginally more interesting conversationalists than village women. The educated women had spent their lives inside compounds rearing children, with virtually no exposure to the outside world, and they seemed more depressed than the village women I had visited during the Taliban regime. In Kabul and other large cities in Afghanistan, women had been more repressed and restricted by the regime than village women. Village life was naturally more in line with strict Taliban rules and so had required less "surveillance."

Competition with women

In 2005, I attended a Kabul wedding with one other foreign woman, held in a large room in a hotel. The room had been divided by a panelled curtain, one side for the women and the other for the men. Through slits between panels, male eyes watched the women dance. One man crossed the divide to dance with his wife. We, the two foreign women, acquiesced to insistence that we dance. Camera flashes appeared in the curtain slits. As usual my partners were women, until suddenly an erotic young man with gyrating hips, reminiscent of John Travolta, bolted onto the dance floor. Maybe he had seen *Saturday Night Fever* on DVD? The women scattered. Now I was surrounded by expectant faces. Only a foreigner would dance with a man, so we became dance partners for a song. Afterwards, wondering what they thought of me, I sat down. Could they fathom that I was just a normal Western woman, or had they relegated me to the category of whore? Within seconds of sitting down, a beautiful woman in a red flamenco dress approached me, challenging me to a dance. In disbelief, I was pushed out to the floor and we danced to the fast-paced modern Iranian music. Was this for fun, or had I inadvertently seduced her betrothed and was now in a competition for his affection? These wild thoughts were only appropriate in the time warp in which I lived. My enthusiasm lagged and I let her outshine me. I never understood what she won.

Escaping

One Friday, I found myself longing to escape to the hills or paddle in the ocean, to roam free from thoughts of work, and the pain, suffering and worry of these people. But Afghanistan is landlocked and much of the land is mined. As compensation two co-workers, Nasrat and Nasim, offered to take me to Doghabad, Nasim's village on the outskirts of Kabul. Nasrat and I had spent several days in villages where every spare moment we had shared photographic techniques and practised the art of seeing through the lens. We parked in a wheat field and took photos of flowers with the ruins of the Queen's Palace in the background. As we climbed, my spirit rejuvenated. The sun sunk into the haze of Kabul's polluted air and the sky lit up with colour. We spoke of the Kabul that had been, pointing out famous geographic icons. We climbed higher and noted how beautiful Doghabad was, having been newly rebuilt. We reached the cemetery where Nasim's father was buried. He stayed a moment. The call to prayer floated across the distance and someone lay down their *patu* (cloth) for the ritual prayer. We took more photos, and hoped that the spirituality of the moment had been captured.

Mike

Mike Frastacky, a carpenter who died while building a school in Afghanistan, was a good friend. We often shared our understanding of the country and culture, as well as the challenges of the work we did. Not everyone has the courage to go to a country like Afghanistan. People often ask me why he spent his own time and money in a place that put him in danger unnecessarily, and which ultimately cost him his life. In many ways Mike's reasons were similar to my own and those of many others who repeatedly return to the country. Afghanistan is a place of poetry and beauty as well as treachery and violence. The beauty of Afghanistan is not captured in the media, but it captures those of us who visit. It is a place where caring, family and friendship run deep, sustained by a marvellous sense of humour. I hope I have conveyed some of this complexity.

> *In the shambles of love, they kill only the best,*
> *none of the weak or deformed.*
> *Don't run away from this dying.*
> *Whoever's not killed for love is carrion.*
>
> —Rumi

Mike Frastacky was an independent aid provider who worked as a volunteer in Afghanistan from 2002 to July 23, 2006, when he was shot to death. Born and raised in Toronto, he spent his adult life in Vancouver working as a highly skilled finishing carpenter. Through his attraction to exploring remote areas of the world, Mike found himself trekking in Tajikistan, Uzbekistan and the Pamirs in the late 1990s, and eventually travelled to Afghanistan in 2001. His goals evolved to a philanthropic purpose, initially sponsoring projects in an orphanage in Faizabad, then focusing on establishing and building an elementary school in the Nahrin Valley, a remote area northeast of Kabul. He worked unaffiliated with any aid organization, donating his money, his organizational skills, and his design and building expertise for several months of each year from 2002 to 2006. These are some of the many emails that he sent home; they have been reprinted as they were sent, though edited for length, with the permission and assistance of his friends, represented by Grant Tomlinson and Jan Rooks, and his sister, Luba Frastacky.

June 23, 2003

Subject: Greetings from Kabul
Hello to all of you from the dustblown, fly-infested streets of
Lovely Kabul, the open gutters send you their very best wishes as

do the innocents in this den of wolves . . . And YES! As a matter of fact I DO call this fun! I guess that we're not in Kansas anymore, eh? . . . What was that mutt's name, anyways???

I can't say that the streets have changed that much since I was here last, though Kabul now has its first traffic signal which everyone dutifully ignores of course . . . There are still great heaps of refuse at their designated locations on every residential street . . . heaven help those whose houses border these piles; a young boy who was rummaging through the debris on our street yesterday was bitten by a poisonous snake.

Jamshaid Kator and his cousin met me at the airport. The Kator family are the former Princes of the Nahrin Valley, where I will be working. It is located about 9 hours drive north from Kabul. Last year, they had a very bad earthquake there in which about 1600 people died. Jamshaid is the youngest of 12 children. His family emigrated to the U.S. about 15 years ago. His father Hamayoun will be arriving in Kabul in about 10 days but I will be leaving for Nahrin in 4 days to settle into the place. Both father and son are driven to be here, I think, out of a mixture of wanting to do their part to restore their area to its former glory as well as seeing a lot of opportunity here to get in on the ground floor of what can only be described as a booming economy. Three months ago, Jamshaid bought 6 tents from an earthquake rescue aid group and started a school. It has 400 students already and he says that 1500 would enroll if the facilities were in place. I may or may not become involved in this project but I do see some very encouraging signs. I have heard from different people that Hamayoun is a very astute business man who will get 10 prices for something rather than pay too much. This is the kind of man that a little lamb like myself needs in this den of wolves, at this time . . . but you couldn't find a more interesting den of wolves . . . so the prospect of partnering up with someone of Hamayoun's stature and temperament is attractive. Also, he is legacy motivated and although that can have its dark side in a feudal society like this, if I can keep a sense of autonomy then I may well see a redeeming reason to collaborate. If nothing else, I will learn more in 3 months here than I would in 3 years in Canada. I kind of arrived with a "hit the ground running" sort of theme . . . sort of like jumping off a moving freight train as it's turning a bend . . . Within 3 hours of clearing the chaos of Kabul International, we had driven 60 kilometres east of Kabul to a small Pashtun village because 3 very successful Afghan expatriates were returning to their former village for the first time in 25 years to participate in a village council meeting to discuss what changes were possible for them if they wanted them. Over the next 24 hours, we sat in on 3 meetings . . . one of which was held in a beautiful old grove of mulberry trees (Afghans have this poetic streak running through them); we all ate together and slept together and that night the village brought out their drummers (the strongest one was 78 years old) and for 3 hours the men danced the traditional Pashtun War Dance in celebration. I felt VERY fortunate to be that little fly on the wall (and yes, there were a lot of other tiny flies on the wall). By the way, in that Pashtun village virtually every farmer was devoting at least 20% of his land to growing opium. I got the impression that both the ISAF (International Security Assistance Force) and the Karzai government are saying, "Let's put as much money in as many people's pockets as we can to win the hearts and minds of the average Afghan during these first few years and then we'll slowly clamp down, once the warlords have made their first 100 million and want to go legitimate" . . . it is the warlords who are in control of the Kabul land prices though there are a few exceptions—one of the Afghan expats from that Pashtun village literally owns a 3-block-square of land in central Kabul. Typical shop rents in that area are now US$1000.00 a month! Afghanistan is like that Pashtun celebration, if you let the wind blow you in its chosen direction, before you've come up for air, you find yourself in a remarkable place with some very wonderful characters . . . it's just that you've got to be willing to swallow some dust and hit more than a few bumps in the road, along the way. Being comfortable with the sight of heavily armed ISAF patrols doesn't hurt a bit either. In a few days, I'll be going up to Nahrin and I'll update you in a week. I hope that all of you are well. I might add, "Wish You Were Here," but I guess that you might not feel that way inclined! Please feel free to email me anytime because I really do look forward to keeping in touch with all of you and as long as you don't email any photos or attachments, then my satellite email system downloads all of the emails within a minute.

Love and Kisses, Mike

Sunday June 29, 2003

Subject: Tucked In at Tabakan
Hello,
Well, I am nicely settled in at Hamayoun's new house in Tabakan. We (Jamshaid Kator, my translator Liaquat and I) came up here a few nights ago through the Salang Pass which is scheduled (in a week or so) to be closed for the next 4 months because a Russian company got the contract to rehabilitate this tattered mess of a major transport connector between the North and South . . . and if that isn't ironic, I don't know what is! The fact that we were able to drive up here at night (the Salang is only open from 6 p.m. to 6 a.m.) is, I guess, a reassuring sign that safety on the Northern roads is fairly good. Tabakan is about 7 kilometres northwest of a town called Narin (also spelled Nahrin on some maps). As I mentioned before, there was an earthquake throughout the Nahrin District last year which killed about 2000 people.

There are ruined mud brick villages everywhere and most people have been living in military-type tents for the last year. We get an average of 2 aftershocks a day which are stronger than anything I've ever experienced but they are very short in duration . . . but one does keep their pants and flashlight within easy reach at night just in case.

A group named "Shelter Now" has been providing some materials (a dozen roof beams) and funding for people to rebuild their houses, and so about 50% of the people are living in simple one-storey houses, which Shelter Now gives them US$100.00 to build themselves. By the way, Shelter Now is acting as a subcontractor for the UN which gives Shelter Now US$400.00 per house built and that, folks, is the name of the game. The Italian Government has built a simple 10-bed hospital in Nahrin and a group called "Concern" has put in hundreds of wells throughout the district. Last year, UNICEF distributed a lot of heavy-duty white plastic semi-circle tents to be used as temporary schools.

They are about 3 metres high and measure 20 feet by 20 feet (5 x 5 metres). I've seen up to 75 kids crammed cheek-to-jowl in one of these units, sitting knee-to-knee on the floor. I guess that you could throw a dart at a map of Afghanistan and within 15 kilometres of wherever it struck, you could justify the building of a clinic, well, school, bridge or irrigation project.

The Nahrin valley is semi-arid, by and large. The average temperature these days is 95 degrees F. Hamayoun Kator's property is an exception because it has 3 natural springs within it. These springs are incredibly clear, wonderfully cold in the summer and hot enough to bath in during the winter.

The NGO "Concern" people get their drinking water here because it tested so clean after the earthquake. Hamayoun is scheduled to come up here in a week or so (Afghan Time . . . give or take 12 days!) so I will be making some initial contacts with other Non-Governmental Organizations here, as well as having casual conversations with village elders and the farmers.

Hamayoun has about 300 acres which are looked after by 9 farmers who hire help as they need it (usually a couple of guys for the season). Each farmer is entitled to half of what he grows, with the rest going to the landowner . . . by all accounts, it's not a big money-maker for anyone concerned. They grow wheat, potatoes, cucumbers, tomatoes, onions and rice and each of them have their own vegetable gardens as well. They have their own flour mill, which is a simple water-driven stone wheel. A wide river, oddly referred to as "The Nahrin River" for reasons beyond my comprehension, runs along one side of the property. During the spring, it can be a raging current, a half a kilometre wide, but these days we can hop over the 3 small streams that remain. Across the river from us on a man-made raised earthen mound is a pre-Buddhist archaeological site referred to as "The Monastery" or "The Fort." Artifacts are found by anyone who spends a day digging around there. An old Kuchi (Koochi) nomad is living on the northern promontory of this primeval site, so around sunset yesterday Jamshaid and I went over to say hello. He laid out a carpet for us and before long regaled us with his stories of the war and the slyness of wolves. His camels can carry from 700 to 900 lbs, depending on the terrain.

Most of his tribe have gone further north, but will return come September. Apparently, there is an eight-year-old girl in the tribe who tells people's fortunes by reading their faces as well as their palms. The word *koochi* means "What, Where" and so they are known to have their summer and winter pastures for their sheep, goats and camels. This Koochi man stays in this area keeping it reserved for his tribe and shifts his flocks about every couple of months. I hope to take his oral history if I can fit it in and he doesn't change sites.

I did drop over to the school which Jamshaid donated the tents to and there were close to 300 kids (half girls and half boys) between the ages of 7 and 10 (grades 1 and 2 only) dutifully sitting on the ground. During my survey (some of which I hope to do on horseback) I will be assessing the realistic numbers which would attend a school if an elementary school was built.

There is no doubt in my mind that the elders, the government as well as the average farmer here see education as a necessary staple to their future. In any area of Afghanistan there is tribal animosity. It may be due to wartime-related reprisals between families or individuals, political manoeuvring or just plain drug related. In Nahrin, however, because of the need for the community to pull together after the earthquake, there is more cohesiveness because everyone here lost members of their family.

Jamshaid's driver, a former Commander (of 400 men), with the eyes of a lion and the gentleness of a lamb (especially with children), lost 20 members of his extended family. It's as if they have been shocked out of their war footing (this was the front line for a long time near the war's end) and just want to get on into the future, so my first impression is that they have the initiative to leave the feuds behind (except of course when the feud is REALLY important!). There are no opium fields on Hamayoun's acreage which is unusual, and when we went over to have dinner at one of his friend's houses yesterday, Jamshaid refused to shake the hands (or leave at the same time) when 5 opium growers/smugglers showed up. They came from the Pakistan frontier area south of Jalalabad near the Tora Bora Mts. He also insisted that we sit at opposite ends of the floor at dinner. They were noticeably quiet during dinner and would never look us in the eye. Apparently, his friend wanted to buy a large transport truck and borrowed money from the Commander in that frontier district (read Loan Shark) and to pay him back, he is growing opium on his fields outside of Nahrin town. These unsavoury characters are here to protect the commander's investment, supervise the harvesting and transport it back for refining/smuggling into Pakistan—they are the insurance policy! This is one of those boomer years for opium here because neither the ISAF or the Karzai Government are in ANY position to even try and make a dent on production. I feel quite safe from the politics in town and from the feuds that arise . . . it helps that Jamshaid's father, Hamayoun, has been away in America for almost 20 years and is most famous for killing 3 Russian soldiers, stealing their tank and driving it up to the mountains. So, I hope to slowly, quietly go about my work and cultivate my sense of humour in the process!

I hope that all of you are doing very well. Love and Kisses, Mike

September 5, 2003

[Excerpts from] Subject: Chapter 8 Random Anecdotes
I thought that I would put a few incidents into words to illustrate just how odd and amusing some days can be in a country like Afghanistan.

4—One night, long after I had spent all of my money which was marked for the school, I was speaking with Noor about the possibility that we may need some more pieces of wood to finish the school. At this point, it was Hamayoun's money which was being spent on mostly labour costs. Noor responded that Hamayoun had some spare wood and we can likely get that. I responded by saying, "But will he want to give it to the school?" . . . Noor said with a twinkle in his eye, "Don't worry, Mr. Mike, we'll pay him for it!!!" which really amounts to paying Hamayoun for his own wood with his own money . . . to make

him feel better!!! and I thought to myself, "Ahhhh, so THAT'S
how the Afghan mind works!"

5—Just before I skedaddle back down to Kabul, I thought that I
would tell you one last story which I would like to call, "Learning
to Cha Cha around Corruption." It reminds me of dancing poodles, rabbits, a fox and the way battery acid eats its way through
your trousers. Dancing Poodles, you stammer . . . "How is that
pppossible?" Have you ever seen an image of trained dancing
miniature poodles wearing bright Scottish plaid skirts with red
berets on their heads, topped by pom-poms? . . . It's a revolting
image, to be sure and one that can keep an otherwise sensible
person up at night, desperately trying to clear this kind of mental debris from their psyche. For some reason, I equate the Cha-
Cha with this exact image and though I am not at all proud to
admit that I am not, on the other hand, the least bit embarrassed
by it either. Noor is the wonderful Afghan man who is the site
supervisor for the classrooms being built. Last year, just after
the earthquake, he was chosen as the people's representative by
the surrounding 10 villages because the previous reps were
stealing (and selling) a lot of the emergency supplies which the
NGOs were handing out to them to distribute to their local
Communities, so Noor was chosen for his integrity, his good
judgement and his ability to relate to different kinds of people. A
rare gem in these parts.

Recently, I asked Noor if I should go myself to get a letter
from the Nahrin Director of Education verifying that I am
indeed half way through building a school and asking anyone
reading that letter to co-operate with me (such as the Afghan
Embassy in Canada, next year). He said that he would take care
of it, but after meeting with the Director he looked kind of glum.
When I asked him how it went, he said that the Director was
angry with Noor and I for a few reasons. Firstly, although I had

had a couple of meetings with the Nahrin Director laying out what I might do and where, I went to the Provincial capital (with Hamayoun and at his suggestion) in order to get approval for the construction at the particular location, which they quickly gave me. By doing this, I, unwittingly, didn't allow the Nahrin Director the chance to delay the process and negated the possibility of him demanding a bribe from me. The first time that I met him, I could see that he was quite a selfish and self-serving incompetent. Unfortunately, there was nothing that he could do if his superiors had granted approval. He also lectured Noor on why I had not given the money for the school to the Director himself, so that his department could build the school. Then, he said that Noor could have at least provided some benefit to the Director for the school being built in his district . . . Noor and I had done all the building independently and had not "involved" them. In every district, certain construction NGOs have very cosy relationships with the Directors of different Ministries and provide kick-backs for work. This is all called "BAKSHEESH," and it leaves Noor in an uncomfortable position, so Hamayoun has promised to sit down with the Director and try and appease him. The Director was pleading poverty to Noor, but Hamayoun's reaction is that anyone here could easily plead poverty, and if you start giving out money to one, then everyone wants some from you. I can vouch for that, I regularly get pleading village women following me on my way back from the school. My personal impression is that the Director is pining for a Russian motorcycle (a US$450.00 value) because his was recently stolen and I'm sure that neither Hamayoun nor I are going to indulge his ego. I offered to buy him a pen, some toilet paper or give him my Swiss Army knife (a $49.99 value!!:) but Noor just laughed.

My best wishes to all of you, Mike

September 18, 2005

Subject: The other side of the news

I thought that this time I would try and describe some of the atmosphere here on the days leading up to the election. I thought that it was oddly funny that the full moon last night looked like a spotlight over the landscape on the eve before Afghanistan's first parliamentary elections since 1969. Having a full moon to help the soldiers guarding each polling station and its electoral officers was a smart move by the ISAF Forces. Of the 130 candidates in this province there are 14 women running and no shortage of posters with the ladies putting their best face forward. I was greatly relieved by this because it seemed to me that it would be a daunting choice to have to make if all of the women candidates were wearing burkas. Looking back at a prospective voter as she/he opened their one metre-by-one metre voting sheet were 130 photos of severe-looking Afghans (in Kabul there were 4 voting sheets with over 300 candidates), each with their own symbol to help identify the individual. One lady had a television as her symbol, another gentleman had a flamingo, there were scissors, sailboats, soccer balls and one lucky sod had a waving hand. I asked the carpenter, who is doing some work at the school, just whom he was thinking of voting for, and he said that his village was going to vote en masse based on who their village elder told them to vote for. When I asked why he chose to do that rather than voting according to his own preference, he answered that their village elder was a pious man whom they trusted. This may help explain why there has been a flurry of luncheons given at the local mosques by aspiring parliamentarians for the teachers, merchants and elders for the last 2 weeks . . . sounds similar to our style of campaigning, except here there has been A LOT of money being paid to people who are willing to carry their villages into a candidate's camp. There has been much money being handed out in this way because the candidates assume that if they win, then the spoils of that achievement will easily make up for their investment. This is a primitive form of democracy, the rules are blurred and definitely open to interpretation. I suppose that we went through the same process a hundred years or so ago . . . maybe more. But it's a start.

An interesting thing has developed at the school. There are 5 of the 16 staff who have stepped up to the plate and initiated changes . . . for the good of the school. YES, I know . . . it's difficult for me to believe too, but they actually keep demonstrating that in small but important ways.

The librarians now have 20 boys at every recess who clamour for books pointing their hands up in the air and shouting to be chosen to be allowed to pick a book. The girls are much more civilized and demure. They wait till the boys are done, then quietly go in and make their choices. The 2 sports teachers are clearly becoming comfortable with handing out equipment and getting it back after recess is over, and have helped dig holes for the steel posts which we needed to put into the ground. The headmaster is being more assertive and the *Chowki* [custodian] has days when he is conscientious and ones when he just has no motivation . . . which I put down to him likely being a hash smoker like his brother. The rest of the teachers really just go through the day with minimal effort. I really do not believe that this situation with this school is any different from the vast majority of government schools in countries such as Afghanistan. There is bound to be a moderately to mostly corrupt bureaucracy in place, complacent teachers some of whom will respond to direction, the majority of whom will not, suspicion of foreigners' intentions especially by power-craving elders, justification of opportunism based on self-importance rather than being motivated by the greater good, a casual (indifferent/complacent/apathetic) approach to student security, safety and maximizing their potential, and a basic resistance to changing the status quo. After observing the way that first aid was administered, I have arranged for a doctor to give 3 volunteer teachers a one-day orientation in basic first aid, to avoid them infecting the students by their lack of knowledge of the fundamentals.

The playground equipment which many of you contributed to will be finished on Wednesday and installed securely. It includes a set of monkey bars and a small climbing form modelled after a set which I photographed at a school in Vancouver, a really good slide which I never thought that they could make here and they not only did that but made it strong as could be, and a curved steel structure which is 4 metres long and 2 metres high and has rails and steps all over it, and I do want to thank all of you for the contributions which you made towards this. I have had 2 large plaques made up listing everyone who donated towards the school over the years. One is in Dari and the other is in English and they will be mounted in the schoolyard this week. Another plaque, which I brought from Canada, will hang in the headmaster's office. The ground beneath the playground will have lots of sand on it to soften any bad landings . . . though with all of this added activity, there is going to be a need for first aid, now and then . . . and hopefully the teachers will not discourage student enrollment by their imitation of Florence Nightingale. It will be very interesting to see what changes the teachers have integrated into the school after a year or two. I think that more than a bit will have lasting power, only because there are a few teachers here who understand the importance of books, sports and basic discipline. There are definitely moments when an affection for this country is not at all difficult to conjure up. Almost

every night, I can listen to the call to prayer coming from 3
local mosques simultaneously, sung without amplification.
Every sunset, a family of orange-winged hummingbirds comes
to feed in Hamayoun's flowered garden. The smallest is 1 inch
long and the largest is 1 1/2 inches.
Mike

July 5, 2006

Subject: Let's talk about Security . . . and insecurity
Hi,
I think that I'm starting to get a fuller picture about the state of
the nation here and what I see ain't that pretty. Certainly there
are hopeful signs, such as the new British General in charge of
the ISAF forces here admitting that there has been some critical
mistakes made here, such as not deploying more troops in cru-
cial areas and not listening enough to the Afghan government
about strategies . . . but it is much more complex than that and
though he made an excellent media soundbite, it's the complex-
ities that give the FULL picture. On the up side, the electricity
grid in Kabul is a lot more reliable than the 2 hours a night which
we had in March of 2002 and there are actually high-voltage
towers being erected from the North where the Afghans are
going to be importing power from Tajikistan. There is more food
in the markets as the free trade economy takes over and most
everyone that I meet here in this neck of the . . . desert . . . looks
a lot healthier than they ever have. The local hospital is func-
tioning well and there is a good immunization program in place
around Nahrin. The roads have improved since the days when
the Salang Pass Tunnel system looked more like Dante's inferno,
with its suffocating fumes and people running for the exits when
one vehicle blocked all of the traffic because it was stuck up to its

axle in the icy ruts and 10 of us were trying to lift it out. The Turks
rebuilt and paved the whole highway from Kabul to Mazar and
did a splendid job, though some Chinese workers working on a
northern section were killed because a warlord didn't get the
contract that he, deep in his heart, thought that he deserved. So
there has been progress, and at the same time, there have been
setbacks and resistance to creating a society approximating
egalitarian reality. There is definitely more of a mood of "hun-
kering down" even for many Afghans here, not just the foreigners. The government changes Governors of provinces whenever
another family member of a new minister decides that his relative requires recognition or a hefty bribe is handed over. More
often than not it's about tribal and family loyalties and jockeying
for power in a region or province. So the top tier of the power
structure is heavily weighted towards nepotism. That in itself
isn't unusual in Asia, is it really, but the trouble is that these
political players are in direct competition with the local commanders of the districts, who, though left over from the war, are
still enjoying being the major movers and shakers in any region
because they have a lot of connections and cash (hence they are
the money lenders for anything from marriage contracts to
trucks to buying more land), they have a lot of opium rights to
fields (in return for having their men train the farmers in the
finer aspects of maximizing production for their cash crop) and
they also have political sway among the more minor district
players of the towns and villages. Then there are the police,
which really are the laughing stock of every average citizen
because they work in concert with the criminal element because
their wages are so low that they look to other means for supple-
mentary income. This means that if a thief is caught red-handed
and taken to the jail and if he or his relatives have enough money
to buy his way out of jail, then he is let go without recourse. This
of course makes for a very awkward judicial system where

accountability is not exactly at the top of anyone's agenda because if you start talking culpability then EVERYONE in the political structure would be implicated and isn't a thoroughly corrupt system better than no system at all, I ask you!!!!

The police are funny here . . . they man their checkpoints as if they are in friendly meetings with one another, joking at the side of the roads while ignoring the cars passing by and seemingly oblivious to any sense of self-consciousness . . . meaning their superiors have no sway whatsoever or the bunch of them are just putting in time. So the free flow of arms and explosives would not be difficult under these conditions. I found it amusing though that my impression is that about the same percentage of police as teachers in the school are able to demonstrate initiative and interest in what they are doing and that this 20–25% of the police are pretty preoccupied dealing with the insurgents and giving protection to the powers that be. It's just that at the grassroots level there is not much to have faith in because crime tends to be holding sway without consequences and that does not win "The Hearts and Minds" of the common people. I have to admit that after hearing some of the recent incidents here I am seriously considering arming myself. Of course, we do have our own high-efficiency Afghan Security System here on the ole homestead. Our first line of defence is a motion detector named "LUCKY" who is a puppy with a soprano bark, a bad case of the mange and who is overearnest in his diligence to protect . . . whatever . . . he tends to bark a lot at the birds, who I am convinced are laughing at him, and his intellectual prowess leaves something to be desired, but by golly what he lacks in experience, he makes up for in sincerity. I named him Lucky because he was left here by Hamayoun and almost died as a result of being given some bad meat by Noor, and if he lives at all, then he is nothing if not "Lucky." I have tried feeding him a number of different things but he insists on meat and, since most Afghans

do not eat meat more than once a month and when we have it there aren't any "leftovers," I think that his days are numbered. I think that when the birth location Karmic lineup was being put together, he got into the A's lineup thinking that he'd land in America and he got Afghanistan. Our secondary line of defence is a bodyguard named Nawab who sleeps in the hallway in front of my bedroom with a single-bore shotgun at his side. This is a comfort. But . . . I think that it's the idealist in me . . . I would still prefer to arm myself with a combination of a revolver with spare clips and a pump-action shotgun for when things get "up close and personal." The benefits of wide dispersion of shot and quick reloading really appeal to my sense of self-preservation, I guess. I haven't quite decided if I need to go that route but I sure am tempted and then, whenever I visit again, I would feel so much more at ease! The revolver is a VERY likely acquisition. We all know that to travel right you've got to pack light! Next week, we'll be going up to Kunduz to buy some more sports equipment, blackboard paint and chalk and then I'll decide whether to buy some insurance.
Mike

July 10, 2006

Hi,
There have been some truly bizarre situations here lately but I thought that I would start with the most amusing. As I mentioned before, Luckie/Luckee/Luckey (Afghan pronunciations—NOT spelling mistakes!) was not exactly looking like a splendid example of canine splendour BUT he is a keener. I thought that since no one here had ever washed, shampooed and combed a dog north . . . or I guess . . . south of Kabul, we might as well break the records and clean a puppy for humanity. Oddly

enough, he seemed to kind of like the attention since no one was really interested in touching him in the state he was in. Mind you, he did look almost as dirty 2 hours after his "grooming" as he did 2 hours before we took the plunge, but at least we cracked the cultural taboos and today . . . I figure we'll do it again!

He is not adapting to the heat very well at all so I thought that I would take him to the local spring for . . . SWIMMING LESSONS!!!!! and see if he likes the idea of cooling down that way. I have hosed him down every afternoon and he liked that, so we'll see what he thinks of the dog paddle.

I have still not armed myself though if the opportunity presented itself, I would not hesitate. I am looking into "renting" a Kalashnikov while I am here but no one seems to want to part with theirs for some reason . . . Mmmmmm, now why would that be??? The cost of new Russian handguns has skyrocketed this year as well. Mmmmmm, I wonder why????? They cost in the neighbourhood of US$800.00, which is too pricey for me. Jeepers, there was a time . . . oh well, forget it.

I am fairly convinced that my connection with the school offers me—and I use this word loosely—some protection. I'll give you an example. A few days ago, 8 men from a village which "allows" some of its children to go to the school (but only up to Grade 4), decided to pay a social visit to a family from another village served by the school. A gentleman from this group sat down with that family and insisted that their 15-year-old daughter marry his son and when the family declined his offer, he went outside, got his Kalashnikov and threatened to kill the mother of the family if they didn't agree to "his" marriage proposal. I was stunned by this incident because it is one of the most barbaric—and I cannot think of any other word for it—which I have heard of in this village group. I have heard every year that I have been here that the village from which the perpetrator comes is considered a rogue village which does not abide by the present government, and I have never been allowed to set foot in there even though it is only 2 kilometres away. I had always felt that they were likely responsible for some of the banditry in this area and that the only reason that they have not stolen money from the easy Canadian mark is that some of their younger kids go to the school . . . and I guess that you could call that "protection" in a really loose way! Then there was an incident in central Nahrin town last week where 10, count 'em, 10 armed men surrounded a money changer's house in town and while 6 kept guard, 4 guys entered the house, beat the guy up severely and ransacked his house. Now there ARE police in town at night and for them NOT to see a group of 10 men on the streets kind of defies the imagination, so the general conclusion is that the police most certainly were involved. . . .

In spite of the staff's apathy, I will still go ahead with sinking a well down to 55 metres and having the compound wall put in, including a swinging metal double entrance door, and I may even negotiate to buy another playing field but I will leave it at that. The Library books have been supplemented this year with more Afghan-focused folktales which are very popular, an excellent Dari dictionary, and since they will be starting to teach English this year, we even found some good English/Dari books on grammar/spelling/curriculum for the school, so I have no hesitation in saying that the staff have all of the tools in place to operate this facility at a functional level. There are Dari textbooks being handed out to the children by the Ministry so the only missing ingredient is the teachers' attitude. The Ministry of Education is even providing teaching seminars this summer to elementary teachers in this district, so the momentum is building. There are encouraging signs of change, but there are also equally obvious indicators that cultural entrenchment (am I really trying to find a substitute word for "lazy"?) is resisting the essential shifts which are necessary to create an educational program which will produce students who have been exposed to a curriculum that will prepare them to make choices that will improve their lives. Ten years from now, we could see small changes and be very grateful for that! I promise not to say anything more on the subject. . . . Otherwise, things are peachy. I will be here for another month, suntanning in Dubai for a few days and then gradually I'll make my way to Toronto on August 16th. Thank you for reading this far and not deleting after the word . . . Luckie.

Mike

July 18, 2006

Subject: Yes, it's kind of like a mangy puppy here . . .
You've got your floppy ears and bright eyes on top and then you've got your dark, scruffy underbelly underneath. So . . . when we first got here, "Lucky" was mangy over 3/4 of his body and now after a few weeks he is just 1/2 mangy and that is a fairly accurate analogy of the way that some things are here, though in a lot of other sectors there is a regression receding the other way which makes you wonder whether the country is coming or going! If you are confused, then you are in tune with things just fine. Also, considering the positive response which I have received about Lucky, I am seriously considering integrating an animal sub-theme into all of my future exploits . . . kind of a Monkey on My Back thing. As far as the school is concerned, it seems to be maintaining fairly well. There are about 540 kids attending classes regularly out of a total of about 610 registered students. Numbers fluctuate due to swollen rivers in springtime, harvest season and kids' ailments. I might mention though that people's health here has really improved and that I see no overt infections, which is a big change since 2002.

The school has been designated as a secondary school now so it will add another grade, which it teaches every year for the next 3 years, meaning that it will teach all the way to grade 9, which secures its role here nicely. We took a day trip up to Kunduz on the concussive road between here and the main highway and bought replacements for the used and tattered sports equipment ($100.00), some paint for the steel wall railings and a visit to the renowned "All Cans" exotic imports store there, purveyors of fine ketchup from Dubai and cookies too! The essentials—in other words—to sustain the gastronomically-challenged like myself. The teachers might be cycling through their lessons in a repetitive pattern BUT there is mounting pressure from the Ministry on them to structure their teaching according to the new curriculum books which are being issued this summer. The new Headmaster is firm and experienced and respected by the teachers, who seem to have a healthy fear of his authority because he has a lot more experience than any of them. One incident which I found gratifying was that the new Headmaster had approached Noor for some money to help him get to Kabul because his wife had a gynecological problem that was looking serious. Actually, a friend of the Headmaster had asked for a loan on his behalf (US$30.00), which Noor had given him, and when I found out, I offered to pay Noor the money back. But Noor explained that the teachers had decided to "take up a collection" for the headmaster and give him the money. Considering the fact that neither the teachers nor the Headmaster have been paid their US$50.00 a month wage for 4 months, I thought that this was a formidable gesture on their part and showed real solidarity. I was also delighted to see that the most competent teacher was chosen by the Headmaster as his substitute while he was away. This guy has taken very good care of the Library and has demonstrated to me that he actually cares about his students. The books have been very well used and looked after by the kids, though next year I may get Liaqat to buy replacements for the more popular ones for the $200.00 that it would cost.

To get back to the situation around the headmaster's loan and the teachers' collection towards it, let's not also forget that when the teachers do get paid the District Head of Education slips $10.00 of that into his pocket, and in a country where life can be pretty cheap, I am amazed that he hasn't been taken care of. His brother holds a high position of respect in Baghlan, unfortunately. Of course, my life is not cheap . . . to me or to Osama . . . and the going rate for foreigners' heads seems to be hovering in the $100,000 range, though so far there haven't been any reports of this occurring. Since that has been in effect since I travelled in Tajikistan (2000), that is just one of those things which you store up top and out of the way. A few nights ago though, around 2 a.m. there was a staccato of automatic weapons fire on the main road a couple of kilometres away. The Police (Ha!) had seen some men distributing flyers denouncing the government and threatening violence so they made a show of pursue and abandon. A couple of days later it was a comfort to see 4 heavily armed jeep loads of ISAF soldiers come to Nahrin for their weekly discussions/investigations with the District Administrator. By the way, the ISAF people dropped by the school last spring (at night, no less) to document the buildings and so all of you donors whose names appeared on the Commemorative sign out front are duly registered with the CIA, NRI, CSIS and probably the National Rifle Association as well.

There have also been helicopters scanning the terrain in our direct area, though I imagine that this has more to do with opium production than anything else. Yesterday, ISAF got serious in Baghlan and arrested a former commander who had been the opium kingpin of that province. The funny side to that story is that President Karzai had just chosen this cretin to be the

Administrator of Nahrin District, but the Elders of Nahrin got so upset that they went down to Kabul in protest and had him removed as an appointee. This Commander had been chosen by Karzai because a former Defence Minister named Fahim, whose nickname is "The snake under the blanket!" put his name forward to Karzai. This commander had been commanding the Taliban in Nahrin during the war and had surrendered to (please read "been bought out by") Fahim when the CIA came in, so his reward was to be given the power within Baghlan province. I wonder what on earth ISAF will ever do with this guy. Why is it that we do not have Gulags for people like this? Because we kid ourselves into thinking that to be "just" we need to forgive, or are we living in desperate fear of characters like this? . . . I do not think that that rule holds true at all when you are dealing with former Taliban commanders who set out to rule provinces. I call Karzai "The Castrato" with my Afghan friends. This country is nowhere near ready for Democracy, though a form of benevolent dictatorship would be an excellent transitional state towards a more democratic form with Afghan pillars. There will be 900 more British troops coming here, which should help stem the flow of fighters crossing through Iran from Iraq, where they get their basic training. I suspect that this disreputable Commander will be released soon and just cause more antagonism towards the government while rebuilding a power base, financed by his control over the opium fields.

A bright spot around the fields is that there are now more water-drilling rigs up here. For the last 4 years, they have been busy drilling wells for the opium fields in the South, and now that those are done they are coming to the North and that is why we can finally have a bored well at the school (God willing!). The perimeter wall, all 200 metres of it, is coming along really splendidly. It is a source of continual amusement to me how important this wall is to the elders of the villages, who have all thanked me for putting it in. I just put this down to traditional concepts where some measure of purely physcological (I never could spell that word) protection is afforded by the compound walls that proliferate in these parts. It has a mountain-stone base and then a grille of steel rods that will allow the wind to pass through. I have held meetings with the Elders in about half of the villages and they have gone well. I enjoy these meetings immensely because of the age-old tradition behind them and how they evoke a kind of basic government that is still a model for us today. We sit cross-legged in front of the mosque after sunset prayers and talk about their sense of the school and what their ownership of it means. I am not sure that I can count on them to replace broken windows when even their mosques do not have glass in their windows, but I feel that it is important to ask them to look after the minimal maintenance if asked by Noor (who has supervised the construction and is the political representative for many of the affected villages). I have said that I will not likely return for a few years but that when I do, I hope that they have "looked after their school" (in my dreams!). I have added that Liaqat will visit yearly to monitor the school and that if he asks for their help, then I would ask them to co-operate.

I have had to adjust my expectations about a lot of things here . . . the time it will take for the teachers to upgrade their teaching skills and motivational levels . . . the willingness and aptitude capability of the villagers to participate in their children's progress (most of them cannot read or write and there is always water to fetch, clothes to mend, fields that need looking after and animals to tend) and the capability of the local educational authorities to demonstrate leadership (upgrading standards/minimizing bribes/accountability about pay/distribution of books and nepotism). Wow! That's a handful!!!! So, it really is sort of like a mangy puppy, ain't it? I hope that all of you are well. Mike

Epilogue

In 2006, Mike's work at Maktabe Hazrat Usman school was drawing to a close. He wrote of his intention to leave the operation of the school to the villagers, and was considering returning in a few years to see how it had fared. On the night of July 23, 2006, Mike Frastacky died of gunshot wounds in the home in which he was staying close to the town of Nahrin. His translator, his bodyguard and the school superintendent were falsely accused of his murder and incarcerated for several months before being released. The subsequent report by investigators to the Afghan Ministry of the Interior concludes: "It seems that the murder of Mike Frastacky was planned by anti-government groups and practically happened through armed criminals . . . This murder was a political one."

As of mid-2007, a new well had been drilled for Mike's school; however, the perimeter wall that Mike had started in 2006 was yet to be completed. Maktabe Hazrat Usman school continues to provide education for nine villages in the area, in nine grades, to more than six hundred boys and girls.

—Grant Tomlinson and Jan Rooks

AGILITY AND ENDURANCE:
TASK FORCE ORION IN HELMAND
BY
LIEUTENANT-COLONEL IAN HOPE

Lieutenant-Colonel Ian Hope joined the Canadian Forces in 1980 and has served in the West Nova Scotia Regiment, the Canadian Airborne Regiment and the Parachute Regiment (U.K.), and with his parent regiment, Princess Patricia's Canadian Light Infantry. He has an honours degree in history and a master's degree in military art and science, and is currently working on his doctoral thesis in history through Queen's University. Lieutenant-Colonel Hope has deployed to Afghanistan a number of times, most recently from January 2006 to August 2006. As the commanding officer of Task Force Orion, he fought numerous battles against Taliban forces, and, on occasion, assumed tactical control of American and British forces. What follows is an excerpt from Dancing with the Dushman: Command Imperatives for the Counter-Insurgency Fight in Afghanistan, *being prepared for separate publication.*

Captain Steven Wallace had his 150-man company of U.S. Army infantry positioned with two platoons facing west. The right flank platoon was clearing compounds in the village of Heyderabad. The left flank platoon was deployed along a narrow ridge that ran through the centre of the village, with the troops firing into a series of compounds and orchards from which the Taliban had ambushed his forces. One of his Humvees had been damaged by RPG (rocket-propelled grenade) fire, inflicting minor shrapnel wounds to one soldier. Wallace was in fine spirits when my tactical command convoy (called "Niner Tac") arrived, the captain and his men happy to be engaging the enemy in a full-blown fight. His company (D, or "Devil," Company of the Second Battalion, Fourth Infantry Regiment) had been under my operational control for seven days now—the first U.S. Army infantry under Canadian control in combat in fifty years. His soldiers had been relegated to economy-of-force tasks, producing only fleeting contact with insurgent fighters. This had frustrated Wallace, who wanted action, and he was very pleased to be having it as my LAV and that of my artillery battery commander, Major Steve Gallagher, joined his command vehicle atop the narrow ridge that formed the firing line for his left platoon.

Wallace gave me a quick target indication and I passed these to my gunner, Corporal Greg Davis, who began to engage Taliban firing positions about one hundred metres away. It was approximately 3:30 p.m. After only minutes of our fire, the enemy began to withdraw, giving us brief glimpses of dark-turbaned forms running between compound walls and into the "green belt." The compounds from which they had fought were at the edge of the fertile area of green cultivation that lay astride the Helmand River, and comprised a complex of farms, fields and villages, highly compartmentalized and hardly traversable to us because of the narrow roads, high walls, and wide and deep irrigation canals. Its lush green orchards and fields, growing bountiful poppy crops, stood in stark contrast to the desert that rolled up to its edges. Both Wallace and I knew, from a previous fight in this location, that once the enemy entered the green belt he would easily escape.

Wallace ordered a platoon to chase the enemy on foot. The U.S. infantrymen alighted from their Humvees and began to muster in files to assault into the first compound. My LAV provided intimate support, covering their movement with fire and acting as a moving armoured shield to the vulnerable infantrymen as they walked forward. To give these soldiers an easy breach into the compound, we tried to blast a hole into the closest wall with cannon fire. The thickness and hardness of the wall prevailed. Regimental Sergeant Major Randy Northrup dismounted and used an M-72 anti-tank weapon to try to produce a hole; nothing. U.S. infantrymen began to grin at our impotence, but gave a cheer when my LAV driver, Corporal Hayward—a.k.a. "Stitch"—slowly rolled forward and battered a hole in the wall the perfect width for the infantry squads. They ran in. The height of our LAVs allowed us to maintain visual contact with them as they began searching the compounds and orchards for the enemy, finding weaponry, blood trails and body parts—severed by Davis's 25mm cannon fire.

We continued to give support to the dismounted American infantry as they cleared the western portion of Heyderabad, between the village and a deep canal to the west. Several times, the Americans came under intense enemy fire from the north and from the opposite bank of the canal. We used mortars and direct fire from small arms and from our two LAVs to destroy both groups. I jockeyed Niner Tac from firing position to firing position on the right flank of the U.S. infantry, engaging the enemy as they attempted to establish ambush lines in front of the Americans. Suddenly, when rounding a narrow corner between a compound and a house, we were hit by RPG fire. The first round passed between the cannon and the driver's hatch and struck the wall beside me. It disabled our communications in the turret so that Davis and I could not speak to each other. Stitch reversed a few metres. Over a wall, I spotted the enemy's firing positions, but could not communicate a target indication to Davis. A U.S. Army sergeant with two dismounted squads was just behind the LAV asking directions from me. Frustrated at the inability to yell to him over the noise of firing, and wanting him to see where the enemy was, I grabbed my rifle (always placed beside me in the bustle rack of the LAV turret) and jumped out of the turret and down behind the LAV. I yelled for the sergeant to follow me, and in single file we began to work our way around the compound on our right, attempting to find a place to flank the enemy. We skirted the compound and entered an open rice field. Once exposed, we came under heavy small-arms fire from the same enemy. The U.S. soldiers needed no orders from their platoon leaders or me; they immediately spread out into two squad lines and began to advance, firing all their weaponry into the enemy. The exchange of fire was about even, but the enemy's passed over our heads whilst ours found the mark. The swift action of the American infantrymen—a result of many hours of battle-drill training and the efficiency of the sergeants (all now four-year veterans with multiple tours in Afghanistan and Iraq)—was very effective. The enemy fire slackened.

I was proud of these Devil soldiers. Later, as I reflected upon this, I realized that, at some point in the past decade, we have had a fundamental shift in the culture of the Canadian infantry, making us identify most readily with American, and not British, soldiers. D Company was easy to work with, reliable, and very professional. Perhaps the biggest similarity was that they wanted to fight, unlike the soldiers of other allied countries who remained very risk-averse, too shy to stand and fight the Taliban. When firing began, the American leaders demonstrated decisiveness and tenacity, and the American soldiers performed battle drills quickly and with great effect.

A young American platoon commander arrived and took charge of his men. I told him to continue his fire but not to advance forward, as I intended to finish the enemy with LAV and artillery fire. He agreed. As I made my way back to the LAVs, I attempted to make myself as small a target as possible for the bullets zipping past and hitting the wall behind me. I heard more RPG fire farther west. Niner Tac was still without communications when I returned, so Major Gallagher took our place in the firing position. The combined effect of LAV and small-arms fire from two directions forced the enemy to stop and withdraw. Captain Wallace asked if he should attempt to chase the enemy into the green belt. With the oncoming darkness, I told him no, but reminded him of our policy of remaining on the battlefield after each fight, until it was clear to both the enemy and to any non-combatants that it was the Taliban, and not us, who had given ground. Our withdrawal would occur after darkness, and after our superiority of arms was made clear to all. Wallace understood this. Maintaining the initiative was as much a psychological matter as anything else. It required a moral ascendancy over the enemy. He busied himself sorting out his troops and assisting in our attempts to chase the withdrawing enemy with close air support and artillery fire. Two groups of enemy were observed and tracked as they withdrew from Heyderabad and crossed the canal, moving into a fairly prominent yellow building. Gallagher brought aircraft and artillery onto that target. These were effective, and the target building must have housed a considerable weapons cache, for we could hear and observe the secondary explosions for more than an hour after our strike.

I met Wallace as the light was fading, thanked him for his support and service, and said goodbye. His company was scheduled to move back to his parent U.S. battalion early the next morning. I regretted losing these troops. We gathered the Niner Tac convoy and proceeded slowly and carefully back to A Company's position seven kilometres away, travelling off-road and without light to avoid IEDs and ambush. We arrived at A Company's position at 11 p.m. I was exhausted. We had been on the go since 4 a.m. and the post-combat adrenalin slide was occurring. I asked my operations officer—Major Mason

Stalker—whether we were ready to begin moving back to Kandahar Air Field (KAF) the following day. He assured me that the orders had been sent and acknowledged, and that he would coordinate the rest. This was welcome news, as I felt the need for deep and prolonged sleep. I went back to Niner Tac to find—characteristically—the boys already snoring, and the back ramp down and the bench ready for me to curl up on, with a folded raincoat for a pillow and a ranger blanket to ward off early morning chill. I had just finished loosening the laces on my boots (we slept fully clothed, but had to loosen belts and laces to allow circulation, otherwise we'd be woken up by the pain) and was on the brink of instantaneous sleep when a duty officer climbed onto the back ramp and informed me that the brigade commander would give me radio orders in five minutes. Shaking the cobwebs from my brain, I walked blurry-eyed to the command post.

The tactical command post was an approximately five-by-seven-metre rough tent attached to the back of a Bison armoured vehicle, and it contained three radio sets on tables, satellite phones, a satellite laptop, a map table and chairs, and—thank God—a coffee pot, always full. I sat by the command radio and after a few minutes heard the brigade commander's voice. Receiving radio orders was a rare occurrence—I knew that something important must be happening. Normally the brigade commander approved our plan before an operation commenced, and we simply got on with it. I knew we could forget about going back to KAF for a shower.

The brigade commander came on and relayed to me that the district centres in Nawa and Garmser had fallen to the enemy that day. President Karzai was very concerned, as were the U.S. and British commanders and the governor of Helmand. Lashkar Gah, not far north of these district centres, was exposed. The brigade headquarters surmised that the Taliban were deliberately moving on to Lashkar Gah in an effort to stop our operations in Sangin. Task Force Orion was ordered to retake the Nawa and Garmser district centres by 4:30 p.m. the next day.

"Are there any questions?" "Roger, sir," I said. "Just one. Where are Nawa and Garmser?" "They are in southern Helmand," he said. "Roger," I said. "But we have no maps." The following silence conveyed his understanding: without maps it would be impossible to do this, and the production and distribution of maps for a whole task force would take hours. "We will get maps to you as soon as possible" said the brigadier. Helicopters were ordered to bring maps to us by first light, with one to take my command team on a reconnaissance at the same time, so I could get the lay of the land for our coming assault.

There was obvious tension after the radio orders were sent, as everyone knew that we were staying out in the heat and dust and danger for another week; it had already been eleven days. We had manoeuvred over 350 kilometres and fought in over twenty intense firefights. We had rescued the beleaguered British garrison in Sangin and continuously put pressure upon the Taliban over a frontage of seventy kilometres. The sentiment was, "Isn't there anyone else they can task to do their hard work? We're tired of rescuing everyone." This normally "can-do" organization was feeling very victimized. I gathered a few key folks and told them to get over it; this operation was obviously very serious and good people were looking at all the options—and those good people had determined that we were the best option. I then had to deliver more bad news to Major Mason Stalker. I needed him to relay the warning order to the company commanders by radio, to concentrate our three companies (dispersed over the seventy kilometres) for orders, and to organize re-supply for us before we advanced south in the morning. I told him that I was going to bed. I was still overcoming the post—adrenalin rush and the brush with death. I knew that we were in for a longer haul, and that as a commander I needed to be "in the zone" when making decisions in the next few days. I went back to my bench and fell into deep sleep.

I awoke prior to first light at just past 4 a.m., tightened my boots and went looking for a coffee. The reconnaissance helicopter had arrived, but the maps hadn't. A Company commander Major Kirk Gallinger and I jumped aboard the bird and asked if they had any maps. The aircrew had only aerial maps, but they did inform us that Nawa and Garmser were south of Lashkar Gah on the Helmand River. Further complicating matters was the fact that the headsets on the helo were not working, and I was the only one able to communicate with the pilots. Major Gallinger sat behind me without a map and without sound. We flew to pick up Captain Wallace. I was happy that he had been ordered to stay with us for the next phase, and his smile as he boarded the bird revealed he was just as happy to stay. He liked working for an organization that let him fight. We proceeded south.

Without a map and with no real knowledge of where Nawa and Garmser were, I took out a pencil and paper and began to sketch our routes. I had been to Lashkar Gah before and knew that much of the journey. From Lash we would have to proceed south following the wide Helmand River. On both sides of the river stretched three to five kilometres of farmland and village, with a maze of roads and trails winding between them. I needed two routes traversable to LAVs and heavy vehicles. I observed the main roads and the prominent tracks and tried to memorize details of major intersections and choke points, then quickly sketched them. Several times, a track I was following disappeared into nothing, and I had to ask the pilots to backtrack to find an alternate route. We then flew over the Nawa district centre, thirty kilometres south of Lashkar Gah. The villages were empty—meaning that the Taliban were present. Garmser, sixty kilometres farther south, was the same, but I could see it would be harder to retake. It was on the east bank of the Helmand River, and we had to approach from the west. There was only one bridge over the Helmand south of Lash, at Garmser, and it was five hundred metres long, single-lane and about nine metres over the river and very vulnerable to fire if we attempted to cross in the face of the enemy. I had no doubt that the enemy were present in the otherwise empty town.

We had no maps, and only sparse intelligence of Taliban activity. We received a grainy air photo of each of the district centres and a half-page written report and hand-drawn sketch of Garmser. This, coupled with my hand-drawn sketch of the two routes we would take, was rather less than I expected to have in modern warfare in 2006. But I was confident. We returned to the task force and all of the companies began to muster together—150 vehicles—to resupply and to conduct a brief "face-to-face" before starting. I found Warrant Officer Armstrong and the Tactical Command Post with maps, and we taped together a number of sets. Using my sketch, I traced the routes on the map with a yellow highlighter, and then gathered the company commanders together for quick orders. I dispatched Gallinger (with Reconnaissance Platoon attached) on the long route that would take him more than 120 kilometres from our location, well west into the desert area southwest of Lashkar Gah and then south and east towards Garmser. This allowed them to circumvent Nawa and the thickest part of the green belt, and we hoped the Taliban would report this movement and that their forces in Nawa would start to panic about being flanked. I then instructed Devil Company to proceed straight south from Lash to Nawa, with 1 Platoon, A Company, attached to give them a LAV vanguard. I would go between the forces, accompanying the artillery and ensuring that our guns were in range of both forces at all times.

I had arranged to stop just west of Lashkar Gah—on the west end of the bridge over the Helmand River—to meet with the Helmand deputy governor, the provincial police chief and liaison officers from the U.K. forces. When I arrived, we conferred for thirty minutes. They provided good information, confirmed the substantial fear in Lashkar Gah about the possible Taliban attack and offered approximately one hundred Afghan National Police (ANP) to support our operations. I divided these police between our companies, agreeing to escort those dedicated to A Company (already moving southwest) and deliver them that day to Gallinger. Wallace took his ANP south. C Company organized themselves in Lashkar Gah to protect the U.K. Provincial Reconstruction Team (PRT) and the town, and to be prepared to escort our resupply convoys when they came. I then proceeded southwest in pursuit of A Company as Devil Company (with 1 Platoon leading) proceeded due south on the west bank of the Helmand River. It was past noon and we had only a few hours left.

By 4:30 p.m. 1 Platoon and D Company had stormed into Nawa unobstructed. There were minor skirmishing and IED finds, but the enemy had clearly evacuated in the wake of A Company's western flank manoeuvre and before D Company's advance. At the same time, A Company was on the west bank of the Helmand across from Garmser, ready to assault across the bridge into the district centre. The enemy was present in strength, firing dozens of RPGs across the river at our forces. Gallinger would have proceeded but for two delaying events. Our convoy had had a vehicle breakdown with the artillery troop that was to support his fight, and at 4:30 p.m. we were still out of range to provide the necessary fire support; also, locals had said that the Taliban had mined the narrow bridge, and it would be very difficult to find and clear those mines after dark. In radio discussions with Gallinger, we agreed to wait until first light to attack. Once our vehicle problem was sorted out (the Canadian soldier is a master at improvising vehicle repairs and recovery), we established an artillery-gun position at a location that could provide the best support to both A and D Companies and protect our resupply routes and from which we could coordinate the transfer of casualties and detainees. By 6:30 p.m., we began to fire in support of A Company, who spent the entire night firing at groups of enemy on the east bank, Taliban fighters who were unfamiliar with the night-firing capability, accuracy and penetrating power of LAV 25mm cannon rounds.

By first light, A Company and Reconnaissance Platoon were advancing into Garmser. They skirmished all the way through the town, forcing the Taliban out block by block. Gallinger maintained a very deliberate and balanced approach, never extending his soldiers so far that small groups could be isolated, ambushed and cut off. Instead, he always presented a powerful front to the enemy so that they could not hope to ambush anyone and survive. Because of this, A Company suffered no casualties, inflicted dozens and broke the enemy's resolve to defend Garmser. By 8:30 a.m., A Company owned the empty town. I arrived shortly after that to deliver about forty ANP and the provincial chief of police and deputy governor, who were determined to stay there and establish government presence in Garmser once again. I gave them an Afghan national flag to hoist above the district centre. This they did, to the satisfaction of A Company and Reconnaissance Platoon soldiers, who knew they had achieved something special.

Our forces stayed in the Nawa and Garmser districts for the next four days until U.K. and Afghan National Army (ANA) forces were sent to relieve us. In that time, there were more than fifteen substantial firefights with the enemy as A Company continued to push the security bubble farther east and south. A Company was fighting at the end of a 240-kilometre supply chain overland from KAF. This required a daily drop-off of ammo, water and fuel, but we never wanted for any of these commodities. The dedicated folks in our maintenance, supply and transport platoons performed yeoman service for days on end, without sleep, to keep our forces fighting, enduring bad weather, worse roads and several terrible Taliban ambushes.

On July 22, we handed Garmser and Nawa over to U.K. forces and ANA/ANP and proceeded to move incrementally back to KAF. I knew we had achieved a great thing and was determined to inform the soldiers. I mustered what I could of A Company, C Company, the Guns, and the National Support Element in a field in Helmand to personally inform the troops of their achievements. I requested a media reception for their arrival back at KAF. I wanted to get into the press some coverage of their remarkable feat of arms, very much overshadowed in the news cycle by the war in Lebanon, but no less deserving of coverage. I wanted to gloat to the Taliban about our superiority in fighting. I wanted to let the Afghan people know that we were here to do whatever was needed to give them a chance at a secure future.

All my wishes were moot when I received the radio message—while driving into KAF—that our support convoy had been hit by a suicide IED in western Kandahar City en route back to the airfield. Dead were Corporals Francisco Gomez and Jason Warren; ten others were injured. I spent the night in the hospital and writing letters. My initial instinct was to avoid the press conference scheduled for the following morning. But I came to realize that night that it would not be wrong to explain the success of the operations. The achievements were indeed overshadowed by our late losses. But I knew Gomez (we had been in the Airborne Regiment together); he and Warren would want Canadians to know what Task Force Orion had achieved for Canada and for the Afghan people.

It was a story I would tell with solemnity the next morning during the press briefing. It was not a decisive military victory, but rather a superb example of the type of operation we needed to continue to perform. It was one of twenty-seven continuous offensive combat and non-combat operations that we had conducted to keep the enemy off balance. These tactical military actions were conducted not to inflict casualties, because the enemy had a phenomenal capacity to reconstitute, but instead to continuously increase Afghan confidence and to keep the enemy disrupted. Only by doing so could we buy time for the Afghan National Security Forces to grow and develop, and for governance and reconstruction reforms to gain traction. This will take many years. That night, as I prepared letters to the families of our fallen soldiers, I reflected on our recent operations and the losses. We could not be beaten on the battlefield, but could only win if we were prepared to remain here for a considerable time. I realized again that this is, indeed, "the Long War."

CIVIL-MILITARY CO-OPERATION IN KABUL
BY
CAPTAIN MARTIN ANDERSON

Martin Anderson was born in 1965 in London, England. His family immigrated to Canada in 1971 and settled in Westmeath, Ontario. He began a career as a financial advisor in 1991, and today works with RBC Dominion Securities Inc., in London, Ontario. In 1995, Martin joined the Fourth Battalion, The Royal Canadian Regiment, as an infantry officer and has progressed to the rank of captain. Martin was the second-in-command of the Civil-Military Co-operation detachment for Task Force Kabul, Operation Athena, Rotation 3, in Afghanistan from February 2 to August 10, 2005.

It's a silly picture, really. It's the kind of picture that people seem to take more frequently now, with the advent of the digital camera. You know the kind I mean: two people lean in together and one takes the picture with the camera at the end of an outstretched arm. I took that kind of picture of me with a young girl named Zaripha one day at the Merman Orphanage, when we were dropping off some food and school supplies. Zaripha's short, jet-black hair falls naturally into a part on her left side, and her dark eyes have squares of light in them from the brilliant sunlight reflecting off the dusty yard. She is smiling. I keep that picture on my desk and glance at it from time to time as a reminder of all the good things that we accomplished in Kabul during the long, hot summer of 2005, and why we did them. A reminder that I was part of something much bigger than myself and that, in some people's lives, we actually made a difference, no matter how small.

In 1995, I joined the Fourth Battalion of the Royal Canadian Regiment (4 RCR), a Canadian Forces infantry reserve unit, as a way of taking a break from my regular civilian occupation as a financial advisor, while at the same time doing something for my country. I felt that even though a tour overseas was not likely in my future, I could at least help to train people who would be in a better position to go. In September 2001, a lot changed in the world. North America was no longer a safe place from those who would wish us harm—those with an ideological axe to grind. I began to think that there were two ways an individual could respond: do something about it, or watch others do something about it. I knew that I could be part of the solution, so I bided my time over the next couple of years as Canada responded to this new threat the way we have responded to the threats in the past . . . by going to the bad guys and stopping them from getting their way.

In the summer of 2004, I applied to be the platoon commander for the Defence and Security Platoon of Camp Mirage, the "secret" staging base located in the Middle East (undoubtedly the worst-kept secret in the Canadian Forces, but if you don't know where it is, you won't hear it from me). While that position eventually went to another officer, I knew that something would come available, as long as I was patient. Fate intervened in early November 2004, during the work-up training at Area Training Centre Meaford, in the form of an injury to the individual slated to be second-in-command of the Civil-Military Co-operation (CIMIC) detachment. Even though I was not trained as a CIMIC operator, my superiors agreed that I could learn as I went along, as well as focus on the administrative aspects of the detachment.

The rest of the work-up training took place in CFB Petawawa, where we focused on convoy movement, first aid, cultural awareness and mine awareness. Training culminated in a week-long confirmation exercise to ensure the lessons being taught were the lessons being learned. My CIMIC detachment flew out on February 2, and arrived at the inappropriately named Kabul International Airport (take a moment and ponder the initials) in the late afternoon of February 4. We were then hustled into some Bison armoured vehicles for the forty-five-minute trip to Camp Julien. Exiting the vehicle in the early evening gloom of the unlit camp is an enduring memory, and I distinctly recall several emotions: I was apprehensive about finally being on the ground as part of a Canadian Forces operation, unsure of how serious the threat level was, overwhelmingly disoriented from being somewhere completely foreign after so many hours of travelling and, finally, wondering why the hell it was so dark. We were met by our counterparts from the previous tour and given a quick, lightless tour of the camp, ending at our bunk space in the tent lines. The camp stayed dark at night, with windows blacked out and no visible white light, because the bulk of the city around it had no power, and the commander felt that we should not present an easy target by being lit up like opening night for a Hollywood blockbuster. Interestingly, this changed midway through the tour, as power was gradually returned to the city.

CIMIC's role is to act as a liaison between the military, civilian and non-governmental organization (NGO) personnel in the area. Our team comprised three operators and three drivers, and all of us were reservists from Toronto and southwestern Ontario. Major Kevin Winiarski was the officer commanding, I was the second-in-command (2IC), and Warrant Officer Jim Kolar was our operation's non-commissioned officer. Rounding out the team were our three drivers, Corporal Andrea Katona-Smith, Bombardier Jordan Murray and Corporal Craig Newman.

Camp Julien was located in the southern end of Kabul (just after we left, the tents and equipment were packed up and moved to Kandahar). There are two distinct sections of Kabul, divided by mountains. The mountains have one small gap in them that allows traffic to pass from one side of the city to the other and, needless to say, that area gets very congested. All of the other major NATO-nation camps were in the northeastern part of the city, about a forty-five-minute drive away. We would travel those roads every couple of weeks to attend coordination meetings with their CIMIC operators.

Kabul itself is divided into smaller sections called Police Districts (PD). We were responsible for PDs Six and Seven and an area south of the city called Chahar Asiab. Each PD has its own mayor and a council of *wakils,* which serves the same basic function as a city council here in Canada. The *wakils* represent the people and are usually the elders of the community or people who are highly respected for past deeds. The mayors are appointed by the mayor of Kabul, making their positions somewhat tenuous.

We spent our first few days settling in and getting acclimatized to both the altitude and the time difference. We met our interpreters, Omar and Abdul, two senior interpreters in the task force who were an invaluable source of information and directions. The CIMIC detachment from the previous tour took us out to show us the projects that were currently under way and to help us get oriented in the community. As our predecessors' time drew to an end, we all attended a luncheon for the outgoing detachment held by the mayor of PD Seven and his council of *wakils.* It was at this meal that we got our first taste of both Afghan food and Afghan hospitality. It amazes me to this day that, for people with so little, they were able to lay on a spread so bountiful. That is the way with the Afghan people. They may not have much, but what they have they will share with you. It was a humbling experience, as most of our experiences there were.

Before the last of Roto 2 left, I was asked to be the president of the Humanitarian Club. This was a club of both military and civilian members of the camp (of any nation, although they ended up all being Canadian) who wanted to get together and dream up ways to raise money for the local community. It was felt that since I was the 2IC of CIMIC, I would be able to help the club find worthy projects to fund. We set a modest goal for our tour of raising US$12,000. Roto 2 had raised US$44,000, with the help of a large, one-time donation of US$30,000 from a Middle Eastern businessman who supplied NATO forces. The previous Roto wanted us to use those funds to build an addition to a local school, the Chehelsotun Girls' School, and we were to oversee its construction. Interestingly, the term "Girls' School" is a misnomer, as both boys and girls go to most of the schools, just not all at the same time.

We quickly settled into a routine, arriving at the office around 7:45 to begin our day. Major Winiarski would brief the task force commander on our activities of the past twenty-four hours and our plans for the next forty-eight hours. While he was gone, the drivers would prep the vehicles, and Warrant Officer Kolar and I would plan the routes and let the transport people know where we were going and when we were expected back. We would confirm with the operations centre that the routes we planned to use were still open and passable, and get a briefing on the transport scenario for the day, including the weather, road conditions and the daily passwords. We would also receive a daily briefing on things for which we were to keep a lookout. This usually meant to watch for a white Toyota Corolla, but given that almost all the vehicles in the city were white Toyota Corollas, it soon became a standing joke. I suppose that in light of the number of casualties that Canada has suffered since our tour in 2005, we should probably have paid a little more attention to that detail.

Once Major Winiarski came back from the commander's brief we would head out into the city. We visited the local leaders at the mayors' meetings, and the schools, medical clinics and hospitals in the area in an effort to determine the needs of the community and to see what we could coordinate to help. Even if we couldn't help at the time, understanding those needs would be useful when dealing with any NGOs looking to contribute to the community.

Unfortunately, our CIMIC tour did not have any funding for the completion of projects, since our role was mainly to be a liaison and to prepare follow-up reports for the Canadian International Development Agency (CIDA) on some of the major projects completed during Rotos 0 through 2. The local community leaders had grown used to the previous teams' having funding with which to pay for some projects, even if they were on a small scale. When we attended meetings at the mayor of PD Seven's office, we would sit in a room about twenty feet by fifteen feet with about twenty or more *wakils* (now I know how it feels to be a sardine in a tin) and the mayor behind his desk. Abdul or Omar would translate for us and tell us what the problems were and we would be left to make some comment such as, "Yes, I can see how that would be a problem for your people, but we will have to go back to the camp and think about how best to help out your situation as well as the others in the community. We can't promise anything, and we will let you know if we are able to help at all." This did little to placate a group of people who were seeing the pace of change brought about by foreign soldiers slowing considerably. I'm not saying that they were ungrateful—far from it—but they knew we were there to help them, so they didn't understand why we wouldn't have unlimited credit on our reconstruction credit card. As February turned into March, it became obvious that we would have to try to find a way to do *something*, as it seemed that our credibility and effectiveness were increasingly in question.

One of the non-funded projects we were able to coordinate was regrading the school compound at the Sarasiab Girls' School, in order to dry it out. Just about every school in Kabul was operating at huge multiples of their realistic capacity, so most had several tents in the compound in which classes would take place. This school's compound was somewhat bowl-shaped, and so would catch the spring runoff water and turn the tent area into a mud pit. By helping reshape the compound floor, we were able to put the tents back up and save the children from sitting in the mud. We eventually brought them desks as well.

The commander of the task force, Colonel Walter Semianiw, recognized the need for us to be able to fund some of our projects, and in March he approached the then Canadian Ambassador to Afghanistan, His Excellency Chris Alexander, to ask for funds from the embassy. We were approved for C$100,000 to be used on minor infrastructure projects. Once we found this out, we were able to go back to the local *wakil*s and let them know that we were going to be able to commit to some funded projects after all. Knowing that the money would run out fast, we helped them to prioritize what they wanted done. The mood in our meetings rapidly improved.

As the 2IC of the CIMIC detachment, I was usually able to observe these meetings, rather than participate. I would study the ways in which people interacted with each other and compare notes with Major Winiarski and the interpreter afterwards, to make sure we had caught the various nuances of the meetings. I remember a few of the *wakil*s with considerable fondness. There was the *wakil* for Gorzaghah, who had a wooden leg and who sported nine bullet wounds from his years fighting the Soviet occupation. There was the *wakil* for Wasalabad, a giant of a man who was so grateful to us for helping repair the road in his area. And there was Mr. Amin, the head *wakil* of PD Seven.

Sometime in April, Mr. Amin invited us to lunch at his house along with a couple of mullahs from the local area. I let Corporals Newman and Katona-Smith go in and eat first, and after they came out, I went in to partake of Mr. Amin's hospitality. We must have spent an hour or more discussing religion with the mullahs. It was during this conversation that I realized the vast difference between what the average Afghan thinks of Islam and the way in which the Taliban warps that same religion to provide the rationale for their campaign of terror, both locally and internationally. It was an eye-opening experience, and one that I will never forget.

Fairly early in the tour, we received a call from Afza, a woman who ran a small orphanage for girls aged three to sixteen called the Merman Orphanage. This orphanage was located just north of the PD Six boundary (it has since moved) and really didn't fall into our area of responsibility, but it was close enough to make an exception. During our first visit, Major Winiarski was speaking with Afza while I was keeping off to one side. The room had no furniture and, at one point, one of the girls brought in chairs for us to sit in. This was my first meeting with Zaripha. After a time, I decided to get up and stretch my legs a bit, and moved over to the other side of the room. I had been bringing my camera out on most of our trips and I wanted to get some pictures of the room and general conditions. As I moved to the other side of the room, Zaripha picked up my chair and moved it over to me and motioned for me to sit down again. I was completely taken aback. I smiled at her and motioned to her that I would take her picture. As soon as I did, the rest of the girls in the home crowded around and I got a picture of about ten girls all vying for the camera's attention.

We returned to the orphanage a number of times during our tour. I took a fellow Humanitarian Club member, Sergeant Peter Warford, out one day to have a look at their two generators, both of which had ceased working. When he determined that he was unable to repair the second generator, he and one of the other members of his section bought the orphanage a new one, with their own money. This kind of selflessness was quietly occurring all around, yet would never get an opportunity to be recognized (until now, that is).

The Humanitarian Club met every Monday night. We continued to raise funds through a variety of means. In a few cases, members wrote home to their families, explaining what we were doing, and asked them to hold fundraising efforts for our cause. The club held two trivia nights that turned out to be spectacular successes, with fifteen to twenty teams vying for a fifty-fifty split of the entrance fees. The prize money ended up totalling US$450, but in both cases, the winners just turned around and, without batting an eye, donated the money back to the club. We put the money to good use by using it to dig wells and to buy school supplies and desks. The Merman Orphanage also received some of the funds in the form of a washing machine and three or four months' worth of food.

The remainder of the tour revolved around project management: getting bids, engaging contractors, monitoring progress and ensuring quality control. By the time we left in August we had completed seventy-eight projects in total. The Humanitarian Club had raised a little over US$24,000, more than twice our goal. We combined this with the funds from the embassy and those left from the previous tour, and spent US$148,000 in PDs Six and Seven on minor infrastructure projects and a six-room school. We conducted thirteen quality-of-life distributions (distributing clothes, shoes and bedding), delivered 250 new desks and 175 repaired desks (many repaired by Humanitarian Club members on their one morning a week of free time), installed twenty-eight classroom tents in school compounds, resurfaced nine kilometres of roads, drilled twenty-three wells, refurbished eleven other wells, delivered tons of school supplies and helped out two orphanages with school supplies, toys and food.

Our greatest sense of accomplishment, however, came when we accompanied Colonel Semianiw to an unofficial opening of the Chehelsotun Girls' School (it wasn't quite finished before we were due to leave, so our replacements held the official opening). The dream of two rotations of Canadian soldiers and civilian employees came to fruition with the completion of that project. Roto 2 had raised the funds and developed the plans, and we had hired the contractor and overseen the construction from May to August. To see the building almost complete and know that in a week or two it would be filled to overflowing with girls and boys all ready to learn was something I will never forget.

Zaripha was always happy to see us when we went to the Merman Orphanage. Every time we visited we managed to arrive while her age group was home from school. Afza, who was more or less fluent in English, had been teaching the girls, so I was able to talk to Zaripha one-on-one a couple of times, although we weren't able to communicate much beyond exchanging pleasantries. Zaripha represents, to me, the future of Afghanistan. As trite as that sounds it really is true. There is much discussion these days about the mission in Afghanistan and the efficacy of our involvement there. I believe that the answer lies not with the adults—who are already entrenched in their views of the world— but with the children. The children will be the ones to inherit the nation that we are helping to build, and it behooves us to make sure they receive the best possible preparation for the job. I think that our focus on education, with the Humanitarian Club and the main CIMIC projects we completed, was a small step in that direction. Hopefully, it will help the children there realize that a better future awaits them, and that the international community won't turn its back on them as it has in the past.

Zaripha loves going to school and I hope that she continues to take advantage of her ability to do so, and one day perhaps become a doctor, a lawyer or a teacher. Hers is the first generation of girls that has been allowed back into the school system after the fall of the Taliban. Today you can see girls by the thousands walking to and from the schools every day: a sea of black pantsuits and white *hijab*s. Her future, while it may not be particularly bright by Western standards, is at least considerably better than it would have been had she been born fifteen or twenty years ago.

Towards the end of the tour, it was obvious that we needed to go home. All of us were exhausted from working six and a half days a week. We had come to Afghanistan with no idea what to expect and we had been given a job to do and we did it to the best of our ability. Along the way, we were able to make it a little easier for cars and city buses to use the back streets, a little easier for people to get clean drinking water, and a little easier for young Afghan boys and girls to go to school.

One day in late July, when we had dropped by the Merman Orphanage with some food supplies, I had the opportunity to sit with Zaripha and some of the other girls on the front steps of the orphanage. I took out my camera and held it at arm's length and captured the moment in time that now sits on my desk. I often wonder how and what she is doing, and I hope that she is okay. Today, sitting in my office on the nineteenth floor of an office tower in London, Ontario, I look at that picture and think back to a time when I was part of something bigger. Like the others who came before me and those who followed after, I am forever thankful to have had the opportunity to be a part of this mission. Churchill once said: "We will have no truce or parley with you, or the grisly gang who work your wicked will. You do your worst—and we will do our best."

CHRISTMAS ON TV HILL

BY

MAJOR (RETIRED) DAVE WHITTIER

Dave Whittier retired from the Canadian Forces in January 2006 at the rank of major, after twenty years as a communications and electronics engineer/signal officer. He has served overseas in Cyprus and Croatia, and was in Kabul as part of Operation Athena, Roto 2, from August 2004 to February 2005. Dave is presently director of telecommunications with the Vancouver Organizing Committee for the 2010 Winter Olympic and Paralympic Games. An aspiring writer, he currently has two published short stories to his credit. Dave is married with two children and lives in Maple Ridge, British Columbia.

Christmas can be bittersweet for a soldier deployed overseas. It's normally looked forward to as a time to come together as family and friends in the spirit of giving. On an operational tour such as ours in Afghanistan, however, that's simply not possible; family and friends are of course left far behind. And so, as has been the case since armies first set foot on foreign soil, officers and non-commissioned members (NCMs) take part in a number of activities designed to lift spirits and capture even a small part of that feeling of family.

One of those activities is known as the "Men's Christmas Dinner." It is a great military tradition dating back to antiquity that gives the officers and senior NCMs an opportunity to show their appreciation to the troops for their loyalty and service. Designed as a reversal of the normal course of events, here the soldiers dine while the officers and senior NCMs serve. It is standard fare for the commanding officer to trade tunics (and thereby authority) with the youngest soldier at the table, and often the regimental sergeant major trades with the oldest. This inevitably leads to a number of good-humoured (but pointed) comments on the relative fit of the new threads, and a couple of speeches and edicts from the new chain of command, and often ends up with the new CO giving the unit a day off. Woe to those who plan a Men's Christmas Dinner for a weekend!

Christmas of 2004 in Kabul was not much different. As part of the second rotation of Canada's Operation Athena, I was the task force's communications and information systems staff officer as well as the commanding officer (CO) of Task Force Headquarters. Not to be confused with the commander of the task force, my role as CO of the headquarters was largely administrative. And among my more pleasant duties was presiding over one of the many Men's Christmas Dinners that were held during the week or so leading up to Christmas. All of the units participated in one dinner or another: the Reconnaissance Squadron, the Engineer Squadron, the Force Protection Company, everybody was covered off, including Task Force Headquarters. Everybody, that is, except for the soldiers up on top of TV Hill. What to do about them?

TV Hill is a fascinating and critical location. Nestled in the mountain range bisecting the city, it hosts a round, two-storey stone building originally designed to be a restaurant. In its time, it must have been stunning, boasting a panoramic view of the city below. Unfortunately, the Russians invaded before it was ever opened, and ownership then passed from the Russians to the Taliban, and then to the NATO forces. Because of the difficulties the mountains pose for radio communication between the two halves of the city, there has always been a real need for a high point to place antennas and repeater stations. TV Hill has the height, the access road and permanent shelter, so it became very popular, to the extent that the NATO forces placed a permanent communication detachment there soon after arriving.

Canada is only one of the nations contributing troops to the International Security Assistance Force. That December, there were twenty-nine soldiers stationed on TV Hill from four countries—Germany, Norway, Belgium and Canada—of which eight were Canadian. However, because of Canada's position as lead nation from the previous tour, and our Sergeant Freiheit's being many years older than the next oldest NCO from any of the other countries, we agreed with the staff of the Kabul Multinational Brigade, or KMNB, that Canada would take on a lead role in the day-to-day operations on TV Hill. Christmas of 2004, therefore, would be taking on a decidedly Canadian flavour.

Our adventure started in the early afternoon of the twenty-fourth. The team was ready to go: Warrant Officer Hamilton, the Task Force Headquarters chief clerk and sergeant major; Warrant Officer Whipps, our foreman of signals; Warrant Officer Birch, our chief communication operator; and me. We loaded up two G-Wagons with a feast fit for an army: turkey, stuffing, potatoes, corn, buns, cranberry sauce, carrots (with glaze, no less) and Christmas pudding for dessert. Oh yes, and presents. Lots of presents. We then left Camp Julien, having informed my counterpart from the KMNB, a German Lieutenant-Colonel named Brauns, that we expected to be at TV Hill in about forty-five minutes.

Leaving the camp at any time required a fair bit of coordination. Our convoy commander would report to the tactical operations centre (TOC) to file a route plan and notify the duty officer of our expected return time, as well as to receive a threat briefing from the duty staff. This included updates on known Taliban activity outside the wire, routes to avoid, and descriptions and plate numbers of vehicles believed to be operated by suicide bombers carrying IEDs. After the threat briefing, the convoy commander would hold his or her own convoy briefing. To soldiers huddled around a topographical map laid out on the hood of a G-Wagon, it would have sounded something like this:

"Okay, listen up. We're heading to TV Hill this afternoon, a trip that'll take about forty-five minutes. We'll be staying the night, and I expect us to be back by 0900 tomorrow. I've just gotten the threat brief at the TOC and we're at Alert State Bravo in this part of the AO; mags off until we exit the gate. Two suspected IEDs to worry about: one's in a bicycle last seen on Orange route in the area of Brown, and a white Toyota pickup truck believed to be heading from Chicken Street to the U.S. Embassy, plate number is on these sheets.

"We'll be taking a direct route to TV Hill: up Red route to Brown, west on Brown, then off the Main Supply Route at Point Alpha Charlie One. As per normal, no deviations from this route without checking in with call sign zero.

"Order of march: I am the convoy commander and will be riding in the lead vehicle. Warrant Officer Whipps is the convoy second-in-command and will follow up.

"Action on contact: if we get bumped and both vehicles are still serviceable, then we keep driving until we reach a safe distance, assess the situation and report back to call sign zero. If we get bumped and one or both vehicles are disabled, then we stop, return fire if fired upon, extricate casualties and carry on if possible, or establish a perimeter and call for the Quick Reaction Force if not.

"Both radios should be on net with radio checks done by now. If not, we'll wait and establish comms before we head out. I will be reporting our location as we proceed. Password for today:

challenge is Whisper, response is Sunrise. Running password is
Tang-Tango-Tango.

"Questions? Good, we head out in five. Have a good one."

Turning off the main route on to the dirt and stone road that
weaved its way up TV Hill was like going back in time. The first
hundred metres or so were lined with shops, and most of them
were little more than shacks or modified sea containers (steel
shipping containers about two and a half metres high by two and
a half metres wide, usually six to twelve metres deep, with
wooden doors replacing their steel ones). Engines, stacked tires
and unidentifiable parts and pieces were sure signs of local
mechanics, skinned goat and sheep carcasses hung in the afternoon sun outside of butcher shops, and a grey haze of road dust
and smoke covered the entire area. All along the route we saw
children, adults, goats, handcarts and the ubiquitous white
Toyotas, muddled together in a cacophony of horns, bleats,
cries and shouts. We carefully and slowly threaded our way
through this mess, minding the rocks and potholes so as not to
disturb our treasures. Each driver had a short-range radio with
an earphone and mike strapped on his head and a push-to-talk
switch secured onto the steering wheel, and they kept up a constant chatter as they exchanged info on road conditions, traffic
and suspicious pedestrians. As a passenger, I always found the
effect a little bit disconcerting: "Car on the left . . . watch that
bike . . . slow down, you're getting away . . . yeah, I see him . . .
no, probably not . . . really? I see it . . . Roger . . ."

Once out of the "commercial district," we continued up on
a series of half-roads and hairpin tracks carved out of the rock.
The side of the mountain sported all manner of stone houses
and shelters, so close I could have touched them, if the bulletproof windows of the G-Wagon hadn't been sealed shut. We
still passed the odd handcart and Toyota, and here the children

were everywhere: walking along the side of the road, flying plastic bags they had fashioned into kites, playing marbles in the middle of traffic. On an earlier trip, we had driven past a group of kids who were just standing there, each with a medium-sized snowball in his hand. They looked torn between the desire to let us have it and the fear, no doubt learned from the Taliban, that they might get hurt for their troubles. Of course, after we started making faces at them from behind the windshield, temptation overcame both fear and good sense and we found ourselves on the receiving end of a pint-sized snowball fire mission.

At some point in our climb, we passed the last of the stone houses and drove past the Afghan and ISAF checkpoints to the parking area. The Afghan checkpoint simply made sure no unauthorized vehicles got to the detachment. The ISAF checkpoint was a bit more thorough: we stopped at the barbed-wire gate, our names were given to the command post for verification and the outside and undercarriage of each vehicle was inspected to make sure we had not picked up any IEDs during our trip.

When we arrived, Lieutenant-Colonel Brauns was already there, as were a few bottles of champagne. The four of us unpacked, brought the food and the gifts into the first-floor kitchen area, and started preparing.

Now, in all fairness, the actual dinner was not much effort to prepare, at least not for us. A cook had been assigned to the detachment, so we felt properly supervised, and much of the food was precooked, so we only had to warm it up. I remember my wife being so proud of me because of a picture that eventually made its way into our local base newspaper. In it, a couple of soldiers stand in the background while I am busy over a tray of food, looking for all the world like some kind of executive chef. It was months before I told her that I was actually emptying cans of cranberry sauce into little glass bowls, under close scrutiny by the expert!

While we were getting the food ready, some of the soldiers set up tables in the room where they took their meals. They didn't usually all eat at the same time, so space in this area was a bit tight. Unlike the area on the second floor originally intended for dining, this room had thick stone walls and no windows, with the kitchen area on one side and the command post on the other, where all of the radio and computer gear was set up and where the duty radio operator stayed to ensure the nets remained up and running. For tonight, we added four or five rows of tables and set out pretty much every piece of dishware in the place. We all agreed that the mismatched table settings only added to the ambiance. Someone had scrounged up some colourful napkins and candles, and when we brought out the seafood cocktail, served on a bed of chopped lettuce by four well-meaning but kind of clumsy serving staff, the effect was, well, kind of like home.

In keeping with tradition, I traded rank and combat shirt with Private Laflamme, the youngest soldier there, and Warrant Officer Birch traded with Pte St. Onge. "Major" Laflamme really got into the role, and I think he enjoyed himself more than any of us. After we finished clearing the dinner dishes, he had the soldiers from each of the nations represented sing a Christmas carol in their own language. We servers were obliged to throw in a couple of songs for good measure.

After the carols, we exchanged gifts, which was magic. I don't remember all of the presents given out that night, except that Master Corporal Lavallee had picked me up a DVD of *The Adventures of Bob and Doug Mackenzie: Strange Brew*. I don't know how she even knew I liked that movie. Afterwards we sat around admiring our treasures, thinking that this was going to be one Christmas to remember, when Warrant Officer Birch stood up.

"It's time," he said, and left the room, followed by Warrant Officers Whipps and Hamilton.

The TV Hill crew looked at each other with puzzled faces, and they looked even more puzzled when the three returned weighed down with plastic shopping bags and started tossing them at the soldiers.

"But, what is this?" one German corporal asked.

"Open it and see," Birch said with a grin.

The corporal did so, and pulled out a quilt, as did everyone else there. After some excited questioning, they found out the story: Warrant Officer Birch's mother belonged to a quilting group back home in Canada, so unbeknownst to us or anyone on TV Hill she and her friends had decided to make enough quilts for everybody there. They had frantically quilted for months to make sure that their creations got to Afghanistan on time, and the warrant officers had kept them in their own already-cramped bed spaces until it was time to deliver them.

The crew was delighted and started chattering away, pointing out this or that detail for a neighbour or sharing the excitement as one soldier or another showed off a personal theme or signature in his quilt. This went on for some minutes, and in the ruckus I noticed a young Norwegian private who couldn't have been much more than nineteen or twenty, and was almost certainly on his very first tour. Slightly apart from the others, he sat in his chair with a vacant smile on his face and contentedly stroked his brand-new quilt. I could just tell that wherever he was right then, it was definitely not Kabul, Afghanistan.

We then broke out the champagne, enough for everybody to have a toast. Once the little plastic cups were filled, the room stood as one and raised their cups.

"Ladies and gentlemen," declared the young temporary CO to the assembly, "to the soldiers of TV Hill."

To the soldiers of TV Hill. Not to Canada, or to Germany, or the ISAF, but to the soldiers who worked and slept and patrolled together at that place. And they drank, and I saw that they had become like family, and I was humbled to be part of it, even for a few hours.

After dinner, we servers became scrubbers and cleaned up while our soldiers relaxed and arranged their new quilts at their bed spaces. In between trips out back to the pumphouse, I had the chance to see Kabul from TV Hill in the moonlight, which is another experience I will never forget. The lights of the city were like a quilt in themselves, lighting up some patches while others were still dark. There was a thin haze over the entire valley from the cooking fires, and in the moonlight Kabul looked like a pastel painting all in blues and greys, with just a touch of brown.

Once we were all cleaned up, a group of us played Canadian Trivial Pursuit until eleven o'clock. Then we scrubbers became sentries and took turns on radio watch until seven o'clock the next morning. And when our two G-Wagons took off down the twisting road back to Camp Julien soon afterwards, we left behind, at least for a while, a family who had managed to come together in the spirit of giving.

MASCARA

BY

MARIJA DUMANCIC

Marija Dumancic is a journalist from Drumheller, Alberta. She has worked for the CBC in Nunavut, Ottawa and Calgary, and has had pieces published in The Globe and Mail, *the* London Free Press *and the* Calgary Herald. *She worked in northern Afghanistan from February to September 2005, mentoring female journalists and helping develop an all-woman radio station there. In June 2007, she returned to the country to do a similar radio project in western Afghanistan. Photographs taken during her first stint in Afghanistan are part of a travelling photo show,* Voices on the Rise, *documenting female Afghan journalists.*

The women in Afghanistan need one thing. Mascara. And I'm searching Dushanbe, the capital of neighbouring Tajikistan, to get it for them. I've found six tubes of the same brand, but there are eight women at Radio Zohra in Kunduz, just a few hours away from the Tajik–Afghan border. Equality is everything when it comes to makeup. Sexual inequality is a way of life in Afghanistan, but makeup is another matter. An Afghan woman can accept three or more other wives if Allah wills it, but if she feels another woman got a slightly better brand of mascara (or lipstick), she'll make a nasty desert sandstorm look mild compared to the rage that'll rise.

Only about three places in this city sell mascara that doesn't cause your eyelashes to fall off. And I'm counting on my ten words of Dari and my twenty words of Croatian, which I hope will sound like leftover Russian from the Soviet occupation, to convey two things.

I need clumps of mascara that doesn't clump.

And it needs to be all the same brand, not five of one and three of the other. It's eight or nothing.

Shouldn't I be buying books or pens for the journalists I've come to Afghanistan to train and mentor? Nope. Women who live close to death know how to live. They know they can get paper near the centre of town and that pens can be purchased at small stands selling other vitals like pink toilet paper at five afghanis a roll, or individual-use packets of Head & Shoulders knock-off shampoo for twice that. Of course, the packets also get used at least twice. The country is poor.

But mascara is another thing.

Once the women at the radio station learned I was going to Dushanbe for a little side trip after several months in the country, the first thing they asked for was mascara. This after they expressed how very lucky I was to be able to just pop across the border for a few days. Alone. Without a man. Without much more than a visa penned in Cyrillic in my much-valued Canadian passport. This look of envy instills guilt in the hardest of hearts, let alone someone who is personally not a fan of makeup. Thus, my resolve wilted, so that their eyelashes wouldn't. It's a sacrifice any serious journalist would make.

As I scour the wide, tree-lined streets of the sleepy Tajik capital for more mascara, I have just one question.

Is this my contribution to democracy and women's rights in Afghanistan?

It's been close to thirty years of war in Afghanistan. The slow erosion, almost to the point of eradication, of women's rights has taken female Afghans from positions as doctors and teachers

to scraping by with tailoring jobs and housecleaning for expatriates and aid workers. Before the Russians invaded in the late
seventies, the country was moving towards several positive
reforms for women, which was unusual in an Islamic state.
During the conflict, though, close to a quarter of the country
took refuge in neighbouring Iran or Pakistan—many of the
refugees women and children. Women who remained in the
country were known to kill themselves so as not to be captured
by soldiers. After the Russians left, conditions went from bad to
worse as the country plunged further into civil war. The Taliban
were welcomed at first as a way out of the lawlessness that was
making life hell for everyone, especially women. Hope faded,
however, as they closed down schools for girls and would no
longer allow women to work outside of the home. The roller
coaster of hope and despair that so plagues Afghanistan rose
again when the U.S. bombed the country after 9/11, effectively
ousting the Taliban (for a time), but the country has yet to return
even to the level of freedom for women that it had reached in the
mid-seventies. And fighting from these successive conflicts has
left a large number of widows, so it's still not uncommon to see a
woman swathed in blue crouched outside a restaurant, begging
for bread.

The first hint I had that every woman wasn't cowering
under the burka, however, came during my interview in Calgary
for an internship mentoring new journalists at a series of all-
women radio stations in Afghanistan. Expecting to hear how
grateful and happy these poor women would be to have any help,
I instead heard my future supervisor go off on a tangent about
how if one woman at the station in Maimana had a Nokia cellphone, all the other women at the remaining stations would
complain that they needed one too—their Samsungs weren't
good enough. As I stared out my window at the snow, I couldn't
really comprehend women in Afghanistan complaining about

cellphones. Weren't they all starving and eating the bark off trees? Or was that North Korea?

I covered up my disbelief and dutifully babbled on about how I would be the one to bring peace, solace and the Sawatsky style of questioning to, again, these poor women journalists of Afghanistan. My next thought was to wonder what kind of cellphone I'd get. Women across the world aren't so different.

The Canadian non-governmental organization (NGO) must have bought my line, because I was soon hurtling across the Atlantic with just six months to undo what all those years of war had done to a previously thriving society. I got cue cards to help me master the language so that I could make Afghanistan all better in record time. Perfect when you're on a tight schedule for social change. Three other media-minded women from Canada were on the same mission as I was for the same NGO, and we all somehow found each other at Heathrow while awaiting our flight out of civilization and into the belly of a burgeoning democracy. Toni was an Iranian-born diva with a PhD who staggered up to us wearing huge Chanel sunglasses—inside. Mina was the youngest of our new team and in search of her roots, having been born in Kabul but having left the country before turning a year old. And Shelley was a fully committed community radio whiz from Halifax.

Of course we would succeed. We had six months, didn't we?

I ended up sitting next to Mina, who would be my new Dari teacher, for the final leg of the flight. We were on a decades-old Ariana Afghan Airlines plane and it took the crew thirty minutes to somehow wedge the door shut. I guess they hoped the outside pressure as we sped through the air would hold it in place, and we finally got cleared for take-off from Dubai. There were seat designations on our tickets, but as I worked my way to the back of the plane and saw the looks of fear from all the *hajjis* returning from their pilgrimage to Mecca, I decided to take a seat up front with Mina. It would undo all the spiritual work the *hajjis* had accomplished on the trip of a lifetime if they were sullied by having to sit next to an infidel with her head uncovered. Plus, it would have been hard for me to squeeze in between their traditional turbans. Especially with my head swelling at the thought of emancipating my Afghan sisters and possibly lucking my way—and thereby cementing my journalism career—into an interview with the man himself, Osama bin Laden.

My basis in Dari, the lingua franca of the country, was the word *tashakor*. It was my first word and it means thank you. I figured it would be a good word to learn because I would be hearing it so often as I swept my magic media wand over the country and the people began to embrace democracy, equal rights for women and open-ended questions. Mina taught me how to ask if there was beef, if there were bombs and if there was a bathroom. Beef because I am a vegetarian. Bombs because I promised my mother I wouldn't step on any. And bathrooms because when it comes down to it, plumbing can be just as important as democracy.

A week of whirlwind orientation in Kabul had us all ready to get assigned to one of the four outlying stations, and eager to get away from the capital. The cracks in the ruined city and culture were easy to see, but the cracks in the foreign community were the hardest to take. Wasn't everyone here to help the downtrodden Afghans? Victims of wars fought on their soil, with their blood, but not their agenda. Instead, French aid workers, American journalists and adept businessmen were swooping from foreign restaurant to foreign restaurant, UN employees were complaining about not getting reimbursed quickly enough for the R & R (rest and relaxation) that came up for them every six weeks, and devout Muslim drivers were ferrying foreign staff around to DJed parties with camels sitting on lawns, just for the effect. Yes, the outlying regions would be a better place for me to bring this country out of the sixteenth century. To the northeast then. Kunduz it would be.

An eighteen-seat UN plane flew me over snowcapped and possibly insurgent-shielding mountains and landed in a snowless dust bowl doubling as the tarmac of the Kunduz airport. German soldiers stationed here lazed on top of their tanks. Farooq, the driver from Radio Zohra, the all-women's radio station I'd been assigned to, picked me up in what would be my chariot for the next six months—a beat-up Toyota with non-matching doors— and brought me to the station. At first Radio Zohra employed about six women, with several men acting as guards, drivers and gofers. Several of the women I met here came and went during my stay—one reporter's father decided it was too risky to have his daughter's voice on the air and another fulfilled her family's wish of becoming the second wife of a cousin. Many of them, however, were there before I came and remained after I left. The station manager, Najia, was fond of perms and matching skirt-and-blazer sets. Long long skirts that hid any sign of skin, or feet for that matter. Zarghoona, one of the first women to be recruited to Radio Zohra, worked two jobs, as many of the even remotely educated people in the area did—anything to help their large families eat. Zakiah added an Iranian accent to newscasts— much admired by the Afghan people due to their fascination with Iran and love of Iranian music—that made people forgive her for being a minority Shia Muslim. And Siddiqa was the smallest of the bunch, with a shy manner but a firm belief that the burka was good, because for men to even see the eyes of the opposite sex was just too tempting.

The women at the station greeted me warmly, if somewhat warily. The Canadian NGO had set up Radio Zohra the year before with CIDA (Canadian International Development Agency) funds and pretty much left it alone after that. Why would the funders be sending someone in now? Were the women at the station doing something wrong? I blithely assumed they were just shy, and that my year of journalism graduate school and eight months at the CBC would have this station humming along with high-quality, relevant programming in good time, and that together we could prepare the country for the upcoming parliamentary elections.

Before this could begin, however, I first had to find a guest house that would take someone not affiliated with the UN or one of the many German NGOs that congregate around the nearby German Provincial Reconstruction Team compound. After several rejections, my translator found a nice Afghan-owned guest house willing to take in a non-Muslim single female aid worker for the bargain price of thirty-five U.S. dollars a night. Meals were extra, but the house had hot water, a bathroom door that kind of locked (when persuaded with a swift kick) and a guard with a gun. I moved in.

And so began six months of Muslims, mentoring and mascara shopping.

With the zest of a well-meaning Prairie girl, I dove into "capacity building" at Radio Zohra. I put capacity building in quotes because it is such a *pffft* term it makes me laugh and cringe at the same time. It is the buzz phrase people drop when they hand you their (bilingual in English and Dari) business cards and explain how they're going to fix up the place. Literally, capacity building is the altruistic idea that giving equipment to a group of willing people, and training them in the fundamentals of its use, can build a framework that will remain functional/standing once the capacity builder is back sipping cappuccinos in Berlin. Sadly, however, it often represents nothing more than the dreams of aid workers doing six-month stints who, just when they've gained the trust of their local staff, answer the call to the next global hot spot like

Somalia or the Congo. Many people like to bandy the term around to make themselves look good. But just to play the game, I only dropped it into every other introduction to fellow "capacity builders" as I handed over my impressively bilingual business card.

The Canadian NGO had set up four radio stations throughout what's left of Afghanistan and sent volunteers to each one to help it along. Several years earlier, my supervisor had arrived in the country with a mandate to get women's voices on the radio. Progressive-ish cities were chosen, brave and usually single women were recruited, and microphones and mixing boards were set up in cramped, overpriced two-room offices. The new reporters received training in journalism standards, operating recording equipment and programming playlists with the underground Iranian and Indian music that the country's youth adores.

The other volunteers and I were part of a final push to make sure things were running smoothly before funding was to cease later in 2005. When I started, however, I had no idea that one of the biggest contributions I would make to the women would be stronger, longer lashes.

Kunduz is a small city one hour south of the Tajikistan border. It's in a relatively peaceful area of the country but is experiencing more bombings and "incidents" as the situation in the south spills into other areas. Within a week, I had developed a routine of getting to and from work that blew the other aid workers away. I walked. They were probably worried that *I* would get blown away, but I resisted having a driver come and pick me up only to drop me off three blocks down the road, despite the fact that my NGO paid him sixty U.S. dollars a month to do just that. In hindsight maybe I should have taken the rides, but on most days it was fine. Most days.

As I walked to work in the morning, I sidestepped kids on donkeys, rickshaws, horse-drawn carriages, pedal and motor bikes, UN vehicles, camels and men pulling ungodly amounts of stuff (engines, hay, bricks) on jumbo wheelbarrows. I drew some attention, of course, as the only woman on the street not wearing a blue burka, and some of the looks could be a little unsettling. But then a boy would pass me wearing toenail polish, and as I laughed to myself the threat of my hosts passed. Besides that, it was like being in a dusty (dust was invented in this land-locked 'stan) cowboy town from the turn of century—the eighteenth or nineteenth century, that is.

One day on a muddy walk to work, near the beginning of my time in Kunduz, I tripped on my shoelace and hit the ground. Hard. Luckily my camera bag broke my fall. And possibly one of my ribs. As I lay in a puddle, my headscarf half-strangling me, the men nearby did not move to help. They watched me gasp to catch my breath and they almost seemed to smirk. I wondered if, just maybe, they did not want me to succeed in getting women's voices on the radio and rights on the table. But I quickly pushed that thought out of my mind and painfully hauled myself up. Questioning the work the mighty foreigner can do in such a destitute country is for people far too grounded in reality. I soldiered on to work and hoped that I could find the Dari phrase for punctured lung. Possibly it is synonymous with bruised ego. Or growing realization.

My duties at the garage-turned-radio-station included drawing up budgets with number-savvy Najia and visiting local businesses and aid agencies with outspoken Zarghoona in a bid to raise Radio Zohra's profile and sell airtime for advertising. A lot of my time, however, was spent sitting on the cold cement floor making posters of "best journalism practices." Highly useful when the Mini Discs the women were to record their interviews on were constantly jammed with sand, and when the power went out every fifteen minutes, so that most of our time was spent apologizing for having gone off the air, only to go off again fifteen minutes later.

But after broadcasting blips like those and my initial fall in the street, I settled in quite nicely to my self-billed hero role. Najeep, "the boy" from my guest house, would greet me every morning with a gunfire fast and loud "ARE YOU FINE?" I'd fall over and pick myself up, and then he'd hand me a jug of tea. The routine was strangely soothing. As I kept showing up to work day after day, freezing in the non-heated winter and sweltering in the fifty-degree-plus summer, the women slowly let their guard down. They let me know that the headscarf I had bought years ago in Bombay was no good and that fabric with leopard spots on it trumps paisley or flowers any day. *I guess a real media mentor would know this. Perhaps I was learning too, could it be?* These were real women, hear them roar. Najia once told me, through a translator, that if a mountain came she would push it. And I believe her. Najia is from the Hazara minority, which is often maligned in Afghanistan—this in a country where being at the bottom of the barrel is truly the bottom of the world's deepest barrel. She has a sweet smile, a broad back and a will of steel.

All of my translators liked Najia as well—I say all of them because I went through three. The first one was a woman, an Audrey Hepburn look-alike and just as airy; the second looked like the Count from *Sesame Street*, but with a moustache; and the third looked like an angel. Which he turned out to be. The first two left for better-paying jobs with higher profile NGOs, as my budget was only ten U.S. dollars a day. I was happy for them, but it was especially unfortunate to lose the Hepburn look-alike, since female translators are hard to come by. However, the women at the station quickly grew fond of my cherub of a translator, Jawed, and treated him like a little brother. He is an artist who learned English as a refugee in Pakistan, like many of the

translators in Afghanistan, and far too calm to be from such a
war-ravaged country.

For fun one Friday (that is, the weekend in Muslim countries), we headed north of the city for a picnic. Wedged into a car
with eight other women, we raced over the hills while our driver,
Farooq, belted out *"Khub, khub"* ("Good, good") and dust settled
into crevices of my body that should never know dust. When we
hit the site for the picnic, Farooq hit the ground for Allah and the
ladies played volleyball, having pulled off their burkas as soon as
we passed the city limits. They shocked me by acting like foreign
tourists when we happened upon a Kuchi (Pashtun nomads)
camp, barging excitedly into a tent, having me take pictures of a
woman making thread and taking turns snapping shots of themselves holding Kuchi livestock. The Kuchi kids did well with our
picnic leftovers, however, sipping Pepsi and eating city bread as
they gazed with interest at the white girl trying to make sure she
didn't step on land mines, real or conversational, while talking
politics with some of the more strong-minded Pashtun reporters
from Radio Zohra.

Hanging out with the reporters outside the confines of the
station, while interesting, wasn't enough for me to learn everything I could about Afghan culture and the ways I could fix it. A
hero's work is never done. Since the family is the heart of any
culture, I resolved to get to know one.

My chance to probe deeper into the culture through an
unsuspecting family came, unfortunately, when something
uglier than one-eyed Mullah Omar was probing into my intes-
tines. Weeks of working non-stop and sampling street ice cream
(which caused local and foreign doctors to shudder when I told
them I ate it) had finally caught up with me. I had nothing left to
excrete from my body but memories and I was starting to forget
my past. Then Najeep, "the boy," hammered on my door.

"You come my sister's birthday party."

"Can't. I'm sick."

"Ten minutes only."

"Impossible. I need a toilet."

"Only ten minutes."

He took my running past him to the toilet as a yes and my fate was sealed.

So at one o'clock I was bundled across the city to Najeep's real house—he lived at the guest house to work, and his father and his father's two wives ran a household of thirteen kids on the other side of town. I was led through a yard where two cows gazed at me unsympathetically as they chewed grass growing under a decrepit Volkswagen van. They seemed calm, so I resolved to be as well. What's ten minutes anyway?

Ten minutes, of course, turned out to be two hours.

I was led into a typical Afghan living room. Long, fat pillows lined the walls and at the end of the room was the birthday girl, turning five, in traditional birthday garb. She sat perfectly under a mass of tulle and heavy traditional dress, and wore more face jewellery than Dennis Rodman. She was an absolute angel for the whole party, posing for pictures, cutting cake and graciously accepting gifts.

While an auntie was giving her a pair of pretty gold earrings, the girl's mother (second wife) pulled out one of those fun string cans and let it rip over them. Suddenly, part of the not-so-fun string landed on a candle burning on the cake, and a toxic mushroom cloud enveloped the room.

I figured it was time to leave. Not only were my guts about to become more toxic than the fun-string fallout, but I still didn't feel I'd gleaned the cultural understanding that other aid workers lacked.

Then the food mat was rolled away and the dancing began. The birthday girl changed to her civvies and a Donna Summer wig that fell to her waist.

Then I *knew* it was time to leave.

Soon after, I found myself planning the R & R to Dushanbe that I so often made fun of UN workers for taking. Tajikistan is Third World on the best of days but paradise after the constant stress of Afghanistan, which is starting to tire of foreigners in big trucks making big bucks. At times, mentoring the female journalists was more painful than hearing about the continuing deterioration of security in the country. One of my lowest points came when Zarghoona interviewed her sister, who was running in the country's parliamentary elections. Since part of my role was to guide the women in fair, balanced, unbiased journalism, I suggested that one of the other ladies could interview the sister, and that we should give all the candidates the chance for an interview as well. Zarghoona's questionable solution to the problem was to simply cut out her own voice, get another reporter to re-voice the questions, and then mix it back together. No problem. Problem solved.

Defeated, I bumped up my travel plans to Tajikistan for the very next day. Zarghoona is a Pashtun with flashing blue eyes and seven other sisters to back her up. I'm a measly journalist from Canada with strict self-imposed orders to instill the power of solid media in a country where suggestions like this aren't seen as so off-the-wall or journalistically reprehensible. My hero-star was starting to fade.

Then the real hero stepped in. Najia realized this was not right, and suggested we should all talk about it. The staff had a meeting, and although it was tense at times, we all had our say. Finally we agreed that another reporter would do the whole interview again. No problem. Problem solved.

But I still went to Tajikistan. These ladies needed makeup.

And so, in Dushanbe, I dutifully go from store to store (to store— I said there were only three) and get six tubes of mascara at one stand and two at another. Ah, the successful fieldwork of an aid worker. Each tube sets me back around eight US dollars, but I know my brown paper bag full of hard-won beauty bounty will be priceless. Back at the station, the women excitedly flip back their heavy burkas and apply mascara that is burka-proof, fifty-degree-Celsius-proof, and sweat-proof. The women pass around the single makeup mirror they share at the station to bat their newly lengthened eyelashes, and then they put their burkas right back on to head out to interview the newsmakers of the day.

Surrounded by these up-and-coming Afghan female journalists . . . and friends . . . I wonder if I have succeeded in making them safe and self-sufficient in the world of journalism and jihad. Have I ensured the protection of women's rights and the democratic process by drilling into them the value of asking open-ended questions and taking appropriate pauses while reading the news? Hard to say. For now, as I look at them, I think they will be fine without me. And that's what it's all about, the country being fine without us—the mentors, the foreign aid workers, the soldiers. Unfortunately, it's one open-ended question that eludes us all for now.

Back in Canada, more than a year after handing out the mascara, it still doesn't take much to pull me back into that tiny radio station on a dusty side road. A news clip about Canadian soldiers in Kandahar, a flash of that unmistakable burka blue on a website, an email from the ladies. When I left, none of them spoke much English. But from time to time, I get an email that is low on English but high on heart, like much of the country. Here is one of the most recent ones, from Najia:

> You know how much i and we miss you?
> before some days i and zarghona went on a trip to silwak
> (Slovakia) it was wonderful and i checked ur email there

and i sent u an email but i think you didnt recieve it.
in afghanistan nowadays everything is going well and
radio zohra also getting developement and i wish u are
compeletly fine and have great time we are all fine and
having great time.
i dont want to take ur more time my phone number is
XXXXXXX and i dont know ur number to call u and we
alll miss u.

Hmm, in Afghanistan nowadays everything is going well and Radio Zohra is getting "developement," as the email says. I guess they don't read the Western media, because the word "Afghanistan" is rarely in the same sentence as "well." But the message for me is that they are all still alive, making progress, getting training in places like Slovakia, and using the Internet to keep in contact with one another. And with me. And that is fine. To quote Najia, completely fine.

ON A CHILLY EVENING IN MARCH

BY

PETER SHERK, MD

Peter Sherk worked on the Kandahar Air Field at the Multinational Medical Unit during March 2007. He studied medicine at the University of Toronto and specialized in critical care medicine at the University of Western Ontario. He now lives with his wife, who is a pediatric intensive care physician, and their two sons in Victoria, British Columbia. He is planning to return to Afghanistan in April 2008.

"Unfortunately the people in the West think that their lives are more important than our lives.

— General Pervez Musharraf, *The Globe & Mail*, May 23, 2007

It is always disconcerting when someone you don't particularly like tells you something about yourself that is both repellant and true. This is how I felt reading the words of the Pakistani president quoted above. His comment recalled for me the deaths of two young men, one a Canadian army corporal and the other an Afghan policeman.

On a chilly evening in early March, I stand at the back of an old hangar on the Kandahar Air Field. Around me hundreds of young soldiers mill about quietly as we wait for the ramp ceremony for

PETER SHERK, MD 204

the corporal to begin. The night sky is visible above our heads through large holes in the hangar's roof—gaping wounds left by long-forgotten mortar attacks. Two nights earlier the corporal had been shot in his tent in an incident that is known, in the bureaucratic manner of military parlance, as a negligent discharge. An accident. A lapse of judgment. A tragic folly.

There is a squatty yellow building next door to the hangar called "The Taliban's Last Stand," and soon after entering it, one can easily imagine why. In the centre of the building is an immense hole, created by a very powerful American bomb delivered from above to kill the Taliban within. As you walk along its dim corridors, you soon lose count of the bullet holes that have denuded the otherwise solid walls. One thing, though, has been counted. A poster on one wall announces that forty-two American soldiers died of negligent discharges from 2003 to 2004. Elsewhere on camp, particularly at the entrances to the dining facilities, signs remind recruits about the finer points of gun safety: "Always treat your weapon as if it is loaded"; "Never point your gun at anything you don't intend to shoot"; "Do not put your finger on the trigger unless you are ready to shoot."

These admonitions echo in my head as I stand waiting for the corporal's funeral to begin. And then, in the distance, an unseen voice barks out one of those terse, guttural two- or three-syllable commands familiar to quarterbacks and drill sergeants. Everyone else seems to understand what has been called out though I can not. The throng quickly, silently organizes itself into groups according to beret colour or nationality. Sadly familiar with what lies ahead, the soldiers file out of the hangar onto the tarmac towards the waiting Hercules airplane, cargo ramp in the down position, beside the spotlit Canadian flags fluttering in the crisp night breeze.

It is a fair distance to where the ceremony will shortly take place and I am practically whisked along in the slipstream of what must be a thousand marching soldiers. As a civilian, I take up a position in the last row of Canadians beside a phalanx of American servicemen wearing expressions of astonishing grimness. I feel like an outsider. I am an outsider. This is all very sad and very strange. How do all these men and women manage to stand at attention, so perfectly still, for so long in this surprising cold?

The padre has an unenviable job, I think. What can one say under such circumstances? There before an assemblage of youth from some of the world's mightiest nations, there before the flag-draped casket of the dead corporal, what words can make this event appear sensible and decorous? We are told what a fine young man the corporal had been, how full of life and well liked. How decent, how giving of himself and how proud to serve his country. God is extensively invoked. The padre makes a thinly veiled reference to the Taliban—"the enemies of freedom" he calls them, and in this he is certainly correct. He doesn't say anything about gun safety. Some things go without saying.

Then, as the corporal is borne upon the shoulders of his pallbearers into the waiting Hercules, the padre recites Psalm 23. His French-Canadian accent crackles over the loudspeakers: "The Lord is my shepherd . . . He restoreth my soul . . . though I walk through the valley of the shadow of death, I will fear no evil . . . surely goodness and mercy shall follow me all the days of my life: and I will dwell in the house of the Lord forever."

I shudder at the conclusion of the funeral, move off silently and stamp my feet to keep warm. I walk the hundred yards to the hospital to check on one of my patients who is not doing well. He is a member of the Afghan National Police and was admitted earlier in the day, after the Taliban attacked his post with a rocket-propelled grenade. In the fog of war, we know very little about this policeman. We don't know his name or his age but he is young—about the same age as the corporal—and he is from a town called Qalat, to the north and west of us.

One startling thing about many fatal injuries is how innocuous they first appear. Tiny grenade fragments pierced the policeman's forehead with such velocity that they left what seem to be little more than two small lacerations above his right eye. Behind them, however, his frontal lobes have been transformed into a slurry of blood, brain tissue and bone shards. His right hand has been torn from his arm, but he would certainly survive if that was his only injury. As the night wears on, his brain continues to bleed and swell, until the pressure inside his head exceeds all compensatory mechanisms. His pupils enlarge and soon cease to react when light is shone into them. His blood pressure surges, his heart rate slows, events that, when appearing together, are well-known harbingers of neurological death. His breathing becomes erratic. The meagre tools at my disposal to reverse this process—intravenous mannitol to draw out brain edema fluid, propofol and morphine to lower his already declining cerebral metabolic rate, ventilator adjustments to increase the rate and depth of his breathing—all prove themselves no match for the fury of an RPG.

Just like any other person, a doctor often first confronts a patient's impending death with denial. This can't be happening. There is something that I have forgotten to do that, as soon as I remember it, will draw this man back from the precipice on which he now stands. I hear myself thinking these thoughts as another inner voice, at first faint but gradually more insistent, sensibly declares the futility of any further attempt to save his life.

I disconnect the ventilator from the policeman's tracheotomy tube. At home in Canada, there would be family or friends by the dying man's side. It seems wrong that the last people to see this man alive, this policeman who is about to die anonymously on his own soil for defending his country, will be a nurse and doctor from Canada. Rob, the nurse, and I exchange uncomfortable glances and the simultaneous realization that we must tell someone else about this. I restart the ventilator and hurry out of the intensive care unit (ICU) in search of the hospital interpreter.

The hospital has four interpreters who take turns being on duty for twenty-four-hour shifts. They are our connection to our Afghan patients, skillfully translating Pashto into English and vice versa. For this, they are paid the princely sum of about six hundred U.S. dollars per month. For this, they must take risks I would never even briefly consider. Co-operation with the NATO coalition could very easily cost them their lives if the wrong people found out what they do for a living.

They have good, strong Afghan names that, with little practice, anyone can learn to pronounce, but absurdly, perhaps to keep it simple for their military employers, they have come to be known as Steve, Tony, Bob and John Rambo.

It is about two in the morning and I find Bob out on the ward sitting on a metal folding chair watching a movie on a portable DVD player. The flickering light from the tiny screen is all that illuminates the large, open ward where a number of wounded Afghan soldiers lie sleeping. Seeing me coming, Bob tugs his earphones down, smiles in his gracious, kind way and almost jumps up, seeming a little embarrassed perhaps to be found enjoying a moment of leisure.

I tell him about the policeman, about the brain injury. Brain death is a strange concept and frequently hard to explain to the families of my patients back in Canada. How can I explain this to a young man whose cultural, religious and linguistic touchstones are so different from my own? Death in the ICU often happens when we allow it to happen. I don't want Bob to think we've given up too soon. He instinctively senses my unease at allowing the policeman to die without the observance of appropriate customs. He will go, he says, and find the Koran, and offer prayers over the policeman so that his dying will be made easy.

Anxious, fingers trembling, he flips through the sacred text. His nerves get the better of him and several times he has to restart his search. I think he's worried that the policeman is about to die at any second and may do so before he locates the chapter, or *sura,* he's looking for. I try to reassure him that there's plenty of time, while Rob draws the curtain around the bed, giving at least a semblance of privacy. Bob then begins to read from Sura Yasin. His manner is arresting. Leaning low over the policeman's chest, whispering almost inaudibly in Arabic, directing his words, it would seem, at the wounded man's heart:

"It was said, 'Enter Paradise.' He said, 'I wish my people could know of how my Lord has forgiven me and placed me among the honored.' . . . So exalted is He in whose hand is the realm of all things, and to Him you will be returned."

After several minutes he stops, his voice never having been louder than the soft hissing and puffing of the ventilator, which we now shut off for the final time. Paradoxically, the quiet in the room makes me think back to hearing Psalm 23 coming through loudspeakers at the corporal's funeral a few hours earlier. The interpreter presses his lips to the pages he has just read, closes the book, kisses the cover and gently presses it to his own forehead before encircling the policeman's head with the Koran three times. He kisses the book again and passes beyond the curtain. Before leaving the ICU, he waves the book over the heads of the other two patients in the room. One is an Afghan army commander who drove over a land mine and sustained unspeakable injuries, and who, it will turn out, is only days away from death. The other is a seven-year-old Hazara boy who, while shepherding, had a rock thrown at him by another child, causing a severe skull fracture and brain injury.

Later, I ask Bob what he thinks will happen to the policeman's corpse. Once the chain of command identifies the man, his body will be placed in the morgue at the Mir Weis Hospital and radio announcements will be made in the Southwest region requesting relatives to retrieve his body. If not claimed within ten days or so, he will likely be buried in a pauper's grave. How different this would be where I come from. The funeral of a policeman killed in the line of duty is front-page news. I recall images of Royal Canadian Mounted Policemen in their iconic red serge uniforms marching solemnly in the funeral cortège. Why don't we give this man the same honours after death that we accord to our own fallen? Because General Musharraf is right. There will never be peace and justice in Afghanistan as long as our actions demonstrate the different value we place on our lives and theirs.

The next morning I must go to the morgue tent beside the hospital to attend to the paperwork that follows after a death. The regimental sergeant major escorts me. Apparently I need a security escort to fill out the death summary. The policeman's body lies in a white bag on a steel table in the centre of the tent. I write down the injuries and cause of death:

1. Hit by a rocket-propelled grenade.
2. Traumatic amputation of right hand.
3. Penetrating injury to left shoulder and head.
4. Severe traumatic brain injury.

Across the desk, three young American servicemen on morgue tent detail enthusiastically discuss their plans to become morticians when they get out of the army.

FAR FROM CANADAHAR
BY
CAPTAIN DAVE MCALLISTER

*Dave McAllister was born in 1968 in Vancouver, and enlisted in the
reserves during his first year at the University of British Columbia. In
1989, while still a student, he served a peacekeeping tour in Namibia.
Captain McAllister was transferred from the regular forces to the Army
Reserve in 2005, and was immediately selected for service with the
First Battalion, Princess Patricia's Canadian Light Infantry, Task
Force Orion. He deployed to Kandahar in January 2006 and served,
until redeployment in August 2006, as the operations officer for the
Kandahar Provincial Reconstruction Team. Captain McAllister lives
in Squamish, British Columbia.*

I don't really know how to describe what follows, except to say that
it should speak for itself. It is a memoir of an experience that is
impossible to describe, and of which a description is unnecessary
once one has lived it. It has a wide-eyed quality for which I will not
apologize. Wonder has a power and magic all its own. Cynicism is
adolescent; it shuts the eyes, it closes the mind, it dulls the heart.

I'm an infantry officer; my rank is captain. When I left my
home for Edmonton in August 2005 to begin training for
Afghanistan with 1 PPCLI, I had no idea what I would be doing. I
lucked out. I deployed in January 2006 as the operations officer
of the Kandahar Provincial Reconstruction Team (PRT).

An operations officer in an army unit serves much the same function as his counterpart in a civilian business. Like an operations manager, he coordinates the various parts of his organization so that they support the boss's plan, don't interfere with each other and don't waste resources. He is plugged into every part of his unit and into all the other units. He has to know what is going on, everywhere, all the time.

In my case, that meant coordinating patrols, moving VIPs around, working with civilian agencies, dealing with Taliban activity and a whole host of other things. My workdays were at least twelve hours long, every day of the week. Before I left, I knew I would be busy. I had no idea.

I hit upon the idea of blogging about my tour as a means of keeping my family and friends in the picture, because I didn't imagine I'd have the time to call or email everyone frequently. I asked my sister to contribute as well, so that there would be a family side to the story—every deploying soldier has a "from" as well as a "to." The blog turned out to be wildly successful, unfortunately so, since as time wore on I had less and less time to post, less energy to write and fewer experiences that I could blog about. I didn't post at all in the last month of the tour.

This is what we wrote. I've selected the posts I like the best, and I have edited them a bit for clarity. My sister and I have added narrative, but only enough to give it context, to fill in some of the blanks. The story tells itself. It's far from perfect. The first post, in particular, now seems overwrought. The best posts are the ones I dashed off without too much thought. So be it. This is how we felt at the time. I stand by every word.

January 21, 2006

It's here

Posted by Dave

The time has come for me to leave Canada. I'll be in country in a few days. You'll understand if I don't say exactly when.

I would like to describe how the last week has felt . . . but I don't have the words. The best analogy is that THX ad before movies—digital cacophony, growing and coinciding as the volume rises, coalescing in a deafening symphonic chord.

Emotions, rather than acoustics, are rising. My comrades left work early today to take advantage of every last moment with their loved ones. I said my goodbyes last weekend, at my aunt's house in Calgary. Tomorrow morning I will watch the same script play on a hundred faces as we board the bus.

I wish I had the wit to describe how my perception has changed over the past few months. I stood outside last night, and I looked at the underside of the hazy clouds, the slippery steps, the ice crystals in the air; I watched rapt as ambulance lights danced on windshields arrayed in rows in the parking lot. Bundled shapes hurried over the sidewalks. A year ago, my only thought would have been to get inside. Last night, I lingered, and even the cold was powerfully intoxicating.

As I type now, I notice the reflections on a man's glasses, the wrinkles on a woman's sweatshirt, the ebb and flow of conversation in the business party to my right. It makes no sense—I am barely conscious of these things, but I am intensely aware of them all the same. I've never felt like this before. It's as if I am feeling the input from a billion senses at once.

I don't know if others who share my circumstances share my feelings. I hope they do. I've experienced some amazing things in my life. Living, in winter, in an igloo I built myself near Baker Lake in Nunavut. Dawn from a portaledge three thousand feet off the ground on El Capitan in Yosemite National Park. The Akshayuk Pass in Baffin Island with Richard and Jack last summer. But this feeling, even before I have begun to do the business—how intense, positive and apprehensive it is, all at the same time—is different.

AJ Lutes was on the CBC tonight. I've known AJ for many years. He and I were platoon commanders together in this battalion, back when it was in Calgary. We are going to replace him in the PRT. He was talking about the bombing that killed Glyn Berry and grievously wounded three of his soldiers. You can't imagine how much I hope I never have to give my reaction to a similar incident. But we are not going to Bosnia, or Cyprus, or Namibia, or any of those other UN fantasylands. I am coming face to face, after almost nineteen years, with the reality of my profession.

Wish me luck. Wish my soldiers luck. More than anything, support us. Support our fight. There is absolutely no question that it will become painful—and when it does, remember that we are all volunteers, Canadians like you, who believe so strongly in our country and its commitment to this unfortunate land that, in our minds, our sacrifices are as nought compared to what we will achieve.

Remember, always, that the world is a better place the more Canada it has in it.

January 21, 2006

Yellow Ribbons
Posted by sibling
As my brother is leaving for Afghanistan in a week's time, our mum bought twenty Yellow Ribbon lapel pins and a handful of car magnets from the base at Jericho, to give to other family members. The commissionaire was very helpful, but hadn't

actually heard of the pins and needed to ask a colleague for help. I have been wearing mine on my coat since Christmas, and my infant daughter proudly displays hers on her Baby Bjorn carrier. When her uncle returns from Kandahar she will be nearly a year old.

I haven't yet been asked by anyone what the ribbon represents. This is possibly a Vancouver blind spot; in an army town like Edmonton the reaction would be much more positive. Vancouverites are notably wary of aggressive-sounding things like troops and I expect that some of those who do get around to asking what the pin stands for will regret doing so. In the meantime, I can't help but wonder if people here think instead that we're in favour of Third World aid, or against Wal-Mart, or something else they feel better able to relate to. Not many people have to wait at home for soldiers these days.

There also isn't really a dramatic way to send off the few soldiers who do go overseas. My parents said goodbye to my brother over lunch; my husband, daughter and I saw him off at the airport later in the day. Mum apparently held her composure well, while my daughter gurgled and dribbled, and if I sniffled a bit it was probably just a winter cold.

January 25, 2006

Arrival
Posted by Dave
I won't post much today. I've arrived in Kandahar. It's everything I expected it to be and more. Until I get my feet under me here, I'll be brief. For at least the next week, I'll be at the giant base at Kandahar Air Field. This place reminds me of nothing so much as a northern Canadian town, with its gravel roads, continual construction and endless parade of every kind of vehicle imaginable.

Not just military vehicles—those are a kaleidoscope in themselves—but the civilian vehicles would fill a book. People make their way around here in everything from golf carts to tour buses, although most are ATVs and SUVs. Everything is dusty.

I've only got a few minutes on this Internet connection, so I will keep it short, and leave you with this one image. Local delivery trucks are called "jingle trucks," not from the gaudy paint and crazy decorations which crowd the cabs and block the driver's view, but from the way their owners deck them out with thousands of identical baubles that hang from every surface, jangling and sparkling as the truck rolls and bounces along the tracks in the road.

I'll post some pictures as soon as I can.

January 30, 2006

Outside the wire . . . sort of
Posted by Dave

Well, I did get outside the wire yesterday, but not really. The happy part of the story is that I had an excellent helicopter tour of the city of Kandahar, of all of the danger areas, and especially an aerial view of the PRT compound . . . the sad part of the story is that as I was getting on the aircraft, I thought about my camera, and said, "D'oh!"

There will be other flights.

My impressions of the city, from the air: an ocean of single-storey mud-brick compounds. The city is of a very respectable size. Population estimates vary, but the most reasonable have it at 250,000 to 500,000.

The city rises gradually from the desert—all around the city are what pass for fields here, if you can call a roughly rectangular patch of brown in a vast brown wasteland a field—and the fields are usually associated with some sort of ruin or well. Some compounds are more elaborate, consisting of what appear to be deep, closely spaced trenches surrounded by a mud-brick wall, a two- or three-storey rectangular structure, like a granary, standing at the side. Little rectangular windows dot the "granary" walls. People carry loads, swat goats and squat randomly in fields. Children run around excitedly as we roar overhead.

As you get closer to the city, houses appear, first alone, then in progressively larger communities. Some are nothing more than mud-brick enclosures with a tarpaulin over a corner; others look to be built of cinder block, with roofs and little outbuildings. Nearly every house has a wall enclosing a sort of compound or yard, usually with children and chickens running around inside.

In the city itself lies chaos. What appear to be apartments sprout from a mud-brick sprawl. Donkey carts mingle cheek-to-jowl with taxis. Jingle trucks are everywhere. Traffic of every description lines up behind the police checkpoint at the intersection of Highways One and Four, where there is some sort of a double triumphal arch—we have dubbed this checkpoint "the Golden Arches." Brilliant azure mosque domes stand out like sapphires in a creekbed.

Everywhere is the colour of mud. Yesterday even the air carried a sandy hue.

My connection time runs short. The flight was fun but uneventful. Nobody shot at us, not that we could tell, anyway.

February 3, 2006

Outside the wire (really)
Posted by Dave
There was a convoy scheduled to go to the PRT compound and back the other night. You won't be surprised that I dropped everything to get on it.

It rained hard that night. When we went off the pavement, the Afghan soil turned to a kind of greasy goop that would be familiar to anyone who has lived in Alberta—we call it "prairie gumbo." Thank God for big, knobby tires.

When it was time to depart, nobody said "good luck." You never wish anyone good luck. You say, "Let's have a safe trip."

Jingle trucks. That's my clearest memory of the first part of the trip—thinking, Christ, any of these stupid things could have a bomb in it. After a few kilometres, with jingle trucks high-beaming you every few seconds (apparently many of them don't have low beams), I stopped worrying. They actually started to seem kind of comical.

They're not just gaudy in the daytime. I saw what I thought were several police cars a few kilometres away, with all their lights flashing. It was actually one jingle truck two hundred metres away. You know those people who mod up their cars with spoilers, ground-effects kits, spinners, air dams? Those guys are absolute amateurs compared to jingle-truck drivers. Lights blink and flash all over the hood and grille. Their owners build a sort of steel arch over the cab, which they paint garishly and use to mount what look like Christmas lights, strobes and spotlights. Some of them remove their headlights and replace them with a single spotlight right in the middle (if the driver doesn't have too many other lights, it looks just like an oncoming motorcycle. We almost hit two). I saw several trucks with what looked like neon lights along the running boards.

Then there are the donkey carts. More than I expected, mixed in with the regular traffic, right on the highway in the middle of the night. Guys riding bicycles, mopeds, scooters. Taxis. Pedestrians.

We got there fine, except my leg fell asleep and some stuff fell out of my pocket in the vehicle. Never did find it. @#$% cramped army vehicles.

I'll post about the PRT compound later. I'm going to LOVE living in that place.

I spent some time talking to old friends and comrades at the compound, but we didn't stay long. The rain dropped off and we mustered for departure—same skit as on the way out. As we got back in the vehicle, the driver said, "Here's to a safe trip back." Hear, hear.

At one point, the streets were deserted, which caused some concern because these particular streets are normally bustling at that time of night. We passed the site of the other night's ambush. A few bent guardrails, but little other sign. My leg fell asleep again.

Sounds anticlimactic? I don't think so. I sure as hell felt on edge, at least at the start. I noticed every little thing along the way. Until I saw the humour in them, I tensed up every time a jingle truck passed. For such a mundane activity, the drive was pretty intense. And the jingle trucks added an element of surreal humour. There's no way I can do these contraptions justice.

[I finally arrived at Camp Nathan Smith—the PRT compound—on the second of February. And not a moment too soon, as I was growing heartily sick of KAF, its dust, its three-inch gravel, its millions of rules.]

February 13, 2006

Day
Posted by Dave
Kandahar has hundreds of mosques. Not tall, gilt, blue, domed postcard mosques, but neighbourhood shrines barely recogniz- able to an outsider—mud-brick boxes, sometimes whitewashed or scrolled with Koran verses, always the centre of community

life. Each has a muezzin, who calls the faithful to prayer five times a day. The first call is shortly after five. Before modern electronics the muezzin's reach was only limited by his voice, but now loudspeaker systems carry the "Ullaaaaaahu akhbar" far away. I sleep in a tent. I can hear five different mosques. I get up early here.

Two weeks ago, when I first arrived, temperatures sometimes dropped to three degrees at night. What a difference a fortnight makes—last night the mercury dropped to fourteen. As long as I'm not exhausted, it's not hard to get out of bed.

I haven't spent a lot of my life in the tropics, so the suddenness of sunrise and set in the lower latitudes still surprises me daily. The sky seems to go from black to blinding in an instant. The smell of cooking fires is noticeable in the sun's first rays, and by the time the sun is up, there is a big-city layer of opaque smog blocking the view to the horizon. Only the wild, crenellated tops of the mountains and ridges to our west are visible. Above, the sky is blue.

Except when it isn't. When there's a wind, like today, fine dust fills the sky and turns the world khaki.

Other days, the wind sweeps away the smog and brings no dust. At noon, if you have a vantage point over the houses, you will see the whole single-storeyed city out to the fields, the hills and the desert beyond.

The afternoon is warm. But we are from a cold climate, and left home in a blinding snowstorm. So warm is hot. Most of us stay out of the sun—even though it hasn't been over twenty-three degrees. In another six weeks, it will be hot. Hot will be hellish.

Night comes as suddenly as day. The warmth lingers a while longer. Stars come out, not as many as we see from the middle of the prairie, but enough to give yet another indication of how far from home we are. Orion is overhead. The Big Dipper is on the horizon. Stars twinkle little, if at all.

It's eleven o'clock. The muezzin should be making their final calls soon. I worked late tonight, but somehow, for the first time in a week, had the energy to write.

I sleep well here.

[I've always been the active sort of leader, and I've never believed that an officer should send his people into places and situations where he isn't willing to go himself. So for my first few months in Kandahar, I took every opportunity to get outside the wire on patrol.]

February 24, 2006

The Wrist Puck
Posted by Dave
I asked for a watch for Christmas. I've always wanted a watch with an altimeter in it, and a barometer, and a thermometer, and an electronic compass. Not because of a need for frivolous gadgetry (a fault of mine, but the watch wasn't a symptom), but because I climb, and an altimeter watch is an obvious complement to my hobby. The compass and weather instruments are similarly helpful.

I got the watch. I've worn it every day since then, since in this environment it is more practical than the expensive Seiko I got at my high school graduation. But it's a big watch. It's so big, I call it the Wrist Puck. The sleeves of my combat shirts barely fit over it, so it usually sticks out. It's a Suunto Vector, and partly tan in colour, so it isn't really incongruous.

At one stop on patrol today we happened to be near a school when classes let out. As we were standing by our vehicles, hundreds of kids, all boys, filed by. It was certainly the most charming experience I've had since arriving here. They were shy at first, as children are everywhere; the boldest ones said, "Hi, how are you?" in accented English, or something in Pashto that I didn't understand at all, before hurrying along. But most peered shyly at us when they thought we weren't looking and shifted their eyes to the ground, grinning, when they caught a soldier's eye.

At first I said "hello" when the children spoke to me. I don't know why. I've learned a number of Pashto greetings, and I always use them on Afghan adults, to great effect. People everywhere love it when you make the effort to learn their language. But for some reason I didn't think of it next to the school. Then I remembered the simple *salaam*, an Arabic word meaning "peace," and used as a greeting throughout the Muslim world. What a world of difference a word makes.

It shouldn't have been a surprise. Kids like troops. Troops like kids. In an instant I was a rock star. Every little boy wanted to shake my hand, ask my name in broken English, ask for an afghani (the local currency). A few used sign language to ask for pens—holding out their left hands and pretending to write on them with invisible pens held in their right hands. I had no pens to give out, so I took one small child's hand and pretended to write on it with my finger. Gales of laughter. I taught them how to high five and do different handshakes. I remembered more Pashto, but by this time it didn't matter, the ice was broken, and the older boys all tried out their English lessons on me. Afghans certainly do a good job of teaching their kids to speak English.

What does this have to do with the Wrist Puck? I'm not sure they gave a damn about me. Boy after boy asked me, straight-faced, "Can I have your watch?" Afghan kids certainly have good taste in personal accessories.

The scrum soon got to be a little much. One of the master corporals in the convoy came to me and said, "Um, sir, we've got to get all these kids off the street . . ." Oops.

As usual, I didn't have my camera with me. But you can take my word for it that they were as cute as five- to eight-year-olds anywhere.

Next time we go by a school, I hope I have the good sense to bring my camera.

March 5, 2006

Bad news
Posted by sibling
I saw Mum and Dad today. They told me that they had spoken to Dave this morning, and he had told them about the attack on Lt Trevor Greene.

I understand Dave knows Trevor, from the Seaforths. I imagine this latest attack has upset him even more than most.

I've thought of little else myself, since I heard the news. I keep thinking for some reason that this attack was particularly horrific, but my husband has rightly pointed out that a suicide bomber would be no less devastating. I suppose that, of all the dangers we at home assumed we'd be reading about, an axe attack seems so shockingly barbaric. I keep half-thinking: an axe? How could they?

That isn't right—that isn't how we do things in Canada.

Dammit, don't they know the rules over there?

Every attack on a Canadian soldier is terrifying for those of us waiting at home. I hope that Trevor's wife can take a little bit of comfort in knowing that we are all thinking of her, and of him, and of the other soldiers there. And of their families, especially of their families. We here are all counting the days.

March 8, 2006

Posted by Dave

As time passes, and the days grow longer and the demands on me increase, my energy diminishes, and my capacity to write ebbs along with my lyricism. So I post less and less often. I apologize and I will try to find more time. But for now, I can't promise anything.

We held a ceremony at the PRT the other night to remember Cpl Paul Davis and MCpl Tim Wilson. It was brief, it was moving. But the ceremony was for his brothers and sisters in B Company, 2 PPCLI, for those who served with them and who are most deeply affected by their loss. So I would rather not talk about it.

I first met Trevor Greene when I was posted as regular support staff (RSS) to the Seaforth Highlanders in 1999. Trevor was in the process of transferring from the navy into the army reserves, and as I helped him with the painfully slow process, we became fast friends. By a fluke, Trevor trained as part of our company for this deployment. If you've read the articles others have posted on this blog over the past few days, you will have read about how much Trevor genuinely cares about Afghanistan. Trevor is, like me, a true believer. I was by the radio when Trevor was first injured in an IED attack, and I was by the radio the other day.

Head injuries are terrible things because they are so unpredictable. I have spent some very anxious hours waiting for news.

We have all heard about how Trevor's condition is improving, and how his family is at his side in Germany. That news made a lot of people here smile.

March 10, 2006

Pencils and other Implements of Destruction
Posted by Dave

I got an email several days ago. Because of the tempo of the last week, I haven't been able to check my civilian email, so I didn't read this message until today, but it strikes me as a great way to indicate to everyone just how complex the situation is in Afghanistan.

My little post the other week about going to a school sparked a lot more interest than I thought it would. Children are popular not just with soldiers, and I got many more private emails than blog comments. One correspondent asked if he could send Canadian-flag pencils to give to the children, if only as an icebreaker?

Pencils are a great idea. Pencils and writing paper are things that I get asked for every day, not just by schoolchildren but by their parents as well. But you need to understand a few things.

Afghanistan is the second-poorest country in the world. Kandahar is one of the poorest cities in Afghanistan. Even successful, powerful people, unless they are warlords or involved in the drug trade, are very poor by Canadian standards. So if I give a school principal a thousand dollars and tell him to buy supplies for his school, what do you think happens? His house gets a roof that won't collapse in the rain, his children get shod and his whole family becomes less undernourished. If I give him a thousand pencils for his students, the next day they are on sale in the bazaar, and the result is the same.

Could you look him in the eye and tell him he's done wrong?

The natural tendency, then, is to give to the students themselves. But does anyone think we can visit every school in the country, every month, and refill every student's bag?

Schools, police, water, power, sanitation, health . . . the problem is the same for them all. And at all levels, from the lowest manager to the regional director. Are there people who are wealthy enough to survive without embezzling, but choose to do it anyway? Of course there are. Everywhere, and at all levels too. Low-grade bribery is part of the culture here, but the distinction between baksheesh and outright graft is pretty murky no matter where you're from.

All that won't be a surprise to any of you. But let me tell you about other factors that you're probably not aware of.

Afghanistan is peopled by many different cultures. In the north live Tajiks, Uzbeks and Turkmen. In the middle of the country, there are the Hazara, possibly the descendants of Ghengiz Khan's Mongol horde, Nuristanis and Baloch. And in the south, there are the Pashtuns. Ethnic divisions are not clear-cut—nothing is in Afghanistan—and sizable populations of Tajiks live in the south and Pashtuns in the centre and so on. But each province has its ethnic makeup, and in Kandahar, like in Waziristan across the Pakistani border, the Pashtuns predominate.

Pashtuns form the largest tribal society in the Islamic world. They view themselves as the natural leaders of Afghanistan, and despise peoples like the Hazara as a sort of underclass. Their relations with one another are dominated by a tribal code called *pashtunwali*, which values above all honour, hospitality, loyalty, bravery, revenge and fierce individualism. This code has some pretty inexplicable facets—it is perfectly acceptable under *pashtunwali*, for example, to change sides in the middle of a battle for a bribe. You don't have to understand it, but if you are doing business here you have to deal with it.

Pashtuns are hardly monolithic either. One is not simply a Pashtun, one is a Durrani or a Ghilzai; and one is not simply a Ghilzai or a Durrani, one is a Popolzai or a Barakzai or an

Alikozai or an Ishaqzai Durrani Pashtun, or a member of one of dozens of other tribes. It doesn't end there; families come next. And it is a vast understatement to call the interrelationships complex. Don't try building a road through a Barakzai area using Alikozai labour, unless the Barakzai of that area have just concluded an agreement with the Alikozai families. And be prepared for it all to go pear-shaped in a heartbeat, for reasons you will never fully understand.

As the Pashtuns say: I against my brother—I and my cousin against the world.

So you can't give everyone what they need, and you can't give it to their leaders to give to them. And if you give it to them in the wrong way, or in the wrong amounts, or at the wrong time . . .

Add to this soup of ethnic rivalry and ancient blood feuds a weak central government and organized crime. Throw in poppy for good measure.

Notice I haven't even mentioned the Taliban. They are only part of the problem here—a big part, and a part that has proven exceptionally adept at manipulating tribal divisions and ethnic rivalries (not to mention incorporating organized crime). So adept, in fact, that the roles played by any of these factors in a particular incident can be impossible to unravel. But for us to focus on a single enemy when we are fighting so many foes at once would be to guarantee failure.

So what's the answer? Just as complex as the problem itself—but it will be slow. I have written before about the "Long War." We have to attack every problem at once. Not everywhere, not all the time—all of Western society could scarcely muster the necessary resources—but at all levels, from village to national, at once. We must hold leaders accountable—and do what we can to force out the excessively corrupt and incompetent. We must help the intelligent, determined and patriotic to learn the skills of nation building, public administration, policing, education and business. We must target our reconstruction efforts to reward successes. Eventually, we must diminish the influence of tribalism—slow though that process will be. We must build the confidence of Afghans in their own government over foreign aid—which is why we give Afghans Afghan flags, not the maple leaf.

And we must have the patience to stay here, and work, and fight, and suffer, until this is done. Or every dollar spent, every life lost will have been wasted.

So I will do my job. I will organize, and coordinate, and direct, and assist the various parts of the PRT to do the things that they do, all of which attack the problems at different levels and in different ways. I will work from my office, in meeting rooms and on patrol. I will tell Canadians about what we are doing, so fewer will be misinformed by the misguided. I will do this all day, every day, while I am here.

And I will give children pencils and paper.

April 1, 2006

No peace to keep
Posted by sibling
I wrote a letter to the editor of the *Vancouver Sun* the other day.

In my letter I was trying to make it clear that Canadian soldiers serving in Afghanistan are not "peacekeepers." This will be obvious to anyone reading this weblog; however, it is not at all obvious to many Canadians, including many in the media, who often refer, or allow correspondents to refer, to our soldiers as peacekeepers.

This is just plain wrong—peacekeeping is done by the UN, not Canada, and we've pretty much pulled out of peacekeeping these days anyway—but it bothers me especially because of the emotive image of peacekeepers, and of the idea being put into people's heads of Canadian peacekeepers as casualties. The article my letter was responding to was one such confused collection of statements about "peacekeeping personnel" being killed, and asking whether this was the best use of our peacekeepers. I may be wrong about this, but I think that people are more likely to support the Canadian mission in Afghanistan—even with casualties— if they know that those involved are soldiers. Changing them into peacekeepers suggests, to me at least, that there should be less shooting involved—both by them, and by others.

Canadians need to understand that these are soldiers, and that this is a war effort. The term "peacekeeping" implies that there should in fact be a peace to keep, and the recent battle at Sangin suggests that this is not entirely the case in Afghanistan.

April 23, 2006

22 April
Posted by sibling
Dave called this morning. We didn't recognize the number and nearly didn't pick it up. He was understandably subdued after today's attack—he was good friends with one of the soldiers who was killed.

We talked for about twenty minutes and he talked briefly about where the soldiers were killed and I told him about how things are here and how Dad is retiring soon, and that my baby daughter is eating creamed corn and yams and beef casserole (all pureed), and how it was sunny today but cold, and he said it's thirty-five degrees there and very uncomfortable, but they have aircon in the trucks so it's not as bad as it looks. When he comes back for his leave he said he would come to our place for curry and whiskey and such, and he's going to be doing some climbing and hiking and things like that in Squamish, and I marvelled about all the drinking he's going to be doing after being in a "dry" camp for so long, and I told him he's going to be a cheap date, and I told him to try and stay "inside the wire" and he said he's trying his hardest to get outside the wire, and so on.

And after I hung up I finished my coffee and chatted with my husband and played with my baby daughter and then we got ready to go out for a walk and I got the stroller out and put her mittens and her hat on her and then I started to cry. And I cried for a little while and my husband held me and my daughter played with her toys and a bit later, we went out for a walk.

Their names are Cpl Matthew Dinning, Bombardier Myles Mansell, Lt William Turner and Cpl Randy Payne.

June 10, 2006

Back
Posted by Dave
I've just returned from leave. I spent eighteen days at home, most of it with family, or keeping to myself. And yes, as promised, I didn't spare my liver.

Things got pretty hard here for the last month before leave. I won't go into specifics, but I was tired, frustrated and demoralized. I stopped posting, not because I didn't have lots to say, but because I didn't want my frustration and bitterness to show. When I got home, pretty much everyone I knew (and many I didn't) told me how disappointed they were that I had stopped posting. I hadn't realized how many people were reading the blog. I suppose I have lost much of that readership. I can't blame anyone for forgetting about it, but I was not in the right frame of mind.

I returned to a much-changed situation. Again, no specifics—but I am much happier now, energized, focused on the very hard road ahead. I worked hard when I first arrived, but now things stand to become much busier and much more serious.

This is not an excuse for future delinquency. I plan to post. I just don't know what to post. Security reasons prevent me from writing about most things that I do. One suggestion I received at home was to write about what I do during the day.

Here's what it might look like:

0700: wake up. If I were at home, I would hit the snooze bar a bunch of times, but I don't have a snooze bar here.

0730: shower and shave. Maybe swing by the kitchen for coffee or cereal.

0800: in the office. Read emails. Maybe get angry at someone.

0830–1230: fight fires, read things, write things, meet people. Try to get outside even though it is over forty degrees.

1230–1300: eat lunch.

1300–1700: fight fires, read things, write things, meet people. Try to get outside even though it is over forty degrees.

1700–1730: eat dinner.

1730–whenever: fight fires, read things, write things, meet people. Try to get outside even though it is over forty degrees.

whenever—until I fall asleep: either read or watch a DVD. The DVDs we buy at the bazaar are really popular, especially the TV series (*Scrubs, Battlestar Galactica, House*. One of my roommates is addicted to *Babylon 5*). Yes, they are pirated. No, I don't feel guilty.

Repeat ad nauseam.

Can't be any more specific than that, I'm afraid. Every day is both exactly the same and unique.

It's good to be back.

August 5, 2006

At last
Posted by sibling
Dave called me this morning, and as expected he is fine. He's quite low, as he knew one of today's casualties quite well. But otherwise he's still okay, and looking forward to coming home.

I gave him a hard time today for not calling home as soon as there were casualties and letting us know he was all right. But—and I didn't realize this before—he isn't able to. When there is a Canadian casualty, the soldiers in Afghanistan are prevented from contacting home until the next of kin are notified (they are unable to telephone or email—the technology is simply switched off). One can imagine the nightmare scenario otherwise—a soldier's family finding out of his or her death from a well-meaning friend, or worse, the press, simply because other soldiers passed on the name of the deceased while reassuring their families that they themselves were okay.

The above "nightmare" would, of course, be only the first of many for such families. As Cpl Christopher Reid's mother put it, "We are shocked, saddened and we are lonely already."

Dave will be home at the end of the month.

August 25, 2006

What it feels like
Posted by sibling
Crash course: Being the Family of a Soldier 101

1. Watch news intently three times a day, instead of your usual distracted once at dinnertime.

2. Let the air out of your lungs forcefully whenever there is word of "a soldier" dead in Afghanistan, identity to be confirmed pending notification of next of kin.

3. Look calm as your brain sifts through the various ways your family could have been notified, but has not been, so it must be okay—no, I spoke to Mum and Dad a couple of days ago, they're available on the cellphone, it can't be us, it's not us, no it's not us.

4. Hate yourself for being relieved when the names of the dead soldiers are confirmed as being Not Your Relative.

5. Without irony, support the recent deployment of soldiers to Afghanistan. Be angry when Letters to the Editor suggest otherwise. Think nothing of it.

And so on. But as it happens, my family and I no longer have to suffer the above, because Dave is no longer in Afghanistan. He is—as of well before the time of this blog post—on his way home.

We've left the light on.

Epilogue

I returned to Edmonton on August 30, 2006, after a return trip that included five days of decompression in Cyprus. The next day, August 31, I was at home with my family in Vancouver.

After my disembarkation leave ended, I took a leave of absence from the army for six months. I grew my hair—after almost twenty years of soldiering, I felt I had a right. I renovated my house. I did some travelling. I skied. Mostly, I relaxed. I thought about Afghanistan every day.

In December, my friend Jack, an American contractor who lived across the street from the PRT—and to whose house we used to patrol a whole fifty metres in full gear for barbecues—was killed, right on the street between our compounds. A suicide

bomber wearing a vest got him, a few days before he was supposed to return to his wife and kids in North Carolina for
Christmas. He gave me a really nice gift when I left the PRT. I
miss him terribly.

The Afghanistan experience is full of stories like that.

A few weeks ago, I was offered a chance to take the Regular
Force Command and Staff College course. This is the course that
qualifies an officer for senior appointments. So in a few days,
the long hair will be cut and I will put on a uniform again. If I do
well, I may be offered another position in Afghanistan. As long
as it gets me outside the wire, I'll take it.

—Dave

OTHER PEOPLE'S STORIES

BY

ALLISON CRAWFORD, MD, FRCPC

Allison Crawford is a psychiatrist and assistant professor at the University of Toronto. She worked as a psychiatrist in Kandahar with the Canadian military from April 2007 to May 2007. She is the founding and managing editor of the journal Ars Medica: A Journal of Medicine, the Arts and Humanities, *and her principal academic and clinical focus is on integrating literature and the arts with medicine. She is also a PhD candidate in English literature at the University of Toronto.*

I will start where I remember myself standing, though this is an arbitrary entrance into events. I am in the hallway that connects the rooms of the hospital's in-patient section: the intensive care unit, the ward, a separate treatment room that can be closed off for isolation, and the doctor's lounge. I can look into any of these rooms from here. I remember being tired, feeling pulled in too many directions. What catches my attention is a very still moment in the ICU. An Afghan man, wearing a long black shirt, loose black pants, and a black headdress shot through with silver threads, is standing motionless above one of the beds, which holds a six-year-old girl. I can only see the lower half of her in that moment, barely perceptible under the blankets that cover her. His hand lies grazing her naked shoulder. He has not moved for some time, in keeping with her stillness. Her arms are arranged on top of the blankets. Her eyes would have been closed. The ICU is kept quite dim, and I can just make the figures out in the arc of light that illuminates her bed. Very little moves. I want to see where his gaze rests, for it is as motionless as he. I follow his line of sight, strange from my own angle, down her body to where her right leg should have been. I want to tell him to turn away, that it is not his fault; I want him to move something. My own unrest must have disturbed him, because he looks up and, seeing me, nods, a shy smile softening his face.

Just the day before, I had asked John, our interpreter, to help me converse with this man, the girl's father. The orthopedic surgeon had already told him that his daughter would need her leg amputated or she would die. The father had initially refused. There was a furor in the hospital, and great uncertainty about whether he had refused because of his Islamic beliefs about what would happen to the spiritual integrity of his daughter's body, or whether he'd refused just because she was a girl and he did not care if she died. Someone suggested it would be important for us to find out, both for this child and for our work with others. As I headed off to speak with him, one of the other surgeons suggested that he might not want to speak to a woman.

The interpreter was forthright and engaged the girl's father immediately. The man held out his small, hardened hand for me to shake. The interpreter offered, by way of an introduction that I doubted came directly from the man, "He is a nomadic-type person, not a city dweller."

We moved to my office where we sat in a small circle, the father drawing the metal fold-out chair closer to my own. His decisive seating arrangement was at odds with the tentative manner with which he sat on the edge of the chair. He leaned forwards, and as I asked him questions, he watched my face intently, leaning on his knee, nodding solemnly every few words. When I paused, he turned towards the interpreter and awaited the translation. He gave his answers directly to the interpreter, after only a short pause, but glanced often in my direction, expectantly as if waiting for some acknowledgement, which I tried to provide with my own nods, though they likely made little sense. "I asked my sons and my daughter to go and watch the donkey. My sons are now dead from the bomb, and my daughter is hurt. I carry a terrible pain in here," he said, laying his hand on the inside of his shirt against his chest, "but I am okay. It is hard to know what to do, since my wife is not here to be a partner to me, to help me decide what to do. I just want to be sure there is nothing that the doctor can do to save her leg."

"Would you make the same decision if this was your son?" I asked at some point. At this, he turned the chair towards me, and, looking at me solemnly, he held up both his hands in the air. This time he spoke to me directly, not unkindly but with firmness: "You see this hand, the right hand, the left hand, if I lose a finger on either one it doesn't matter. A son, a daughter, they are both my children." He smiled at me and turned back towards the interpreter, "Yesterday I went hunting and I killed a rabbit. I did not know she was pregnant until after I killed her. Maybe this is punishment. Only Allah knows."

Of course, all of this was relayed by the interpreter, who made many interjections and qualifications, seeming to use tens more words than the man had. "Amputation is allowed in Islamic law," the interpreter assured me, "but you have to bury the limb, not incinerate it." The father nodded along as the interpreter continued, "Allah approves of science and learning."

The man thanked me sincerely several times, with his hands joined. The next morning, after speaking further with the orthopedic surgeon, he agreed to the amputation. The father, who had walked for hours carrying his daughter to the gates of the hospital, had no place to bury the limb on the base. It was incinerated.

—

I return the father's smile and go back down the hall, leaving him next to his daughter. An American soldier, sitting with his machine gun propped across his lap, guards the isolation room across the corridor. He swings in his chair, which is tipped backwards on its two back legs. The patient in the isolation room is a Taliban prisoner, a major coup, a master IED maker, and they take guarding him seriously. I can barely see through the crack in the door to the man lying in the bed. I can make out the bandages that cover his head wound, and I'm not sure whether I am imagining it, but I think I see the fearful glint of his eyes, peering out wildly from the bandage edges. I turn away, a little unsettled, to find that I am the object of scrutiny for what looks to be a young British Special Forces soldier, who is leaning against the door frame that leads to the doctor's lounge. He is tanned and muscular, with the telltale Special Forces rugged, unshaven look and casual civilian clothes. He meets my gaze somewhat brazenly and barely moves to allow me into the room.

Walking into the lounge, I realize that he is there talking to the Special Forces physician, equally rugged and casual, who lies sprawled on the incongruent oversized floral velvet couch that fills the doctor's lounge. "Oh look, it's the cute Canadian psychiatrist," the physician says in what I'm sure he imagines is a charming manner. "You won't believe what our boy's been through. Amazing. They had a gunfight with the Taliban last night." He nods almost proudly in the younger soldier's direction, the other leaning himself even more casually against the door frame. "Hey, you should see this guy's gun. Come outside, we'll show you," continues the physician, clearly excited now.

The younger soldier asks me, looking back down the hall towards the isolation room, "Who is that in the room?"

"A Talib—" I do not get the word out of my mouth.

"There are no Taliban here," says the Special Forces doctor, looking hard at me. "Let's show the psychiatrist some real equipment," he says, winking at the soldier and angling him with his body towards the hospital's exit. They wait for me to follow.

Outside, standing at the back of the truck, they pull out the soldier's gun and show me the jammed release. I flinch instinctively away from the rifle, and the physician, who has commandeered it, apologizes for pointing it at me. "Boy, you would have been a goner with this thing. It completely jammed mid-fight. Tell her how it jammed." The doctor's pager goes off. "Oh, sorry, I'll see you guys back inside," and he thrusts the gun into the soldier's hands. We both look at it. I can see deep gouges on the gun.

"What was that?" I ask.

"That was the bullets," he says, tracing with his finger the path that they would have taken through the air and along the metal. By holding the gun up to his chest, he shows me how a bullet had just missed his sternum. I notice for the first time that the finger that holds the trigger is bandaged and that his hand shakes slightly. When he sees that I am looking at his hand, he puts the gun down and clenches his fist as if to stop the shaking.

"I'm sorry," I say, not sure of the extent of his injury, but newly aware that he is still badly shaken.

"Aw, that's nothing. You should see the other guy. Hey, do you think they ever bring Taliban to this hospital? When I came in last night, I thought they brought some guy in. Afghan, Taliban, they all look the bloody same. To be honest, now when I see one of them, I want to just rip their fuckin' heads off. Last night I wanted to just slit all of their throats, but the doc calmed me down." In the bright, hot sunlight, I can see the skin on his face, close up. Completely unmarred, paler under his dark beard. Young. He keeps talking, as if to continue where he had left off in the story, but now seems elsewhere. "Yeah, you should have seen that guy. I barely felt the bullet hit my finger, but I just let him have it. I don't know how many bullets he took, but he stopped moving. It was dark, and once it calmed down, I went over because I wanted to see him. His neck was twisted right around. I bent over and took his vest. My buddy has it. It had his blood on it, and some hair stuck to it, but I think I'll keep it like that. I didn't realize how bad my hand was hurt 'til I saw my blood pour all over his vest when I picked it up." Perspiration now stood out on his forehead. "It was weird, man. One minute he was alive and then dead. Just dead."

I am afraid to touch him, to startle him. We both jump as the doctor reappears and claps him on the back.

"Hey, let's get some photos with the psychiatrist. You can hold your gun."

There is something about the immediacy of the multinational base hospital, which treats both soldiers and Afghan civilians, that cracks open and makes visible the network of linkages between stories that bind us, however tentatively, together. All of these stories are bound so strongly by my own sense of place, a kind of memory device which allows me to put myself *there*. Once back there, I can walk through my memory, allowing the more detailed memories of each story to fill the spaces.

Aristotle wisely thought of memory as sensory, as rooted in the body and in place. This association with place can be traced back to the Greek poet Simonides of Chios, who escaped harm when a hall collapsed. The event made him a revered man, not on account of his survival but because of his extraordinary memory, which enabled him to recreate the seating plan of those at dinner, and thereby allowed the grieving families of the dead to identify the corpses of their loved ones. Simonides founded the *ars memoria*, the Art of Memory, in the wake of this incident. His mnemonic system, used by Aristotle, was based on sight and the powers of visualization. The rules of the Art were quite simple:

one was required to memorize the features of a building and to place images or emblems as memory cues on different architectural features.

As I write, I can wander at will through the places of KAF—the hospital, the streets (including "Enduring Freedom Highway"), the dining facility—and my body, with all of its locked sensations and memories, is back there. The writing process simply reminds me of this felt experience. I have a little video that I took on my last day before coming home. Starting again in the hallway of the hospital, I walk in each direction, through the in-patient ward, through the back of the hospital and down to the flight line where we received incoming casualties, into the outpatient section at the front of the hospital where my office was located.

In my office, with its door decorated with an "Airborne" emblem and slogans left by the Americans who had run the hospital before handing it over to Canada—"Freedom isn't free," "I will never leave a fallen comrade," "I will never quit," "I will never accept defeat"—I was privileged to hear, over six weeks as a psychiatrist with the Canadian Forces at KAF, the stories of NATO soldiers from different countries. Some of these stories were fractured, some closed and overworked, some devoid of feeling, others rich and courageous, life-giving, and of course there were the stories that emerged tentative and new in the rewriting of self and experience that occurs in psychotherapy. Here I have heard stories of war. The young woman who was raped by a fellow soldier. The master corporal who was overcome with panic at the thought of re-entering the hot, claustrophobic compartment of his tank, to face again the threats against his life buried in the road to Kandahar that he would again travel in a few days. The sergeant who, while on leave, almost hit an old man in a parking lot because the man took his parking spot. The lieutenant-colonel, decorated from the Gulf War, whose nightmares of the past flood his experience of this war. The seemingly contemptu-ous sergeant who referred himself to be seen but who could not tell me what was wrong, even after he broke down in sobs talking about his soldier who shot himself while he was on the other end of the phone. So many stories.

As a psychiatrist, I try to listen. It is often the best that I can do, to trust in the fact that putting these experiences into words can have some containing power, can allow the random experi-ences of the body under stress to cohere into more manageable and meaningful memories and find their *place* in the memory of the teller. In the telling and the listening, these experiences become something that can be shared, instead of hidden in shame to attack the body and mind in the quiet of a night at KAF. At the same time, I am learning from them things I never thought I would learn. My perspective is so partial—the mountains visible in the distance beyond KAF's gates and outside of the wire remind me of how far I am from what these soldiers experience.

In the video, I leave my office and return to the point in the hallway that connects all of the rooms. Days before, I stand in the same hallway, watching the area at the back of the hospital, where the trauma bays are filling with casualties. I brace myself. Being a psychiatrist in the middle of a medical emergency is something of a hindrance. I am never sure how to make myself useful. I hear that six people have arrived, but we are expecting more. Someone says fifty injured, maybe a hundred. The in-patient ward has been cleared, all the patients moved to overflow tents just outside the hospital. I look around at the staff's faces, trying to gauge who might need help. Everyone, so familiar at other times, looks slightly different under these conditions. Intent on their tasks, no one smiles. I catch sight of one of the nurses, struggling with the beds, and go over to help. Changing sheets, smoothing the covers, I at least feel I am doing something useful. The ward looks empty and strange, but will soon be filled with the new casualties.

The padre is standing beside me, helping to change the beds. Our eyes meet and he asks me what to do with the dirty sheets. He too is happy to have something to do, and probably knows that, like me, he will be busy soon enough.

With the beds made, the padre suggests that we go out to the trauma bays to see if anything needs to be done. He strides out, comfortable in the ongoing, highly organized chaos beside the beds. I hang back. I am caught up at the foot of one of the trauma bays, staring at a bed that seems large for the size of its new occupant, a tiny infant who lies under an enormous warming blanket. Awareness of the mass casualty comes to me in fragments from around the room. This is different; these casualties are mainly children, hit by a bomb dropped on their village. The small child in front of me looks perfect, his face turned slightly to the side. I can see the symmetry of his miniature features outlined in sharp contrast to the harsh tubing, needles and tape that are keeping him alive. The surgeon lifts back the blanket and I can see the child's major injury, extensive damage to his penis, but above the gaping wound I can also see his tiny abdomen moving up and down with his breath, and I try to focus on that hope.

Everything seems to settle into organization. The casualties are numbered and prioritized. The surgeons, nurses and medics will be up late, but things will move forward. The word comes down that we will receive no more casualties. We try not to speculate on what that means. The padre and I find ourselves again standing together. "Let's go for a coffee," he suggests, and I am happy to agree. I have been wanting to speak with him. Usually jovial, his first meeting with me ended with him putting his earphones on my ears to listen to Power Station's "Get It On (Bang a Gong)." I was not sure how to respond to "You're dirty and sweet, oh yeah." But that memory now mingles with the many moments when I have heard his lively voice turn quiet and reflective.

As we sit on the patio in the darkening night, drinking lattes that are eerily reminiscent of home, I ask him why he joined the military. After telling me how his abusive upbringing made him leave home at the age of fifteen, he shares how, after years of being a roadie in the 60s, he found God, first abstractly in philosophy and then in a profound mystical experience during which he was "wrestled to the ground by love." I am very quiet, hoping that he will continue his own story. "Oh, I have lots of problems, Doc," he says, now jovial again. "I guess I joined the military to get some structure."

I am puzzled. "How does all this fighting and death fit in with that love?"

He answers immediately and unsentimentally. "We've had war since the very beginning; it's part of human culture, part of social life." He sounds like he is talking about something pragmatic and everyday, which I suppose for him it is.

"Why do so many of the soldiers I see, then, struggle with the meaning of all of this, why does war bring them so close to meaninglessness?" I ask him, genuinely shaken myself by all I have seen that day.

"I consider my role as padre, and maybe your role as a psychiatrist, too, to be a signpost."

"A signpost to what," I ask skeptically, "the road to nowhere?"

"A signpost back towards humanity." I admire his certitude, but then he surprises me. After a few minutes of silence, he tells me, "I was in a dark night when I first got here."

"The long dark night of the soul," I echo.

"Oh, you know John of the Cross," he says, and continues: "I was sure I would die here." There is nothing to say.

Two women sit across from us, soldiers from Australia, and it becomes clear they have been listening. One woman asks the padre if he is a priest. I get up and excuse myself.

Walking back to the shacks to sleep gives me some time to myself. The dust of the streets settles at night, and it is mercifully cool. The stars are so clear and bright here, and yet they are evidence of my own disorientation and displacement. The crescent moon is oriented sideways, its ends tilting upwards, and the stars and their constellations are not in their usual positions.

The next morning things have settled down somewhat, though the hospital staff look weary. One of the girls who came in, a fourteen-year-old who had just been married before her village was bombed, is causing problems on the ward. She had had surgery to remove shrapnel from her right hip, and was healing well. "There's nothing wrong with her," insisted one of the nurses. "She's being a real handful, spitting at us, peeing on us, acting like she can't do anything for herself." We agreed that I would see her and also speak to her brother-in-law in the next bed, to find out if this was typical behaviour for her. I was distracted because we were standing at the door of the ICU and I could see the infant boy from the night before staring up at the ceiling. He did not protest, but lay there depressed, all of the life you would expect in a ten-month-old gone from his face.

"Where is his mother?" I ask his nurse.

"She died in the bombing, but that's his father on the ward." I make the connection that his father is the brother-in-law of the fourteen-year-old I am about to interview. "She was holding the baby, apparently, that's why the front of his body was exposed like that. Who knows who'll take care of him now," she muses. "I guess his father will have to get another wife."

On the ward, I approach one of the interpreters to help me interview the girl. She is lovely, her hands covered in henna. She also seems impervious to the strangeness of her surroundings, and to the men in close proximity. She reaches out, dramatically arching her back to the interpreter, asking him to help her move up in bed. He discreetly reminds me that he cannot touch her, though periodically as we speak with her, he lifts the sheets to cover her large breasts that spill over the covers, visible through the thin material of her nightgown. She greets me at the introduction, but quickly turns her head to the side and moans dramatically in pain, twisting on the bed.

The interpreter makes several attempts to ask her questions, but she calls out for pain medication. She keeps talking, apparently not in response to the interpreter's questions. He says, "I think she's too tired to talk," and sure enough her eyelids are drooping, but she continues to speak. Something makes me ask the interpreter what she is saying. "She keeps talking as if she is not here. It doesn't really make sense." I ask him to translate anyway. "In the house. We need to move to a different room. They are outside . . . shooting . . . shooting . . . we need to run out of the house. We are in the river behind the house . . . cold . . . they are planes in the sky. We feel safe now from the Taliban who have been shooting around the house. But it is dark and the planes start to shoot at us in the river. No, no," he translates haltingly, then adds, "It really makes no sense now. She is talking to her mother as if she is here." The girl's eyes are closed and twitching, but she no longer speaks.

We go over to the next bed where her brother-in-law lies on his side, facing the girl, with his right arm bandaged and fixed with pins. He raises his eyes when we approach, and they are an arresting shade of pale green in his tanned, lined face. Despite their great beauty, his eyes are flat and barely reflect the light. Through the interpreter, I ask him about his sister-in-law. He agrees that she is confused and that some of the details she is yelling out are not quite correct.

"She is upset," I suggest, and he nods in agreement.

Without looking back at the interpreter, he tells me, "She lost five people last night." And of course her story then makes perfect sense, having needed a translation that went beyond language, its meaning previously lost in the many demands of the hospital's operation. He does not mark these losses by the pronoun "we." When I look back at him as I stand at the nursing station, he looks startlingly like his infant son. He stares at the ceiling, his face devoid of expression.

The following day the hallway is bustling. There is a revived energy as I walk onto the ward. A screen has been placed around the girl's bed, and her aunt who is visiting, an unusual occurrence in the hospital, is demonstrating propriety to the girl, averting her eyes and holding a veil over her face whenever the doctor or another male enters. Another young boy sits in bed, blowing bubbles through a hoop, thrilled with himself and his audience. Then I see what this renewed energy is about, and the smiles. The brother-in-law is propped up in his bed, tentatively cradling his son with one arm. He is playing, trying to catch his son's eyes, both of their faces newly lit. Some of the nurses have cameras and are taking pictures. The father motions for the interpreter. "Could they take a picture of me with my son that I can have?"

These are just moments out of a multitude of moments, brought together through war, through the hospital's corridors, through my perspective. Their meanings swirl for me now like the blood of the Taliban and British soldiers mixing on the war-trophy vest, so partial was my intersection with the trajectory of their stories. How does the young soldier's bravado answer the father's guilt, the Taliban soldier's wild fear, the infant boy's loss of his mother, the padre's guidance, the fourteen-year-old's suffering lost in translation, and my own imagining of it all? Meaning is an accrual of this democracy of stories, is provisional and is open to reinterpretation.

I wonder what it would be like to see these Afghan children instead in the fields around their homes, on the streets and in the markets of Kandahar. I am made sharply aware that this is their home, *their* place that I am remembering as my own. The stars and the moon that look so unfamiliar and disorienting to me is the sky of their world, and I realize I have not yet been to Afghanistan. I am still some place in between.

LOVESONGS FROM A LIEUTENANT
BY
CAPTAIN CASEY BALDEN

Captain Casey Balden grew up in West Vancouver, British Columbia. He attended the Royal Military College of Canada in Kingston, Ontario, and graduated in Honours English, Class of 2004. In September 2004, he was posted to the Second Battalion, Princess Patricia's Canadian Light Infantry, in Shilo, Manitoba, as 1 Platoon commander. He was deployed to Afghanistan in August 2006. He currently lives in Brandon, Manitoba, and is set to redeploy to Afghanistan with Task Force 1–08 as a LAV Captain.

Winnipeg, Canada

It's July 2006 and, in typical Winnipeg fashion, the summer sun is scorching. I walk along Portage Avenue amidst the riff-raff of the city streets and I blend in seamlessly with the crowd. No one is aware of the task I am about to embark upon. I'm sporting a mohawk; it's more of a fashion statement than anything else, but I do get some looks. The thin blade of remaining hair seems to channel my energy and focus it upon others, and they can feel my contempt. Blood, or ketchup, smears the sidewalk. I no longer feel at home here; I'm a stranger in a strange land, a voice in a foreign language.

I watch from a coffee shop as an anti-war protest marches by. It's funny: I've always considered myself a pacifist. I grew up proud to be a Canadian, in part because we were the peace-keepers. We didn't pick fights; we helped resolve them with our intelligent, skillful and somewhat self-deprecating diplomatic skills. Yet as I watch the protest march on Portage Avenue, it's all I can do to stop myself from physically assaulting someone. Ignorance prevails in the crowd. I doubt that many know the difference between Iraq and Afghanistan. I doubt many are aware of all the good things Canadians are doing in Afghanistan, or the atrocities committed by the Taliban regime. The words that come to mind: weak, worthless, petty and feeble. But political science, international relations, government policy—these are not my specialties. My own ignorance is something I hope this tour will reduce. I leave the decisions to people more educated than myself. I simply do what my country asks of me.

Camp Mirage

A voice: "Cabin crew, prepare doors for arrival." Before we disembark the aircraft, we are told that today has been a particularly bad day in the war—four Canadian soldiers are dead. Some motivation upon arrival. The doors open and heat like a tidal wave assaults my body. The sound of combat boots on metal as we walk efficiently down the stairs: *clink, clink, clank*. Someone on the ground takes charge and begins barking orders. For now, we are content to do what we're told; in a few short days, it will be us giving the orders.

We are told we have one hour to be processed. Our plane has another flight scheduled. It's got to fly somebody home—a body. We get our baggage and the first items we need are our fragmentation vest, tactical vest, magazines, helmet and ballistic eyewear. We are broken into three groups and move on to weapons issue.

"Line up by section! Once you have your weapon, file by and pick up your ammo!" Amidst the order pure franticness seems to prevail. The sense of excitement is caught by the humidity in the air, caught and consumed like water vapour. Sweat runs down my nose.

"Quickly now—get a move on!"

Magazines—rounds: *Snap. Shraaaap! Click*. (Repeat.)

This is efficient militancy. The reality, the gravity of the situation begins to set in.

Kandahar Air Field, Afghanistan

When we arrive on the ground in Afghanistan, we step off the plane into a dingy old aircraft hanger. Its hollowness and echoes are eerie; pigeons, or some other birds, line the ceilings and there is bird shit everywhere. This structure has the marks of battle written all over it and you can feel its history in the muggy air. The next morning, I begin to see the physical landscape that makes up Afghanistan. The sand is like moon dust, and the alley to one dining facility is named as such. The trees seem to grow from nothing. The sky is a brilliant blue. And as I look to the southwest, a mountain has sprouted from the desert. Everything is strange, yet slightly familiar. It takes a while to get used to the heat and we drink bottled water from Saudi Arabia all day long. We spend one week receiving briefings in KAF before we commence our handover. We are going outside the wire. As an oncoming force handing over with seasoned soldiers who have been operating for six months, you just listen and learn and ask as many questions as you can. In this regard, rank does not matter. Every soldier holds a wealth of information that you need to extract.

We leave KAF in a company-sized combat convoy, en route to Patrol Base Wilson. Immediately it gets intense. Imagine you're driving on a Canadian freeway. It's only a two-lane freeway with an unpaved shoulder. Now imagine that every time you pass a car, you must assess that car to determine if it is a threat. Now imagine this freeway is lined with people, like the tail end of a city parade. Some are on cellphones, and you must assess each one of those to determine if he is studying you or counting your vehicles. Imagine one hundred ice-cream vendors on bicycles and insert those people randomly along the road. Imagine each old white Toyota Corolla is packed with a family of six or seven and everyone is in a hurry to get where they're going. Now mentally visualize a jingle truck: a double-decker bus, like one you'd see in London, painted a wide array of circus colours designed to catch the eye. Tie random shit onto every conceivable part of this vehicle and cram more people inside it. Imagine dozens of these jingle trucks throughout traffic. As we drive, dominating the road, vehicles yield left and right. It's an ever-changing mosaic of cars, bicycles, jingle trucks, men, children and very few women. And all of these things must be assessed as threats because somewhere on that street someone wants to kill you as violently as possible. This is driving through Afghanistan.

Kandahar province

The landscape of Kandahar province is varied. Black and beige mountains spontaneously emerge from the dusty soil. I've read that Afghanistan was once the heart of Asia, through which all roads passed, but it seems devoid of a heartbeat. Pot fields abound, with plants so tall the insurgents can use them for cover. So many pot fields scattered in the countryside that even a B.C. farmer would be jealous. In the tiny markets, there are street vendors selling meat and vegetables. Many families live in simple mud huts, the walls of which are constructed with a mixture of mud and straw. They bathe in muddy waters. I see crumbling walls of broken brick, like an ancient abandoned castle. Afghanistan used to have a monarchy and was once a respectable country. The people now exist as kings of nothing, without throne or crown. This place is a wasteland, a bridge to nowhere. There are grape-drying huts and orchards of grapes and pomegranates. And poppy fields. *Papaver orientale*—the oriental poppy. There is something remarkable about the image of a poppy; perhaps it's buried deep within our collective unconscious. Poppies produce opium; opium produces a deep and dream-filled slumber; poppies bob their sleepy heads in the breeze. The poppy, our chosen symbol of remembrance, grows out of these desolate gardens of dust and dirt. A field of poppies is absolutely beautiful in full bloom: a sea of green gently iced with pale pinks, whites and magentas. Such a beautiful flower to be responsible for so much misery and money, while at the root of it all is the poor Afghan farmer who simply harvests his crops in order to feed his family. Yet Afghanistan is not unlike Canada. Just as we have many distinct ethnic, cultural and linguistic groups, so too does Afghanistan. Their history has been heavily influenced by other nations, as has ours. The physical landscape alternates between the awesome and the awful, as does Canada's, from beautiful orchards and gardens to lonely mountain ranges and the unforgiving desert. Afghanistan, like Canada, is a nation in search of identity.

Convoy operations

In my initial days outside the wire, I conducted several convoy operations and vehicle checkpoints. I'll share with you a military term that gets overused: situational awareness. In ordinary language, it means having the common sense to know what's going on around you. Afghans driving in Kandahar City lack this process. I've heard it said that Afghans are never in a hurry, unless they are driving somewhere. All day long they can sit and smoke hash, relax, drink some chai, but when they get behind that wheel, suddenly the sky is falling.

Let's take a step back and remember the typical driver's examination. You'd study your booklet, ensure you knew the rules of the road and which sign stood for what. Well, Afghans don't have graduated licensing and they sure don't share North American rules of the road. They have some sort of system, with some form of rules, that probably works for them. But when the greatest threat to us is a car laden with explosives, we cannot afford to be timid. We dominate the road. They will yield. They will move. Or we will continue with escalation of force as our rules of engagement allow us.

It's a powerful feeling standing up in the turret of a vehicle with a 25mm cannon at your disposal and a 9mm pistol readied with the safety off. Standing fully upright, legs firmly planted, both arms fully outstretched and flexed, left hand wrapped tightly around the right, finger on the trigger, ready to fire into the engine block if that vehicle stays on the road for just one second longer.

Convoy driving requires a tremendous amount of mental concentration. Every vehicle is suspect. How do you know? There are combat indicators, yes, but how do you really know? A forty-kilometre drive can exhaust you, mentally. You must be ready at all times, ready for the unexpected. This is the reality of what we fight. The nature of an insurgency.

I feel the helplessness of my situation and it engulfs me.

On our drive west from KAF along Highway One, I witness the first shots fired in defence. We arrive at Patrol Base Wilson.

Patrol Base Wilson

On August 9, Master Corporal Jeff Walsh is killed several kilometres north of PBW. The leadership of A Company was still in

the midst of the handover with B Company, and the remainder of
the platoon had yet to leave KAF. I was not present at the scene,
but rather at PBW, and can still remember with perfect clarity
the moment when my company commander told me the news.
Jeff was a soldier's soldier. He was fit and intelligent, with a great
sense of humour. He had a deep sense of compassion about him.
He believed in Canada's mission in Afghanistan and was a true
warrior poet. He had tattooed on his arm the word "OVER-
COME." He told me he had this tattoo to remind him that no
matter what life threw at you, you could overcome any obstacle.
One day in the platoon lines, he told me he had written a poem.
Within the company, I had a reputation as the English Guy,
which more than one person had gotten a smile out of over my
two years in the battalion. But as such, I was fortunate enough to
be presented with Jeff's poem, which he asked me, in all sincerity, to read and edit. I made no major changes—maybe a comma
here or a semicolon there. He was proud of his piece and I was
more than happy to read it. This is Jeff's poem:

MONSTERS IN THE DARK

I know that they are out there;
I will not be ignorant anymore;
Pulling the blanket over my head will not keep them
From coming ashore
Instead I choose to confront them;
As afraid as I might be
Because if I don't stop the monsters
Our children can never be free.

The news of his death was devastating. The padre came to
speak to the company and I did not believe in his God. Death is the
tragedy that all must face but I, being young, had not experienced it

like this—it was too real. When in KAF, I found this quotation from Jeff regarding the death of one of his friends from his previous tour in Kabul: "You get a sick feeling in your stomach, and then it's hard to believe it's happening to you." That was exactly how I felt: it was just too hard to believe it was happening to me. So one evening, feeling alone and pensive in the Green Bean café in KAF, I composed this poem, structurally modelled after an old World War One poem, and the first lines I wrote overseas:

IN MEMORY OF MASTER CORPORAL JEFF WALSH

O Brother, we have shed our tears for thee:
If only Time may heal
Our grief for you, be it Eternity,
This emptiness, which words cannot reveal.

Patrol Base Wilson was our home outside the wire. An Afghan National Police headquarters compound, it is essentially three small buildings surrounded by a high wall of concrete. Located to the west of Kandahar City, it sits just north of Highway One, while to the south lie many of the areas within Kandahar province controlled by the Taliban, including the district of Bazaar-e-Panjwayi and the Arghandab River. The first day we arrive there, we examine the living arrangements: modular tent, cots, a TV or two. There are two pot plants sitting predominantly in a small garden near the entrance. There is a dumpster near the gate where we stash our trash. When it fills up, a local on a contract hauls our garbage away, driving eight hundred metres in any direction and dumping the trash all over the earth. A mangy-looking wildcat stalks the premises. His slinking movement startles me more than once. We are not there more than an hour when the first mortar round lands outside the camp.

I jump in the G-Wagon of the platoon commander I'm shadowing. As the oncoming force, we rely on the tactics that B Company has developed over the past six months. We push out of the compound, south of the highway, towards the bad land. South from the highway, there is a kilometre of desert broken by a thin treeline, behind which runs a canal. The Taliban use these canals as entrance and exit routes, as the treeline offers concealment for their movement. Anything beyond the treeline and canal is not safe for us. Over the radio, we hear that our observer has seen smoke, indicating a mortar baseplate position. He spools up a counter-fire mission and friendly mortars return fire. The G-Wagon I'm in has a .50 calibre machine gun mounted in the turret and it rains down fire. An entire company's worth of vehicles on a firing line opening up with direct fire is truly an awesome sight. No direct fire from the enemy comes our way. Indirect fire, however, is a different story, and we are harassed by mortars constantly. With indirect fire, there must be an enemy observer who is able to see the target and adjust the rounds by relaying corrections. When under attack, it is more likely you'll be able to spot the observer than the actual baseplate itself. Thus every local national becomes a suspect and you look for the combat indicators: is he observing us? Does he have a cellphone or a radio? I've tried to capture what it's like to feel that vulnerability, but of course words are a poor medium. I recommend you try the real thing some day.

> they've zeroed now, the data's set.
> mortars crash in our camp, like gambling with the Devil.
> shattered windows, sheared sheet metal and
> fragments,
> fragments everywhere.
> concussion rings your ears and you cower

closer to the ground, terrified.
like ants after a disturbed ant hill,
we scatter to our stations.

WHHUUUUMP!

quickly now, move;
commanders conjure up a plan.
ramp up, hatches down.
optics: binos, thermal imagery, scan your arcs.

he's the enemy without a face:
everywhere and nowhere,
blending flawlessly, faceless,
every person a suspect.
suspicion creeps down like oil,
blown barrels stain the walls, rocks.
like oil, they seep deep down into the ground
back to the depths from whence they came.
we wait.

After the mortars stop we wait; vehicle movement is halted on Highway One and some local nationals are questioned, to no avail. Once it has been quiet for a while, we return to the patrol base.

On September 18, a few short days after our handover is complete and B Company personnel have departed for KAF, there is a prolonged firefight atop the Masum Ghar mountain. My platoon was tasked with camp security at PBW while 3 Platoon and Company Headquarters rolled out to the mountain at dusk. What followed was a twelve-hour firefight at night in unfamiliar terrain, including artillery. 2 Platoon was called in as the Quick Reaction Force. To get a detailed account of that battle, where a

reported seventy-two Taliban were killed with no friendly casualties, you will have to speak to members of 2 and 3 Platoons and
to members of B Battery, 1 RCHA. 1 Platoon remained as camp
security; with no one able to sleep, we watched tracer fire rico-
chet through the night sky and listened to the battle unfold on
the radio.

> go atop the roof, past the smell of piss and dirt
> and cultural differences I can't quite reconcile.
> up the stairs—treacherous like the ruins of some old castle
> besieged so long ago—to the observation post,
> fortified with sandbags. look down to the south
> past the highway, the grape-drying huts,
> the treeline, the culverts, canals,
> and into the Panjwayi district,
> toward the mountain side so sharp it cuts the air
> and out of its wound it bleeds tracer fire:
> red droplets in the sky, ricocheting in all directions
> like an insurgent's scheme of manoeuvre:
> all encompassing, three hundred and sixty degrees.
> the battle rages on still and I wake up scared, strange,
> the sound of friendly artillery piercing the night
> like a bass drum on steroids and we sit here, detached,
> shirtless, as sandflies flock to the light.

A close call

The following night, after receiving enemy mortar fire, 1 Platoon
is tasked as the surge platoon. We roll outside of Wilson before
dusk and set up in a defensive posture observing to the south.
Previously we've witnessed farmers moving bundles of hay to
and from their fields. We suspect, but cannot confirm, that they
are in fact distributing and emplacing weapons before our very

eyes. For one thousand metres, we have a clear field of view; beyond that, there is the treeline and culverts, which we know the enemy uses frequently. At night, we have the advantage of thermal optics. This particular evening we have placed our vehicles within the broken-down brick castles that seem to sprout from the dirt, observing, waiting. We sit for an hour, possibly two, and adjust our posture. By now it is completely dark out. Nighttime operations are always trickier than daytime operations; they require more concentration, more focus.

My gunner spots something in his sights: a man. His movement is odd; he gently rocks back and forth in an oscillating motion. His posture seems calm yet alert. From my thermal view screen, it looks as though he is atop a roof, standing near a wall and peeking out from it. We lase him to determine a grid; a second vehicle from within PBW sees the same image and confirms the grid. Suddenly, our laser warning receiver goes off within the LAV. Someone has lased our vehicle to determine a range, as we just did to the potential threat. All I can think in my head is that someone atop a roof is aiming an RPG at our vehicle. I confirm with my platoon warrant officer and make the decision to take a warning shot. I pop down in the hatch and tell my gunner to lay on the target, and to aim low. I give him the command, my command alone, to fire. A short burst from the C-6 coaxial machine gun pierces the silence of the night. In an instant I have clarity, but what I see fills me with horror. What was only moments ago an insurgent on a rooftop, peeking out from behind a wall, is now a Canadian soldier reacting to incoming fire. What appeared to be the rooftop was actually the top of a G-Wagon's gun-shield kit, obscured by a building directly in front of him. I come over the radio with the only words I can muster: "All call signs one-one, this is one-one. I confirm that is not enemy, I confirm that is not enemy." I can't bring myself to say the words "friendly"; I cannot admit to anyone listening what has just occurred, although everyone knows. My warrant officer was in that G-Wagon, unable to confirm his exact grid because the memory battery for his GPS had just gone down. I inform the company commander we are done for the night and are returning to the patrol base. How I became disoriented, how I did not know the exact locations of all my sub–call signs, I do not know. Upon return to PBW I examine the gun-shield kit mounted on the G-Wagon and see the impact of a single 7.62mm round. No one was hurt, but the psychological effect of nearly killing one of my own lingers with me still.

Living in the moment

You hear about it in sports. That time when you exist purely for the moment, right here, in the now. When, in an instant, you decide it's time to launch your body in mid-air and watch upside down as your laces contact the ball and your kick sends it to the top corner in the back of the net. People try to achieve this feeling through meditation, and when they do, it's called enlightenment. Well, from my experience, that's what it's like over here when shit hits the fan. You are always in the present, always focused on the task at hand. There is no other way to exist. This feeling is what soldiers speak of when they refer to the intoxication of battle. The problem is, what do you do when you're not in combat? You are the superhero in between phone booths. You become the bumbling reporter, passed over, ordinary, mundane, unrecognizable. That is why soldiers exist on the fringe of society. They are unable to reconnect with this feeling; they are lost, like a tourist in a foreign country where no one speaks your language: the language of war.

First contact

On August 22, 2006, 1 Platoon was tasked with escorting an empty fuel truck back to KAF while also dropping off some Special Operating Forces personnel at Camp Nathan Smith, the base out of which the Provincial Reconstruction Team (PRT) operates. CNS was renowned for its luxurious qualities: air conditioning, a Canadian-run kitchen, a swimming pool (with no water), bathroom facilities and other minor creature comforts. This camp was in stark contrast to what we had at Patrol Base Wilson, where the words "austere" and "spartan" came to mind. At Wilson, the company was running low on fuel, a necessity for a mechanized organization. As the convoy commander, I issued orders for the upcoming move. Present were the platoon warrant officer, the section commanders and the drivers of the fuel truck, as well as a representative from the SOF (Special Operating Forces).

We travelled east along Highway One through what is known as Ambush Alley. Every metre we travelled we were watching for signs of an enemy ambush and looking for likely places of cover, natural places to fire from. We made it through the countryside and into the city. We were only about eight hundred metres from the PRT when we approached a dogleg left turn we had to make onto a narrow street. As we neared the corner, a van was driving down the road towards us. He slowed and stopped. He was close, too close, but what I saw led me to believe that he was just another "right-out-of-'er" Afghan driver. I conducted a threat assessment; I looked into his eyes and, as he stopped, I determined he had not seen us earlier and was now trying to yield. Stationary he sat, right there on the side of the road, as we made our left turn. To my recollection, the G-Wagon to our front had just passed him when he detonated himself, either in between my LAV and the G-Wagon or closer to us. And he was close: from vehicle to vehicle, the distance was less then three metres. How does something turn to nothing? How does a life, a thriving, breathing life, in an

instant, turn to nothing? "There was a van there," I remember
thinking, "now there is no van there." This attack, a suicide
vehicle-borne improvised explosive device, is the platoon's first
direct contact with the enemy.

The explosion

For a second, you cannot perceive anything; your senses, sight,
touch, smell, hearing, are all rendered useless—but only for a
second—then you begin to piece it all together. I remember black
stuff, soot and dust and ash covering my face and my goggles. I
remember the intense heat of the blast although I didn't register
the flash. I don't remember hitting my shoulder, just a dull pain
that the adrenalin took care of, for a time. Somewhere in the
sequence of events came the voice, the tone, pitch and urgency
of which I still replay in my head and will likely never forget:

"Sir! Braun's down, sir, Braun's down!"

I sent in a contact report: "One, this is one-one. Contact:
grid Quebec Romeo five-niner-six-niner, zero-one-seven-
four; we've been hit by a suicide bomber, we have casualties."
That is what I recall saying, a textbook contact report, a testa-
ment to the success of repetitive training. My first thought was
that everyone in the G-Wagon in front of us was dead. Someone
came over the radio and told the G-Wagon that they were on fire
and had to evacuate the vehicle. I watched from the turret of my
LAV as everyone got out of the G-Wagon. I remember the soot and
the look on the sergeant's face. He was shaken, clearly; but within
seconds, he started manoeuvring his section away from the vehicle and under cover of the ditch to our right. Perhaps it was his
grace under fire that prompted me; I told everyone to get out of the
LAV when I realized that we too were on fire. The panel marker,
which was kept just behind my gunner and me, had caught fire;
jerry cans of fuel, too. My gunner, Private Kozakiewicz, looked

over at me and I could see a trail of blood running down the side of his face. He was shocked from the violence and proximity of the blast. As the platoon commander, my next thought was to take command of the scene. I dismounted from the LAV and thought, "I must get to a radio" so I could control the scene. The G-Wagon behind me told me their radio wasn't working; I realized I was walking around with no weapon, and grabbed a C-9 light machine gun from their passenger seat. When and where I put that weapon down I have no recollection. For as soon as I looked back at our LAV, I saw the fire raging atop the turret. The jerry cans full of fuel had leaked down and the fire was quickly consuming the rear of the vehicle. Master Corporal Mador and the medic, Corporal Comeau, were applying first aid to Corporal David Braun in the back of the LAV. The ramp was down; by the time I went from the G-Wagon to the LAV, the opening at the back of the LAV was bordered by flames. I went in and told them we had to get Dave out. Mador, Comeau and I began to move him out, grabbing hold of whatever we could: his tac vest, his flak vest, his shirt. Several times something ripped or we lost our grip. It's at this point I first remember hearing the cook-offs (a cook-off is when ammunition begins to go off due to intense heat igniting the gunpowder). It was like listening to a bag of popcorn in the microwave; a few at first, followed by an ensemble of tiny "pops." I remember thinking someone was going to get killed by our own rounds, and then realized that most of the platoon had dismounted to take up perimeter security. Dragging Dave out of the LAV and to safety was the most physically demanding task I've ever undertaken. In the ditch, with water up to our knees, Mador, the medic and I struggled to keep moving, even as our legs gave out and we fell over into the mud. I cursed and realized my shoulder was in pain. Comeau and Mador carried on with first aid, while I went back to the next LAV to again try and get on the radio.

Sergeant Dunwoody was there, already coordinating the medical evacuation on the radio.

There was an SOF soldier in that carrier. He had taken up a good fire position and did not seem fazed by the gravity of the situation. He looked seasoned, and I was comforted by his presence. He asked me if I was injured and told me I had to do a self-assessment. I knew something was wrong with my shoulder at this point. I took a seat in the back of the LAV; very quickly, both legs went numb from my groin down and both arms shut off as well. I was parched. In the back of the LAV, an interpreter gave me water and tried to get the blood going back in my legs. Once or twice I closed my eyes and my vision went white. By now I was combat-ineffective, unable to think clearly and unable to get my legs working. I would later learn that, while my legs remained numb, one of my soldiers, with a blank look on his face, walked slowly through the debris with his head down, kicking the dismembered leg of the suicide bomber.

When the Bison arrived on the scene, it took me a few minutes to stand up because I couldn't put any weight on my legs. We loaded up: me, Pte Koz and Pte McDonald. McDonald had suffered burns to his arm and hand, while Koz had a large slice on his cheek and burns to his arm. Dave was loaded up on a stretcher with the medic in the back. It's funny how the brain works: I don't remember anything wrong with Dave, even looking down at his face not more than a metre away. I knew there was blood; my boots and shirt were evidence enough of that. And I knew some things were out of place: his upper torso and head. But to this day, I can't recall anything wrong: it's the brain's way of fitting puzzle pieces together. Later, much later, I would hear what actually happened to his flesh and bones, and I would have terrible nightmares filled with these images. I was taken to the medical facility in the PRT and quickly flown by American helicopter to the Role 3 medical facility in KAF. Shortly after I landed, I asked if Dave had survived, and the answer brought with it the first of many tears.

Did I pay attention to the combat indicators? Could I not have read that man's intentions in his eyes? Will I be the hero of the day? Can I count myself amongst what Shakespeare called "we few, we happy few"?

On board an American transport aircraft, flying out of Kandahar, I asked the pretty nurse attending me for a pad of paper and a notebook. A line had come to my mind, something about a Saskatchewan plain, as I was thinking about Dave's funny smile and how we used to drink coffee and smoke in the field. This is what I wrote on that plane, recent events still swirling in my head:

> *Your quiet confidence,*
> *possessing a rare quality*
> *of kindness to others,*
> *a gentle caring.*
> *Your thin smile stretches on*
> *like a Saskatchewan plain,*
> *then curls slightly at the edge.*
> *Too rich a life to take,*
> *too cruel a thought to kill.*
> *I cannot forget your unfailing character,*
> *I am sorry I have failed you.*
>
> *Dave, this coffee is for you.*

The unconscious mind

The best way to describe what goes through one's mind following an explosion is that it's like looking at a picture that contains many events happening simultaneously and trying, like a detective, to figure out everything that is going on by considering each individual clue. Following the explosion, I recall my thought process going something like this: there was an explosion; we have been attacked; there was a van there, it's not there anymore, it was a vehicle-borne suicide bomber; I am alive; am I hurt?; my toes are okay; my body is intact; my shoulder hurts. This thought process took me all of two seconds. The first second was pure nothingness, like a moment frozen in time as you become a slave to reality. In the next second, it all comes crashing forward and you experience great clarity, although the mind, later, has trouble recalling this clarity.

Americans

We land in Bagram, an American camp north of Kandahar. I am the lone Canadian in an American camp, insignificant in the larger campaign of war. I'm struck by the vastness of the American grasp, and by how everything they do is bigger, better, faster, stronger. I'm amazed by their stories. I've seen one IED; he's seen four. I've spent three weeks in theatre on my first tour in Afghanistan; he's been to Iraq on a year-long tour and is now serving his second tour in Afghanistan. Canadians normally spend six months overseas, although some do a nine-month tour, with a minimum of a year off between deployments; Americans normally spend twelve months overseas and often find themselves redeployed inside of a year. I know why I'm here (or I think I do); he's not so sure. The default answer: terrorism.

When I left the Role 3 hospital in KAF I was given a red T-shirt with the word "CANADA" proudly written across the front. It was a shirt from the Hudson's Bay Company used for the line of Canadian Olympic clothing for the 2006 Olympic Winter Games. I thought of the fur traders and the *voyageurs* and how odd it felt to be in a foreign land. I felt a surprising sense of patriotism building inside of me. Walking around Bagram with this T-shirt on sure did make me conscious of my identity. "Hey, Canada!" a female private yells at me; "Are you really from Canada?!" another soldier asks. The sincerity in his voice is comical, as if I am a rare species or mythological being only ever read about in pulp fantasy novels.

Landstuhl, Germany
After departing Bagram, I made a quick stop in Ali Al Salem, an American air base in Saudi Arabia, before leaving the next day for the Regional Medical Centre in Landstuhl, Germany. The days I spent in Landstuhl are a blur, like when you wake up from a dream and can't quite remember what you had just been dreaming about. I can't remember the exact number of days I spent there—four or five, perhaps. I was given cocktails of morphine and Gravol through an IV, and while the drugs eased the pain in my shoulder, I could not shut out the brutal reality of what had occurred. Even sleep offered no respite. I had suffered a broken right acromion from what I can only surmise was the force of the blast sending my shoulder into the edge of the turret ring. I had a deep line of bruising in an arc from the back of my shoulder blade to the front, and lesser bruising of various ugly colours down my right arm and bicep. My ballistic eyewear saved my eyes from general debris and I was otherwise more or less uninjured.

> I wake up and my shoulder throbs,
> not like some injuries, threatening life, or limb,
> just a dull throbbing sensation, always something there to remind me.
> and in my dreams I have little choice but to

remember
   re-live
      recall:

there we are—my driver, my signaller and I,
and we have lost the pack.
alone, isolated, we make our way
west, traditionally such a safe direction,
but safe no more:

(you hear "west of Kandahar" or
"Southwest Asia")

but no one wants to go west, they are afraid
of what's out there, along that alley of death to the west

and he does what he does best:
make the radios work

      —cut off—

he provides us a means to communicate,
yet in my dreams I struggle to talk

            —loose wire—

is someone trying to talk to me?

"You must monitor these means at all times!"
we must return to the others,
there's strength in numbers

            —another uneasy sleep—

we are in an American compound,
a mechanic's shop—things get fixed here
and we are assured of our security.

My return: Winnipeg

Returning to Canada was emotional. The most difficult thing was landing in the same spot I took off from only three weeks earlier. Yet so much had changed in those three weeks. I could not restrain my tears. I was greeted by high-ranking officers, but can not remember any of them. All that mattered were the comforting arms that were wrapped around me. But my story does not end here: you've heard the rising action and indeed the climax of what I have to tell you, but the aftermath is just as important, for this is what you will see and have to deal with. There is a new generation of Canadians returning from war, something our country has almost forgotten. I had in front of me five months of checking the CBC, CTV and BBC websites daily. And I understood what it was like to have people overseas that you cared about.

Agonizing.
it's the waiting that is the hardest part.

I am every wife, every mother,
every sweetheart, every brother,
every sister, every father,
every cousin, aunt and uncle.

I'm your average Canadian:
ignorant in my bliss, content in my distractions

they are my sons, my friends,
mentors, comrades and all I do is wait.

—attend—

attend moi, mes amis
j'suis ici pour vous.

A night on the town

It's Wednesday night in Brandon, Manitoba, and usually I'm not out, but tonight is karaoke night at the North Hill and we live in a dull city. A Company has returned from overseas. As usual, I am the silent observer, but what I see in these soldiers is chaotic: the desire to apply focused violence; the outrage at being helpless; the shock of our silly North American culture; the attempt to deal with deep pain. The local boys who decide tonight is their night to be tough are beat down and I feel satisfied. Shirts are ripped, noses are bloodied. So many fights break out it's difficult to keep count. "One-handed, motherfucker! I'll kill you one-fucking-handed!" screams one soldier, who had busted up his other hand during decompression leave following the tour. Police arrive and the same feeling of animosity is projected upon them, they who bear arms but many of whom have not fought in this war. My feeling of satisfaction, my deep desire to reconnect with the group of soldiers I was severed from, is overcome by a feeling of pathos and sadness. People have come back from Afghanistan and have changed. Relationships fail. Personal safety is ignored. Identities are fragmented. Ordinary Canadians, those who have not been to war, do not and cannot understand. The American soldiers have us beat there—their fellow citizens have a better understanding; Americans have a better regard for the soldier, I think. While we Canadians love to take the moral high ground, we fail to realize that when you choose to sit on the fence, you sometimes end up with a rusty nail in your ass.

THE THINGS WE TAKE FOR GRANTED

I take pleasure in simple things now,
just a new variation on an old theme.
I avoid crowds; jubilation seems dishonourable,
joy just not quite right.

I'm comforted by the night air,
content in its brisk coolness,
thankful that I no longer struggle
to fall asleep in my own sweat.

The roar of traffic on the city street also calms me,
because this is normality.
This—this right here—is where I dreamed to be
some short weeks ago.

What I wouldn't give for one night back there:
one glance at a herd of goats,
one photo beside a camel,
one flash of a welder's torch in the street.
One jaunt down Moon Dust Alley,
one drive along Angle Road,
Tech Square, Highway One.
One walk through a field of poppy.
But more than all of this, I wish to see my people:
my brothers and sisters.

We played hacky sack in the most militant of
circumstances.
What a sight to see: grown men, professional soldiers,
combats and boots, pulling off the sweetest of moves.
I can still see you all as plain as day,

As we sip Tim Hortons coffee, so Canadian.
I think of you always,
my comrades in arms.

I walk a lonely road.

AUGUST
BY
CORPORAL GORDON WHITTON

This is the third of three edited excerpts from the journal Gordon kept while in Afghanistan. He was deployed from January 2006 to August 2006.

August 1, 2006

We waited until nightfall to make our move out to Camp Wilson, we drove in blackout drive once we cleared Kandahar City. Ambush Alley runs for about six kilometres along Highway Four, so you don't want to be the one all lit up with headlights and brake lights. The drive is scary as hell because you're driving into oncoming traffic with your night vision on; you're basically blinded when oncoming local traffic has their headlights on. We reached Camp Wilson along with the CO (commanding officer). The small camp was packed tight, it looked as if we were about to commence a larger-scale operation, and the fact that we'd ordered more than two hundred Afghan National Police (ANP) told us the bad guys knew we were coming. That night we just went to ground beside our vehicles. It was so hot and humid, and of course there were sand fleas, my sleep was the shits.

We sat around the morning of the second waiting for word on the operation, we heard all kinds of reports of the ANP not co-operating, and we also heard they may have tipped off the

Taliban. Most of us thought the Taliban would be long gone, seeing us build up for an attack, and that may be a good thing. We heard our CO spoke to the ANP and told them we would pull out completely if this continued; at least that's what was going around the camp. I got hold of a satellite phone and called Nikki, knowing it might be my last chance for a few days, she was happy to hear from me. We spoke mainly of refurnishing the front room of all things, but I didn't care, I just love hearing her voice. After I got off the phone, I handed it to Sully and sat in my G-Wagon, pulled out my iPod and started listening to music. Pte Barnes joined me with another set of earphones. We were scrolling through the songs listening to anything we could both agree on, which ended up being 50 Cent, "It's Your Birthday," when all of a sudden an RPG burst right over our heads, Barnes was gone in a flash. I remember Sully running back to our car with the satellite phone in his hand, I also remember laughing at the look on his face and the way he was running, like he was running in a four-foot trench, he had just hung up the phone with his new fiancée, Kristi. The RPGs continued with enemy machine-gun fire, they were attacking the camp but they hit it just as another convoy was entering it. We put all of our PPE (personal protective equipment) on and waited for word to counterattack. We had OPs (observation posts) and snipers already in place, they were identifying targets and engaging them. We also employed mortars and the artillery was positioning a 155mm gun, not to fire from the camp but dragging it out the front gate for some reason. I turned up the radio speaker to hear what we were up to, apparently we intercepted a message from a Taliban leader, he was reported as saying, "We will not leave, we will fight the infidel." As soon as that message was passed over the net one of our commanders sent out a response for all of us to hear, he said very slowly: "Bring it on."

Until this point the mission was up in the air, at least that's how the troops felt, but after the camp got hit, we knew we were going in, some time that night. The Artillery had that 155mm gun outside the front gates of Camp Wilson now and positioned it to fire directly at a grape-drying hut only 370 metres away. The hut was a known Taliban hot spot and we knew it would be empty. It was more of a show of force, but I think everyone was interested to see what damage one of those rounds would do fired directly at such a close target. I'm not sure what damage the round did to the hut but a piece of shrapnel flew back and took one of the gunners right in the leg, he later got a medivac.

Later that day, my platoon finally got orders to secure a bridge and take a school near the village of Pashmul. We were going in with 9 Platoon, C Company, along with engineers and an artillery FOO (forward observation officer), we were being led in by the CO, commencing at 0200 on the third. Of course this was all up in the air because there was some sort of JTF (Joint Task Force) operation going on in the area, but if everything went to plan, we would be able to launch on schedule. Bravo Company was launching in the north end of Panjwayi just off Highway One at first light. Although we would not be anywhere near Bravo Company, we were basically fighting into the same area and taking part in the same operation.

The mission was a go, at 0115 Warrant Officer Silva gave us all a shake to mount up, we marshalled our vehicles within the tiny camp and waited for the CO to lead us out. We had a long drive in front of us, and it was all in blackout drive. We headed out of Camp Wilson east on Highway One, then south on Route Foster; Route Foster leads us right into the Panjwayi district centre and also the back-door entrance to Pashmul. Bravo Company was still scheduled to enter on Route Vancouver through the north at first light. As soon as we got off the blacktop we went completely black, we were driving in dangerous territory and we knew the place might be mined. There wasn't much moonlight so it was getting very difficult to navigate the windy dirt trail with only our monoculars. One of our front vehicles noticed around fourteen armed men in a treeline, as soon as we got confirmation there were no ANA or ANP up there, the LAVs immediately opened fire on them. This momentarily put a halt to the advance, we were just shy of the bridge and the school was in sight. The lead LAV continued on after there was no more enemy movement visible. It was still pretty dark, then all of a sudden one of the vehicles to my front seemed to have been hit by something. I thought it was an RPG hitting armour because it was a strange blinding explosion, but someone else reported over the radio that they thought they had struck an IED, and they were right, the third LAV in the advance had struck an IED. The other 9 Platoon LAVs immediately fired on possible enemy positions and we quickly got some people up to the IED site to help out the injured. The explosion didn't seem loud enough to seriously hurt anyone in an armoured vehicle, but that was just my personal assessment based on the size of explosions I've witnessed in the past. The LAV had hit the IED just over a culvert with cement ledges, it was a choke point. The medics in the patrol quickly moved up to the location to provide first aid. The CO got on the radio and told Reconnaissance Platoon where to establish a landing zone for the helicopter for pickup of the wounded, it was about eight hundred metres back near the district centre.

After a couple of minutes the CO got back on the radio and asked for a SITREP from the IED site, wondering if the injured could be transported to the landing zone. The response from the medic was, "No, one of them can't make the trip." The medics were performing CPR on the driver of the LAV. The medics also stressed to the CO the seriousness of one of the casualties and that we needed to have him extracted from the battlefield immediately, the casualty had become VSA (vital signs absent). A

Blackhawk chopper got there very quickly, it was just getting lighter out when it landed, an Apache escort was circling the entire area for protection while the two casualties were loaded on the chopper. Soon after the choppers departed for the hospital in KAF it became evident that we had just lost a man, Cpl Chris Reid. Reid was a long-time friend of mine and one of the battalion's most-loved soldiers, everybody knew Chris and we were all in shock. We were all in disbelief, I was in shock. We had no time to absorb what had just happened, Sgt Janek and his crew moved to the area where we had engaged those armed men, it seemed like they were just sitting there waiting for us all night. There was ammo, weapons and jugs of water, although there were no bodies there were massive blood trails leading out of there. Sgt Janek then found evidence of multiple IEDs all up that road, and all vehicle movement immediately seized.

All the LAVs and G-Wagons immediately took up defensive positions around the IED site, the CO set up his command post just to the rear of our position in the dried-out part of the Arghandab River. The engineers, who were second in order of march, had their hands full that morning, if any servicemen are worth their weight in gold it's these guys. They had to deal with a road riddled with IEDs, and to make matters worse, one of our LAVs from 9 Platoon commanded by MCpl Tony Perry had already driven over at least five pressure-plate IEDs without detonating any of them. MCpl Perry also drove the only vehicle that had crossed the bridge towards the school before we ceased movement on the road. Captain Hamilton, along with the 9 Platoon commander and the CO, moved forward to come up with a plan to take the school dismounted, there was no way we could wait for all the IED threats to be cleared, and the chance of hitting another one was too high. My section took up a position just to the right of the IED site, I remember MCpl Matthew Parsons engaging twelve to fifteen men with RPGs around the area of the bazaar, which was across a field in Pashmul. MCpl Perry watched his tracer and also engaged, I knew this was going to be a long day. As we were sitting there, the engineer LAV, which was second in the patrol, moved forward to deal with the next IED they'd found. As they slowly moved up they hit a pressure plate only about twenty metres in front of the first IED. The explosion was just fucking huge, it sent Sgt Janek down to his face and everyone else diving for cover. Jack and I were looking straight at the vehicle as it rolled over that IED, I asked him anyway, "What just happened?" and he said, "It was a LAV." We suddenly heard rounds cooking off inside the vehicle and I thought the crew were inside, it was making me freak out listening to all the rounds cook off inside the turret. I wanted to run in there but I knew I couldn't, the medics were in place just outside the cloud of dirt with my platoon commander and platoon warrant officer. The cloud of dirt soon faded away and, to our amazement, the entire crew got out, they seemed to be all okay. I remember five of them all standing to the side of the road hunched over, they escaped with only concussions. The luckiest one in that crew was the crew commander himself; for some reason he was riding on the back deck, and the blast punched straight up through his seat and out the hatch. The driver was the last one to get out, someone opened his hatch to see if he was alive and the driver looked up at the guy thinking his vehicle was being hit by small-arms fire. He was hearing the rounds cooking off inside his turret.

Now that we had just lost most of our engineer assets, I figured the IEDs would be the last thing on our minds for now, we were still waiting for a large group of ANP to show up who were to be the upfront soldiers to take the school. They seemed to take forever, I thought they would never show, then finally a few pickup trucks arrived with twenty-six of them. I remember each of these guys taking a good look at both our destroyed vehicles as they walked on by them forward to Captain Hamilton's position.

Before they even stepped off from the line of departure, there was a contact from the right with at least five enemies, one of the soldiers in the reserve section took a round in the chest plate. After a little while my position and the command-post position were being engaged by harassing enemy fire, mortar splashes were being spotted east down the *wadi*. 2 Platoon was now down in that direction and they spotted and engaged about eight or more armed combatants. Things seemed to be picking up on all fronts, we started hearing massive amounts of small-arms fire from the direction of the school, soon after a bunch of ANP ran right on by me back to their pickup trucks at the command post. I said to Sully, "Can you fucking believe it?" He said, "I'm not surprised." The ANP had fired off all their ammo, which wasn't very much, then ran away. There was another small group of them smoking under a tree near the bridge, I guess if we want something done right we should just do it ourselves. The advance to the school had to continue without them.

The advancing troops from 9 Platoon and Reconnaissance Platoon were being engaged at this area known as the low wall, they had to take a bound into these outbuildings, which were about halfway to the actual school. During the advance, three troops went down with heat exhaustion and they were under an incredible amount of fire. Pte Kevin Dallaire, who was providing cover fire for his section, took a round in his torso. I remember hearing Hamilton send SITREPS over the radio when they all reached the outbuildings, he simply needed LAVs to evacuate the wounded and all the heat casualties, which had risen to five, they also needed fresh troops if they were going to take the next bound to the school. It was a fucked-up situation because they couldn't advance, worse yet, they couldn't withdraw. The roads were so mined there was no getting any LAV near them. I saw soldiers from 2 Platoon move forward dismounted, with stretchers, I figured that would be one miserable hump to do. By now every position in our area was being engaged by enemy fire, some effective and some more harassing. I think the enemy was engaging us from more than twenty different positions in this gigantic horseshoe around us. To make matters worse, the troops at the outbuildings were the primary focus of all the enemy fire. The enemy fire was becoming so intense the odd bullet was hitting my G-Wagon, all turrets were engaging targets of opportunity and dirt was kicking up all around us from enemy fire. In a five-minute period, sixty RPGs were launched at us. Sully made a dash from Jeff's G-Wagon, about twenty metres, over to mine, as he jumped in he said, "Can you tell where it's coming from?" I said, "Everywhere." As he started loading his pockets with M-203s (rifle-mounted grenade launchers), I knew what we were just about to do. We dismounted at the same time at each side of our vehicle, we fired everything we had into that treeline to our front. Jack's machine gun was just over my head and it was so loud; an artillery LAV pulled up to our right side and started engaging as well, everything was so fucking loud I reached into my pockets for some earplugs. Everyone was engaging on all fronts, I watched Sully place his M-203s so perfectly where he wanted them, trees and branches were falling down, it was kind of impressive to see.

I was guessing it had been almost forty minutes since the guys took the outbuildings, we all couldn't help but hear our fire missions continuously get denied over the radio, which was making everyone on the ground just livid. Captain Hamilton came back over the radio, he was yelling, he said "We just took a direct hit from an RPG and we have multiple VSA, we need LAVs here now, guys are dying, I'm hit, everyone is hit, get here right now!" The CO and everyone else for that matter knew what had to happen, we had to get to the outbuildings quickly. The Taliban knew what they had done and they were streaming into the school under the cover of intense fire, Sgt Williams remembers Sgt

MacDonald turning around and saying, "Put a fresh mag on, boys, they're coming around the corner." I heard MCpl Parsons with his Kiwi accent calmly tell the CO he could make the trip, after a little pause I heard, "Good luck." I think Parsons was already advancing in his LAV by that point. I really couldn't believe what I was seeing, we all just held our breath as the LAVs floored it up that dirt road, I made sure I stood on my two feet and watched as these men punched through to our fallen comrades and made history. There was nothing I could do at that point but look on and pray. All of us thought the first LAV was going to hit an IED and the next LAVs would have no choice but to drive right on by them continuing the rescue mission at the outbuildings, but nothing happened, they reached the outbuildings.

MCpl Parsons and MCpl Perry positioned their LAVs on each side of the outbuildings, only a handful of troops were still capable of fighting and almost all of them were wounded. It was a sad sight, guys that were wounded were held up in there still fighting, other guys were giving first aid and applying tourni-quets, almost everyone had someone else's weapon and they were under such intense fire. The enemy fire was so intense Parsons later said it sounded like the drumline was pounding on his vehicle. The most seriously wounded got evacuated back to our CCP (casualty collection point) first, 2 Platoon also made it to the outbuildings, Kris Barker identified heavy fire from the field of pot and put his cannon on HE (high explosive), single shot. He would let another one go every couple of metres all across the field, the explosions were like mini-grenades. LAVs were taking turns moving back to the CCP and forward to the position, I think every LAV in 2 Platoon made two trips. Kris Barker had to do a full upload at the CCP. Sgt Patrick Tower of C Coy was at the outbuilding, he had run across an open field under intense enemy fire when he got the word about the RPG strike. Cpl Brad Kauffeldt, who ran to the outbuildings with Sgt

Janek and Cpl Dusenbury, was helping with the withdrawal. He set his C-9 down to load one of the dead and someone threw his C-9 onto one of the LAVs. He then picked up a weapon off one of our casualties and fired back towards the enemy, he later told me this gun worked like a dream.

As soon as everyone and everything was picked up, our guys got the hell out of there, leaving nothing behind at the out-buildings. There were troops spread all the way from the bridge to the low wall, we pulled everyone back to the position of the CCP and the LAVs took up their original defensive positions to the south of the *wadi*. The remainder of my platoon pulled back to the Arghandab River so we could use the banks as cover while the recovery of the blown-up vehicles continued. My position was now part of our most forward defensive, and we were reacting to a threat that had been intercepted. The Taliban were organizing an attack on our position of four waves of one hundred men each; although they are known to exaggerate, we were taking the threat seriously. The LAVs were engaging targets of opportunity to keep them from organizing anything. I was lying on the bank of the river in the grass looking through my scope at the treeline to my front, the one time I pulled my canteen out and had a drink, the section over to my right engaged enemy movement in the treeline, all I could say was, "He was mine." We could finally see our artillery pounding at all the Taliban locations to the north, something we could have used earlier, I'm sure.

The CCP consisted of one section of modular tent strung off the back of the command-post LAV. Men lay in that tent shoulder to shoulder, waiting for the choppers to fly them out, the most seriously injured first. Meanwhile, at the bridge site, my section was still providing security for the recovery of both LAVs. We were still exchanging the odd bit of gunfire, but things had cooled down. We had to tie a cable to the vehicles and pull them away from the danger area before we could hook on to them properly and drag them back to the highway, where flatbeds were waiting. Two LAVs would back up to a destroyed one and hook a cable up to it, they would just drag the thing as far back as they could until they would have to readjust their cables. The choppers were landing and taking off with all of our wounded, and just about every plane in NATO was taking turns doing fly-bys, including a Mirage 3 and a B-1 Lancer that swooped so low it scared the shit out of us. The buildup of reinforcements at the highway was growing, just in case this battle was to go into the night. A large explosion went off right at the entrance from the highway, at first I thought a plane had dumped its load back there but it was black smoke, which indicated burning fuel. We also thought we heard machine-gun fire just before the explosion. We soon found out that a suicide bomber had tried to drive up behind the convoy at the road and blow himself up beside one of our Bisons. It turned out Lieutenant Thorlakson, who was manning the C-6 machine gun on the Bison, put his hand up to stop the brown Toyota; the suicide bomber stopped long enough for them to make eye contact, then floored his car. Lt Thorlakson opened up with a long burst into the pavement and let the car drive into the bullets, he put a burst through the front wind-shield and the vehicle exploded. The blast was so big it killed twenty-six innocent civilians who were watching the battle from a distance. Lt Thorlakson took shrapnel to the arms and neck, just missing his jugular, the chunk of steel that was meant to kill him was buried in his chest plate.

The recovery of the two blown-up LAVs was slow but we were making progress. We got them back far enough to load them on the flatbeds, and the CO gave radio orders for my pla-toon to escort the flatbeds back to KAF. It was good news we were going back to KAF but we knew every suicide bomber in Kandahar City would be out for us, it was a nervous drive but we made it back with no more bullshit. I was listening to the radio

as the LAV commanders who were still on the position were trying to withdraw, there was the odd vehicle part and spare tire
still lying around, but they had no time to pick up every little
part, so they just commenced their tactical withdrawal with
extreme caution. I remember driving through where the suicide bomber had blown himself up near Pashmul, so many
times I had witnessed this nice little crossroads village living in
harmony and now it was nothing but burnt junk and body parts
everywhere, what a sad day. Before we got back to KAF we
already knew the names of the three 9 Platoon guys who were
killed by the RPG strike, they were Sgt Vaughan Ingram, Cpl
Bryce Keller and Pte Kevin Dallaire.

There was this story going around that a Predator followed
the Taliban fighters home and dropped a JDAM (joint direct
attack munitions—a thousand-pound bomb) on them as the last
man entered a building, that made me feel good for five minutes
but the next couple of days back at KAF were extremely difficult.
I was walking around trying to hold in the emotion and trying to
avoid contact with anyone, I had lots of anger and deep sadness
for everything that had happened on the third. I contacted Nikki
after the communication lockdown was lifted and asked her to
tell Capt Hamilton's wife that he never gave up trying to save his
men even after he was wounded. My platoon and I visited
Hammy in the field hospital and said hello to the rest of the
wounded, it was a sad place to be, full of many reminders and
realities of the Battle. I call those early days after the Battle tender days, because they were so confusing, it's like I was on
another planet, the fact that we had lost four men wasn't even
sinking in. Something set me off and I beat the shit out of my bed
space, sending junk everywhere. I remember standing in the
meal line and noticing that so many members of the next battle
group were on camp, I noticed MCpl Parsons a few people in
front of me talking with MCpl Perry, Parsons turned to say hello

and I told him he did good on the third. He told me, "We all did good," I was holding back the emotion and had to stop talking.

August 5, 2006

The morning of August 5 we knew what the drill was going to be, a ramp ceremony for the four C Company men killed on the third. We marched in on both sides of the rear of the airplane, many from the new battle group were mixed in the ranks with us. C Coy provided the LAVs that transported the men down the runway, the eight men to carry each casket were also mostly from C Coy, many of the wounded were rolled out onto the runway for the ceremony, including my platoon commander; what I'm trying to say is, there wasn't much of C Company standing in the ranks with us that morning. As they slowly marched those silver caskets covered with Canadian flags by us, I didn't have any emotion, I was still in those tender days, I was thinking of something I would like to tell our fallen. "Stand up men, follow the light, you are our heroes, we love you, you will live forever."

Later that day there was another communication lockdown on camp, there were rumours one of our vehicles south of the airfield had collided head-on with a jingle truck, seriously injuring one of our guys, there was also talk that one of our guys had died in the crash. Later that afternoon, when the remainder of that patrol came in, we learned it was all true. MCpl Raymond Arndt of the Loyal Edmonton Regiment had been killed when his G-Wagon hit the jingle truck, the crash also seriously wounded another soldier in that vehicle who was also a Loyal Eddie.

It was becoming evident that I may not have to go out on any more missions, the First Battalion, Royal Canadian Regiment, Reconnaissance Platoon, was all on the ground and eager to sign for all of our kit. Elements of my platoon were involved with the relief in place, which only consisted of driving the new platoon around to different FOBs. I can still remember signing my G-Wagon over to the RCR guy, something I promised Sully so many times we would do. The same G-Wagon I signed for seven months earlier was sitting there with six thousand more kilometres on it, riddled with bullet holes and RPG shrapnel, and the RCR guys just slowly looked at each other when I pointed out that damage and told them, "Don't worry, I already filed the damage report." When they sat inside the front seat, one of them asked what all the ticks were for on the ceiling of the passenger side, I told him those ticks are all the M-203s Sully fired in Battle, there should be 144 of them up there.

August 7, 2006

This morning was the ramp ceremony for Raymond Arndt; his casket was being carried by all his closest buddies. They were all reservists who had probably known Raymond for many years. The reserves are a tight group in Western Canada, so it's easy to say these men were destroyed by the loss of their buddy, judging by the age of MCpl Arndt many people probably knew him very well. Many of the reservists on this tour have been as active outside the wire as our rifle companies, any time I met a G-Wagon full of reservists outside the wire I put just as much faith in them as anyone else, we're all in this boat together.

Some of the guys were lying around the TV tent today watching the news; I was in there as well waiting to see what movie we were going to pop in. The news was playing footage of some of the funerals of our guys who were killed on this tour. The OC of rear party is Major Richard Raymond; I think he was in just about every funeral they showed. He had become the man you didn't want to see, in one scene he was handing the flag over to a family member, it suddenly struck me just what a difficult job this man had to do. Not just him, but all the members of rear party and the duties they have to carry out, all during the tour we kept hearing about the wonderful job these people are doing back in Canada. It's something that never crossed my mind until the moment I watched him hand that flag over to that family member, he had one of the hardest jobs of anyone on this tour. I don't even know the man but I have as much respect for him and the other members of rear party as I do for men like Sully, Jim, Jack and Jeff, or anyone else I've fought alongside.

August 9, 2006

The morning of August 9 I'll never forget, there was this mud trail leading into our tent that went right to Sully's bed, it was funny because the night before we got our hands on some Jim Beam and just got hosed. It was something we all needed to do, just let loose with each other for a few hours. The last thing I remember is Sully sitting on the edge of his bed telling us how much he loves us, which was making us laugh, I must have rolled over and gone to sleep. It turns out that later Sully walked over to our platoon sea container and gained access with his 2IC key; he called home and left the satellite phone in the muck and the sea container wide open. I think Sully found the only mud puddle on camp to crawl through before he found his bed, he doesn't remember a thing. Of course this breach of security was serious enough for the MPs to get involved and Sully quickly admitted to the whole thing. We think this is funny because we love Sully; he got off easy by getting fourteen days of shit jobs.

Later on the ninth we began to hear news of a Canadian death around the area of Camp Wilson, what was really bad about this news was that it was an ND (negligent discharge) by one of our own, this means someone accidentally fired their weapon. We soon found out the name and unit of the deceased, he was MCpl Jeff Walsh of A Company, 2 PPCLI. Jeff Walsh was based out of Shilo, Manitoba, and had only been in Afghanistan for six days, he was from the next battle group and they were conducting a relief in place with B Company. When Jim and I met up with Sgt Gregory that afternoon we asked him if he had heard the news, his reply was, "No, what news?" We told him about MCpl Jeff Walsh and Sgt Gregory said, "No, not Jeff, are you sure it's Jeff Walsh? We were in the RCR together, he just got here with me, we went on tour together, he designed this very T-shirt I'm wearing." Jim and I could only stand there and look on as this man was in shock over his buddy. I looked at him and said, "I'm sorry."

August 10, 2006

Today I used up my entire week's worth of minutes talking to Nikki, she seems to be so concerned about me leaving the wire, I told her to just relax, I don't even have my grenades anymore, I'm done. She says, what about these other guys who were just about to come home, they left the wire. I told her I'm leaving for Cyprus in just a couple of days and they are leaving me alone. It feels good to have that sense of accomplishment, that I have done my duty and I'm going home now; however, I can't relax, I still carry around that tense feeling that I'm going back out there. I know that when I go home I can shake this feeling. I don't blame Nikki for feeling the way she does; I would feel that way, too, if I were her. That poor girl has just had the shittiest seven months of her life; my plane leaves here in just five days and I think she is just as scared now as the times I would call her from the satellite phone during missions.

August 11, 2006

Same drill, get up and rush over to the mess hall to get some food in your guts, then make your way over to headquarters to be formed up by the CSMs. Sling your weapon over your right shoulder, right turn, quick march. As a task force we march all the way over to the runway, which has been shut down until the ceremony is over. The men that carry Jeff's casket are just as new in theatre as he was, it's unbelievable. One of my buddies, who worked on camp as company quartermaster, told me he attended more than sixty ramp ceremonies in his seven months on this camp; he told me he always gets delegated to attend ramp ceremonies of other coalition countries so Canada can be represented, they also delegate personnel to attend ours. Later that day I did my gym routine and hit the showers. The showers are so few and there are so many people on camp right now it's hard to get in when you want to, you must lather up and rinse off, then it's a challenge not bumping into anyone while you dry off. I accidentally rubbed my you-know-what against Cpl Rose from my platoon, he put his hands in the air and yelled out, "Whoa whoa whoa!" like he was telling a horse to stop, and the entire shower started to laugh.

It was in the showers that I overheard some of the guys talking about another VBIED that took out one of our vehicles in a patrol out on the highway, it was yet another Canadian death. This time it was a medic, I guess the G-Wagon they were in was targeted by a suicide bomber who tried to pull out in front of them, the driver of the G-Wagon was able to swerve out of the way but the force of the blast sent the jeep over on its side. The blast destroyed the suicide bomber's vehicle and the G-Wagon immediately caught on fire, the two soldiers in the front seat made their escape just before it became an inferno. The soldier who was still trapped inside was unconscious, the size of the fire made it impossible for a rescue despite many attempts by the soldiers who'd made their escape, they even tried shooting through the front windshield but it was useless, the glass was bulletproof, the jerry cans which were strapped to the top of the

G-Wagon had caught on fire and all the men could do was watch. Cpl Andrew Eykelenboom was that soldier trapped inside; he was a medic with 1 Field Ambulance and was almost due to come home. He was roommates with my platoon medic; Boomer will be sadly missed by all that knew him, and never forgotten.

It's confirmed, August 15 I'm on the first plane out of here. I've already started turning in my UAB (unaccompanied baggage), my bed space is not yet cleaned up and I'm running out of places to put things. I've already mailed home two huge parcels so I guess I'll be chucking some things in the dumpster. I packed just enough things to survive the five days of drinking in Cyprus, let's not forget the decompression training, which is about two hours a day. I won't miss this place much; one of my biggest problems with being deployed with a military unit is that you never have control over yourself, you must be accounted for at all times. There was this sign-out book in our tent we had to fill out even when we weren't on QRF (Quick Reaction Force), there were times when I even had to let Sully know I was taking a piss. So when I get to Cyprus, and then Edmonton, I'll feel like a free man, these past couple of weeks have dragged by so slow it brought back memories of my days in Brookside Youth Centre, second cell on the right in Johnson house, that's another story.

August 19, 2006

I'm in Cyprus, I share a nice hotel room with my buddy Dustin Strazza, air-conditioned rooms and a pool on the roof; I've been walking around with a drink in my hand since I got here. I kind of feel like a zombie, it's hard to explain, but I feel like I have no emotions, like a mobster or something. Carlsberg is my new favourite beer; across the road from my hotel is a topless beach with a panoramic view of the Mediterranean, it's hard to believe I'm even here, I'm a little in shock from the change of environment but I'll take it. Today I was having dinner at a nice little restaurant along the coastal strip, white tablecloth and the whole nine yards. I'm not even sure what I was eating, I noticed Sully walking down the sidewalk with a bit of a stagger, he bumped into my table and I said, "Hey man, what's up?" Without saying a word he reached out for my litre of beer and took a long swig, then nodded his head in approval and carried on as I laughed out loud.

Thinking back on my last couple of days on camp, they were so slow and agonizing, two more ramp ceremonies, one for Cpl Eykelenboom and one the night before I left, for a British soldier. The British do their ramp ceremonies at night, we were waiting to march on the runway when a couple of mortar rounds came in. The sound of that round sent us all diving for cover, I thought for a split second they'd got me. The camp siren went off and after the Apache got up and did its thing, we soon commenced with the ceremony, Johnny Ghostkeeper and I got tasked with it because we were leaving the next day. A British ramp ceremony is as long as any funeral, Pte Kevin Dickson told me we would be standing to attention for over an hour, I told him he was full of shit, but he was right.

When I got on the plane on the fifteenth I said I was going to flip the bird to Afghanistan on the way out, I decided not to jinx myself so I kept my fingers to myself. I was in a rather good mood because every second now is closer to home, the ball is finally rolling and on the twenty-second, I'll be embracing my family. I hope that when I get home I can carry on with family life and forget about all the traumatizing events I've experienced.

I will never forget Afghanistan and I will probably think about it every day for the rest of my life. If it doesn't destroy me it will make me a better person, it's my choice. I know I'll never forget the people we lost; they will always remain in my heart. In my eyes we accomplished more than just the basic mission we were sent there to do. Even though insurgents will continue to flood over the border long after Task Force Orion is gone, we still went beyond my expectations. In Afghanistan, Canada wasn't just another coalition country on camp, we were a dominating force, we stood out amongst coalition countries and by doing that we proved to the world just what kind of military we are, one of the most professional and best trained. Together we made history, just as my grandfather did at Vimy. I can't say I want to go back there in the near future, but I wouldn't trade this experience for the world, for the rest of my life I will hold my head high and stand in nobody's shadow. Every man and woman that goes out that wire, time after time, comes back with a completely different perspective than the next person. One thing is for sure, we have lost our innocence in such a way that Afghanistan will be tattooed on our souls forever.

ACKNOWLEDGEMENTS

The editors would like to thank the families and friends of Mike Frastacky and Captain Nichola Goddard for giving us access to their personal emails and granting us permission to use them in this book. We would like to thank all the contributors for being a part of this anthology.

We would also like to thank Anne Collins, Craig Pyette, Anne McDermid and Martha Magor for their invaluable help and advice throughout this process.

Kevin Patterson would like to thank Shauna Klem and Molly Patterson, as always.

Jane Warren would like to thank Micah Toub, her parents and her brothers for their love and support.

KEVIN PATTERSON grew up in Selkirk, Manitoba, and put himself through medical school by enlisting in the Canadian Army. Now a specialist in internal medicine, he practises in the Arctic and Nanaimo, British Columbia. Patterson lives on Saltspring Island.

JANE WARREN was raised in Toronto and has worked as a literary scout, a literary agent, and a freelance editor. She is now an acquiring editor at Key Porter Books.